D0762300

720.92
S949L
E42L

1787
54.00

LOUIS HENRY SULLIVAN

MARIO MANIERI ELIA

PRINCETON ARCHITECTURAL PRESS

Christian Heritage
College Library
2100 Greenfield Dr.
El Cajon, CA 92019

I am grateful to my wife, Flora Famiglini, for her perceptive and careful advice in the calibration of a number of psychological interpretations.

TRANSLATED BY Antony Shugaar with Caroline Green

EDITED BY
Thomas Forget
Caroline Green
Clare Jacobson
Therese Kelly
Mark Lamster, project coordinator
Kevin C. Lippert, publisher
Sara E. Stemen
Claire Zimmerman

COVER DESIGN
Sara E. Stemen

SPECIAL THANKS
Annie Nitschke

PUBLISHED BY
Princeton Architectural Press
37 East 7th Street
New York, NY 10003

English translation ©1996 Princeton Architectural Press, Inc.
First published in Italian © 1995 by Electa, Milan

All rights reserved
No part of this book may be used or reproduced in any manner without the express written consent of the publisher, except in the context of reviews.

00 99 98 97 96 5 4 3 2 1

Library of Congress Cataloging-in-Publication data for this title is available from the publisher.
ISBN 1-56898-092-2

Printed and bound in Italy

CONTENTS

The history of architecture must take into account, for the distant as well as the recent past, two different sorts of architects: those who write, and those who do not (or whose writings are of no particular importance for an evaluation of their work). This division should ideally have no bearing on the analysis and critical evaluation of the architecture itself; nonetheless, few historians fail to be swayed to some degree by the writings of the architects they study. The motives and persuasiveness of these written texts lead historians to attribute certain intentions to iconic texts.

One wonders why this phenomenon is, or at least seems to be, so much more prevalent in the field of architecture than in other fields of art, figurative or otherwise. The fact is that, historically, many architects have relied not only on design proposals and constructed buildings to establish their relationship with the cultural world at large, but also upon the often abundant essays and texts they have written. The tradition is an illustrious one: suffice it to mention Leon Battista Alberti, although one could go back even further. What is most relevant for a proper historical understanding, however, is an observation of the distinct differences in historiographical evaluation of the two types of architects, whether intentional or not. This is evident in the consideration of the work of Alberti, who wrote so copiously about his own intentions and ideas, in comparison with the evaluation of the work of Filippo Brunelleschi, who is not known to have left any writings at all. The difference, of course, does not appear in our assessment of the quality of the work of the two architects, which is clearly of the highest stature in both cases. Rather, there is a difference in the nature of the critical writings about them: there is a tendency to be more detached, perhaps even more objective, in writing on Brunelleschi's work, unaccompanied as it is by any commentary, versus a tendency toward a greater personal involvement with the work of Alberti, as it is extensively discussed by the architect himself.

The distinction between architects who write and those who do not has always existed, yet it has become more pronounced—and merits greater attention—in more recent periods. This is due both to the direct professional competition between architects and the increase in communication resulting from the larger volume of printed matter. A comparison of Walter Gropius, who repeatedly published his frequently changing yet effective—and eventually famous—cultural message, and Mies van der Rohe, who extended the splendid laconism of his buildings to all of his other forms of expression, offers a particularly apt example from recent history. In any case, it seems necessary to explore this matter to some degree before proceeding with a critical analysis of Louis Sullivan, a figure so extensively studied by those with an interest in modern architecture, a figure who is still seen as controversial, a figure whose two aspects—that of essayist and that of practicing architect—are, or seem to be, intrinsically linked.

In reality, the fact that an architect feels the need to write should not affect one's judgment of his architecture. Certainly, the comparison between Gropius and Mies—considering the excellence of the latter's work—might lead one to suppose that there is a certain creative insecurity or even some sort of lack of linguistic ability at the root of the drive to write about one's own architecture, as was certainly the case for Gropius. Such an observation cannot be made, however, about Frank Lloyd Wright or Le Corbusier, who were both notoriously prolific writers, though both unquestionably produced more architecture than written texts.

In a case like Sullivan's, however, it seems useful to employ a form of comparative evaluation of writings to buildings while still being wary of the possible instrumental or surreptitious use of literary means, employed vicariously with respect to the architecture, or in its implicit support—support for which the urge, or at least the opportunity, can easily be felt. This comparison of writing and architecture should be especially attentive to differences and interferences, to the danger of obligatory observations and potentially misleading statements.

In an essay on Sullivan published in 1970—the product of a course that I taught at the University of Venice in the fervor of the "ideological criticism" that followed the unrest of 1968—I opened with a strong statement questioning the authenticity of the tone and ideas of this American master, who historiographers of the modern movement have seen as the prophet of a new architecture rebelling against the tedium of imported European classicism. I focused especially upon a number of famous essays by Sullivan (read and cited by one and all, but usually without any reference to their dates of publication). Although I respected historical fact, I was also clearly swayed by ideological concerns.

"Just when did Sullivan begin to take his critical stance?" I wrote. "Not before 1900. And when did he openly attack [Daniel H.] Burnham and the Columbian Exposition? In the fifteenth chapter of his autobiography, some thirty years after the fact. And so what survives of his prophecy of half a century of architectural slumber, in light of the distance of those events?"[1] These two statements prefaced a wide-reaching inquiry, yet the former, at least, is not quite correct.

The issues at stake were already evident in Sullivan's lecture entitled "Emotional Architecture as Compared with Intellectual: A Study in Subjective and Objective," delivered in 1894, one year after the World's Columbian Exposition.[2] Here Sullivan first denounced the mediocrity of stylistic obsequiousness in the face of European classicistic eclecticism. The essays he wrote around the turn of the century, when his fortune was in decline, confirm this critical stance, and confirm it in even harsher terms. However, Sullivan's criticism of his colleague and rival, Burnham—who outpaced Sullivan professionally, beginning with the commission to oversee the Columbian Exposition—did not become explicit until 1923. The whole matter, in fact, needs careful chronological examination.

Consequently, as I set to work sorting through all the documentary material, it seemed necessary to verify the chronology of interwoven events and conversations. It was not as if this has never been done before; an enormous volume of documentation has been scrupulously studied and made available to scholars by numerous biographers, especially Robert Twombly.[3] Yet Twombly fell into occasional lapses in methodology, perhaps as a result of his excessive personal involvement in his subject. At one point the biographer expresses himself in rather exalted

language, going so far as to state: "Louis Sullivan's story is one of the great American tragedies."[4] Twombly's emotional absorption, for example, meant that in relating the chronology of events and assembling and interpreting facts, he was not always taking into consideration which events actually were contemporaneous. As a result, many of his comments concerning particular events—and this can be verified in Sullivan's autobiographical writings, as well as in other sources—are taken from texts that were written many years after the events in question, and under substantially and significantly different circumstances.

Many of Twombly's descriptions concerning Sullivan's childhood and youth, for example, were taken from *Autobiography of an Idea*, which was written late in Sullivan's life and published just before his death, at the end of a long decline that had already begun in the last years of the nineteenth century. The beautiful and well-known description of the seventeen-year-old architect's first reaction to the tumultuous reality of Chicago after the Great Fire was actually an invention, the product of loneliness and the weary rancor of a deeply depressed old man. In light of the fact that he did not create his first public works until he was almost thirty, it can be assumed that in his youth Sullivan was probably just as unsure of himself as were any of his contemporaries.

In short, it seems that only a precise chronology of Sullivan's writings and projects in spatio-temporal context, stripped of the rhetorical façade applied both by Sullivan and by his hagiographers, can provide an adequate basis for a thorough understanding of these two principal aspects of the architect's work. Only then can we study the two areas of production together, in order to offer a more complex cultural evaluation, as well as separately, in order to present a judgment less conditioned by specific disciplinary contributions.

Lastly, in connection with Sullivan's unusual status in the history of both building design and architectural language, it is imperative to penetrate the smoke screen that he himself created in architectural historiography. Only then can there be an analysis aimed at distinguishing the characteristics of Sullivan's architecture that were derived from the various teachers he met in the course of his life — some older, others the same age or even younger — from the typological inventions and the compositional devices in which we can clearly recognize his individuality and his original contribution to architectural history. In so doing, we shall arrive at a reasoned justification for the classification of several of his projects as true masterpieces—the Union Trust Building in St. Louis (1892), the Chicago Stock Exchange (1893), and the various smaller banks and other buildings erected after 1908. These structures may well be the truest examples of Sullivan's talent and mastery.

1. Mario Manieri Elia, "L. H. Sullivan, epigono di un'ideologia," in Louis H. Sullivan, *Autobiografia di un'idea* (Rome: Officina, 1970), 10.
2. Louis H. Sullivan, *Louis Sullivan: The Public Papers*, ed. Robert Twombly (Chicago: University of Chicago Press, 1988), 88ff.
3. See the general bibliography in this volume. Robert Twombly's *Public Papers* and his *Louis Sullivan: His Life and Work* (Chicago: University of Chicago Press, 1986) constituted major points of reference for my work.
4. Twombly, *Life and Work*, vii.

More than half of Sullivan's lengthy autobiography concerns his childhood; it may be that the aging architect would have continued with his inspired reconstruction of childhood memories had the readers of his memoirs—published in monthly installments—not begun to express a certain impatience. In thinking back upon the formation of his own complex and troubled personality, Sullivan spent many pages examining his reactions to the difficulties that faced a family of immigrants in laissez-faire America, emphasizing their significance. In so doing, Sullivan was delving deep inside himself, in a typical form of escape from an external world that he feared, or at any rate, that he could not accept. This was an understandable reaction for an old man who had always battled against an unforgiving world from a disadvantaged position, and who was now determined to be victorious in a setting of his own creation, a context of nostalgia and partly-imagined childhood. The clash between a pure, unspoiled individual and a corrupt, fast-growing world is expressed in his autobiography, through the character of his childhood self. The book is reminiscent of Kafka's twisted but marvelous depiction of an America he had only imagined, portrayed through the innocent eyes of a boy, Karl Rossmann, in his novel *Amerika*. In fact, it is impossible to know what the young Louis Sullivan's real reactions may have been when faced with the tumultuous yet exciting reality of America in its greatest period of unbridled growth.

Sullivan's family arrived in America with the vast wave of European immigration that followed the Civil War and preceded the economic crisis of the end of the nineteenth century.[1] At this time, an exceptionally favorable business climate allowed for extremely rapid development, yet harsh pragmatism left absolutely no room for cultural reorganization, at least not until the downturn of the 1890s.[2] Patrick Sullivan, Louis's father, had arrived in Boston by 1847, becoming one of roughly thirty thousand Irish immigrants then living in that city. Patrick Sullivan eked out his living in an unusual profession, one that generally allowed him to support his family for the rest of his life: he was a dance instructor. Louis's mother, Andrienne List, had just arrived in the New

World from Switzerland when, at the age of seventeen, she met and married the thirty-four-year-old Irishman. Together, they embarked on an exhausting journey: New York; Boston; Newburyport, Massachusetts; a return to Boston; then to Halifax, Nova Scotia; with frequent stop-overs at the home of the maternal grandparents, the hospitable Lists, in South Reading, Massachusetts. This unending series of moves made it very hard for Louis and Albert (born in 1854) to adjust. For Louis, at least according to his autobiography, home was the house of his grandparents, so much so that he claimed to have felt liberated when his parents left for Chicago in 1868, leaving him in South Reading. Whether Louis actually experienced this sense of relief is hard to say; that a twelve-year-old boy would experience a new sense of independence, however, is quite plausible. It was at this age that he established a trusting relationship with his maternal grandmother, a well-educated and dignified German woman from Hannover, a skeptic in matters of religion, whose ironic wit verged on cruelty. Their relationship was based on his grandmother's stern yet fair authority, so different from his father's chaotic personality.

Robert Twombly analyzes this juncture of Sullivan's life carefully, observing that Sullivan's admitted feeling of indifference—even satisfaction—to his separation from his parents could be the result of his assuming blame for so painful an event. He may have taken this blame upon himself because he could not stand to put it on his parents, even though they were in fact responsible for the separation, whether or not they justified it with considerations of work or career. This acceptance of responsibility is typical of a child's sense of omnipotence; but the older Sullivan, in his memoirs, is still unable to perceive it as such. Even at an advanced age, Sullivan was profoundly immature in his understanding of the experiences that made up his own life. This immaturity was also overlooked by his very thorough biographer; Twombly went even so far as to state that the reactions of the twelve-year-old Louis made him "more adult than boy."[3]

On one hand, one must credit the elderly Louis Sullivan, looking back on a life that was certainly not

opposite: Henry List, maternal grand-father of Louis Henri Sullivan.

below: Sullivan's parents, Andrienne and Patrick Sullivan.

easy, with adopting a somewhat filtered autobio-graphical reality that compensated for the youthful frustrations that were intolerable to him in light of the sad decline that took place during the last three decades of his life. If he did so, it was to create a self-image full of candor and exemplary vitality, set against the grim backdrop of a world that was any-thing but reassuring—a world through which he adventurously made his way with the heroism of strong faith. This once again recalls Kafka's young protagonist, though any similarities are purely fortu-itous, as the two books were written at roughly the same time. Nevertheless, in the two books sexual ini-tiation occurs early on, in both cases with an older woman. Sullivan's first sexual experience was with his cousin Minnie, who was only slightly older—she was eighteen, he fourteen. Sullivan was profoundly moved by this erotic encounter. Minnie also inspired Louis with her admiration for European literature; Byron, Tennyson, and "the many books she had read, largely French novels." This was an unfortunate con-nection for such a culturally immature young man: sex and Europe were two worlds with which Louis Sullivan was to have problems for the rest of his life.

On the other hand, Sullivan's recollection of his grandfather's harsh frankness seems realistic; Sullivan describes the strong words his grandfather used to paint an unflattering picture of his grand-son, which the autobiography recounts with nearly masochistic precision:

> *'I* know *you.* I know your abominable selfishness—come from your father; and your generosity and courage—come from my proud daughter. You have a God-given eye and a dull heart. You are at one and the same time incredibly industrious and practical, and a dreamer of morbid dreams, of mystic dreams, sometimes clean, brilliant dreams, but these are too rare.

'What you have said, from time to time, con-cerning man's power to do, has astounded and frightened me, coming from you. *That idea* you never got from any of us.'[4]

A sense of power—over both people and objects—is the nearly obsessive theme of the thoughts that the autobiography attributes, with some credibility, to the very young Louis Sullivan. He seeks out power as a form of protection in a world that frightens him so badly that he sometimes feels physically ill. This response resulted from the sexual and literary aggressiveness of his cousin; from the daringly poised suspension bridge over the Merrimac shown to him by his father; and from the metropolis itself, in which he detected a deep and dominant note of fear and anguish.

One day, on Commonwealth Avenue, as Louis was strolling, he saw a large man of dignified bear-ing. . . . Louis wished to know who and what was behind the dignity. So he asked one of the work-men, who said:

'Why he's the archeetec of this building.' 'Yes? and what is an archeetec, the owner?' 'Naw; he's the man what drawed the plans for this build-ing.' 'What! what's that you say: drawed the plans for this building?' 'Sure. He lays out the rooms on paper, then makes a picture of the front, and we do the work under our own boss, but the archeetec's the boss of everybody.'[5]

Architecture and power: these two objectives, naturally linked together, were selected by the young man—in the story that he offers as an old man—as the two great beacons toward which he set his course in search of a safe and edifying haven.

1. According to the documentation checked in Boston by Robert Twombly, "Henry Louis" Sullivan was born at 22 South Bennet Street on 3 September 1856. Robert Twombly, *Louis Sullivan: His Life and Work* (Chicago: University of Chicago Press, 1986), 10. For a discussion of the exact name and address, see ibid., 469, note 22.

2. For a brief summary of the matter, see my essay, "Per una città imperiale, D. H. Burnham e il movimento City Beautiful," in *La città ameri-cana dalla guerra civile al "New Deal"* (Rome: Laterza, 1973), 3ff.

3. Twombly, *Life and Work*, 20.

4. Louis H. Sullivan, *The Autobiography of an Idea* (American Institute of Architects, 1924; reprint, New York: Dover, 1956), 135–36.

5. Ibid., 118–19.

After entering high school in Boston, Sullivan happened to meet another person he would later use to catapult himself toward the goals he had set for himself: Moses Woolson, an authoritarian, aggressive, and dictatorial teacher who is described at length in Sullivan's autobiography. Woolson was the very model of a non-conformist thinker, extremely confident and highly motivated in his work; for the rest of his life, Sullivan attempted to imitate him. In all likelihood, the young man was trying to restore to a father figure—first Woolson and later John A. Tompson—the authority that he had found only on the maternal, German-Swiss side of his family during childhood.

This complex need for a male-female authority figure inevitably led Sullivan to the idea of using architecture as an instrument for gaining power and control. In October of 1872, when he entered MIT at the age of sixteen, William Ware was teaching architecture, and the dominant trend of rational classicism was well-represented by the massive Rogers Hall, designed by William G. Preston and only recently completed. This monument, with its Beaux-Arts rigor, was far more assertive and powerful than the Neo-Gothic Masonic Temple, built by Merrill G. Wheelock, which had so deeply impressed Sullivan as a child.[1] However, there was also a discussion about a new structure: the bell tower of the Brattle Square Church, built two years earlier by Henry Hobson Richardson. This tower was reminiscent of medieval architecture in its sheer mass, while its plastic ornamentation was particularly innovative. Dominating the cultural climate, however, was the renowned master, Richard Morris Hunt, the first American architect to train at the École des Beaux-Arts, who was then working in New York. Ware, along with many other bright young architects working on the East Coast—Charles D. Gambrill, George B. Post, Frank Furness, and Henry Van Brunt—had studied and worked in Hunt's circle. In addition, Ware had written the most widely used manual of classical style, *The American Vignola.*

It should come as no surprise, then, to find the young Sullivan no longer in Boston but looking for work in Hunt's practice. His search was in vain, how-ever, and he had to settle for a job in Philadelphia in the office of Furness & Hewitt. Sullivan's new work-place was an office that tended to reject the approved styles of the day, particularly the increasingly formal classicism in use in New England. In this turbulent period, such an iconoclastic approach was successful in the intellectual climate of Philadelphia. In 1873, the office of Furness & Hewitt was working on the design for the Academy of Fine Arts, and complet-ing the construction of the Guarantee Trust and Safe Deposit Company; there were at least ten other projects on which the seventeen-year-old Sullivan may have worked.[2]

Thus Sullivan's first real contact with the architectural profession and with design was stylis-tically much closer to his first childhood fascination, the Masonic Temple of Boston, than to anything like the formal discipline he had just finished study-ing at MIT. In the autobiography, Sullivan reduc-tively describes Frank Furness as "one of the most picturesque personalities I ever knew." In this, Sullivan is in agreement with more traditional his-torical accounts of Furness. And yet we must recog-nize that this brilliant Philadelphian architect—who has been rediscovered by recent architectural critics including Vincent Scully, who has hailed him as "the first great architect in America after Jefferson and certainly the most original American up to his time."[3]—with his aggressive eccentricity and his Scottish-military bearing, managed to express boundless vitality and indomitable linguistic creativ-ity in his work, nourished by a good sense of the fig-urative and a remarkably fluent graphic skill. Although Sullivan's time in Furness's studio was brief, it is safe to assume that the older architect communicated some profound and important ideas to the young apprentice, perhaps even on a subcon-scious level. Sullivan, moreover, must have been affected by the atmosphere of transcendentalist influence stemming from contact with Ralph Waldo Emerson, a close friend of Furness's father William Henry, a Unitarian minister.

In truth, Furness's work, with its brilliant color, and the unsettling vitality of its figurative and plastic forms laden with communicative tension, falls

below, left: The Masonic Temple, by
Merrill G. Wheelock

below, center: Rogers Hall, by *William
G. Preston;*

right: Brattle Square Church, by
Henry Hobson Richardson, 1870–72.

within a certain genre of nineteenth-century eclec-tic architecture. This architectural current rejected the rules of classicism and the domesticated revival of the Neo-Romanesque and Neo-Gothic styles, and worked instead toward a fresh montage of ancient idioms, assembling selected medieval-style motifs, either redesigned or in some cases newly created. Furness seems to have inherited this attitude toward his work from Eugène Emmanuel Viollet-le-Duc; interestingly, his eager and omnivorous curiosity led him to create work that, as Scully points out, seems to foreshadow the style of Antoni Gaudí, who of course was also influenced by Viollet. This trend in nineteenth-century architecture was close—though not identical—to the formalism of the English architectural and artistic circles of the period that were influenced by the ambiguous anti-classical stance of John Ruskin. William Butterfield, for example, has spoken of a cult of the ugly or at least of a fear of the beautiful that was particularly wel-comed by the ecclesiological community.[4] This may

have been what the elderly Sullivan had in mind when he used the term "picturesque" to describe Furness—"picturesque," in fact, was the literary term that at that time seemed to render art free from the obligation to be "beautiful," orienting it instead toward a search for truth, for unexpected inventive forces.

It is certainly true that unbridled inventiveness and an obsessive pursuit of originality constituted mediocre shortcuts to fame in the atmosphere of professional competitiveness that was shaping the look of rapidly growing cities. Still, this inventive-ness and originality helped overthrow the formalis-tic establishment that controlled schools of architec-ture everywhere, and especially on the East Coast of the United States.

Sullivan left MIT and Ware's tutelage, and began working for Furness; as a result, perhaps even unintentionally, he found himself with a general approach to architecture that he described as "wild" and "iconoclastic." As early as 1869, the *Builder* described the sort of work that Furness was doing as "barbaric." Even Twombly describes Furness as "something of a wild man in American design."[5] These are all reactions to the substitution—evident in the production of the Philadelphia master—of a practice of paratactic montage, using traditional lin-guistic elements (whether adapted from historic models, or reinvented), for a concept of architecture as a language system—in this case, a "French" sys-tem similar to that in vogue in New England.

By so doing, Furness introduced the possibility of experimentalism, the immediate effects of which were offshoots of post-eclectic linguistic innovation. In the long run, his work served to introduce a new figurative approach, one freed from traditional mod-els and tied to a new logic embedded in the concept of architecture as language. This new linguistic logic was to loom largely in the best of Sullivan's work.

Sullivan's brief period in Furness's studio came to an abrupt conclusion when the depression of 1873 forced Furness to reduce staff. This unfortu-nate turn of events disappointed the seventeen-year-old Sullivan and caused him some anxiety; in

Two sketches by Sullivan, after
Vignola, on the Doric order, 1875.

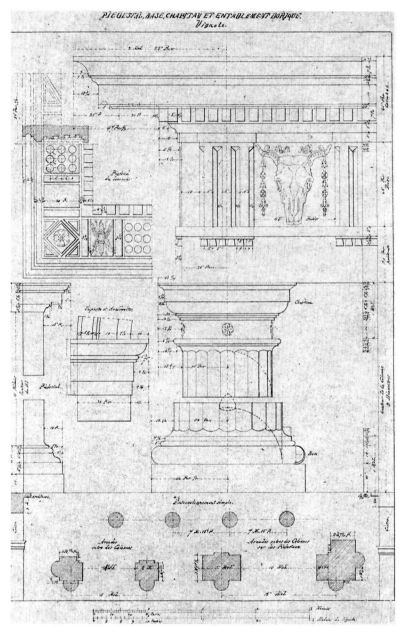

The Guarantee Trust and Safe Deposit Company Building, by Furness & Hewitt, Philadelphia, 1873–75.

response, perhaps, he coldly dismissed his work under Furness as having been of little importance. In fact, it was a highly significant part of Sullivan's training.

The young man had to turn to his parents, who had been living in Chicago for some time; this forced return to his family coincided with the shock of finding himself in a city famed for its brutality, devastated by the terrible fire of 1871, and still in the chaotic throes of reconstruction. This traumatic moment was converted into a heroic tableau by the elderly Louis Sullivan; in a famous—and obviously unreliable—passage of his autobiography, he wrote: "The train neared the city; it broke into the city; it plowed its way through miles of shanties disheartening and dirty gray. It reached its terminal at an open shed. Louis tramped the platform, stopped, looked toward the city, ruins around him; looked at the sky; and as one alone, stamped his foot, raised his hand and cried in full voice: *This is the place for me!*"[6]

Fully adhering to the description offered in Sullivan's autobiography—one that now takes on an inevitable tinge of irony—Twombly follows this quote with a short reference to the possible etymology of the word "Chicago" (taken in turn from John Reps, who traced it to the words "chickagou" or "garlic" and "shegagh" or "skunk"),[7] alluding to the intolerable stench that pervaded the city, which was built on low-lying land, at least until the problem of dumping raw sewage into Lake Michigan had been solved. The solution called for the gradual elevation of the ground on which all buildings were erected: this giant project, begun in 1855, was still underway twenty years later.

1. Robert Twombly, *Louis Sullivan: His Life and Work* (Chicago: University of Chicago Press, 1986), 18, 28.
2. Louis H. Sullivan, *The Autobiography of an Idea* (American Institute of Architects, 1924; reprint, New York: Dover, 1956), 190–96.
3. Vincent Scully, *American Architecture and Urbanism* (London: Thames and Hudson, 1969), 92.
4. Peter Collins, *Changing Ideals in Modern Architecture* (London: Faber and Faber, 1965).
5. Twombly, *Life and Work*, 40.
6. Sullivan, *Autobiography*, 197.
7. Twombly, *Life and Work*, 47.

Sullivan's period of apprenticeship as an architect in Chicago began in the studio of William Le Baron Jenney, whose Portland Block—the "first sky-scraper"—towered above the smoke and soot of the enormous construction yard that was Chicago. And it was reputedly the sight of this building—still incredibly primitive in comparison with the work he had been doing at MIT and with Furness—that drew him infallibly to the studio of his new master. In much the same fashion, according to his autobiography, the sight of a house in Philadelphia designed by Furness & Hewitt had led him to their studio. Whatever slant the aged Louis Sullivan may have emphasized in his literary reconstructions—tending to cast himself as the *faber fortuna suae*, or architect of his own fate—the fact remains that the young Sullivan, possibly at the advice of others, made a number of very strategic moves.

Jenney was an elegant figure. He had been an officer in the Civil War, had studied at the École Polytechnique in France, and still spoke French—though badly. Despite the unimpressive appearance of known works by Jenney, his training as an engi-neer was important to the formation of what became known as the Chicago School. This is demonstrated by the great number of designers who passed through his studio: Martin Roche, William A. Holabird, Irving K. Pond, Howard Van Doren, James Gamble Rogers, Alfred Granger, and John H. Edel-mann. This last designer, a twenty-four-year-old architect of German origin, was to play a crucial role in Sullivan's development.

Edelmann displayed a richness of intellectual breadth that astonished Sullivan, who was easily won over by the idealism that his new friend dis-played toward both politics and art. He was com-pletely conquered by Edelmann's love of music; as a good German, Edelmann knew and loved the work of Richard Wagner. When Sullivan discovered the triumphal dimension of Wagner's music, he immedi-ately linked it to his own childhood ideas of "power," which had been contested by his grandfather but which he had harbored until adulthood.

Sullivan's friendship with Edelmann led him to become acquainted with a number of other young men, all members of the Lotus Club. Sullivan was to become that club's youngest member; he attended meetings every Sunday to swim, run, jump, and wrestle. Louis's brother Albert, two years his elder, outshone him at sports; strangely, Albert is never mentioned in Sullivan's autobiography. Several pages are devoted, on the other hand, to the young Bill Curtis, with admiring mention of his splendid physique. Indeed, Twombly writes, "The extent to which [Sullivan's] enjoyment was sexual, aesthetic, or a combination of both is impossible to deter-mine."[1] It is important to point out that this interest in the body and its vital dynamics was probably nothing more to Sullivan than a reminder of his own father, the dashing and unreliable teacher of dance who, ten years earlier, had introduced his sons to physical exercise, sports, and fishing. All of this, however, stands out in comparison to his apprentice-ship under Jenney, who was instead undoubtedly of considerable importance in terms of Sullivan's tech-nical training. Sullivan chose to tell only of his employer's elegant demeanor, voice, sensuous lips, and *bon vivant*'s tastes.

When Sullivan left for France, it was a sudden interruption of and contrast with the atmosphere that had been created among the young men of the Lotus Club. His decision, not adequately explained in any source, leads one to think he felt a different sort of calling. By leaving Chicago in favor of Europe, France, and the École des Beaux-Arts, Sullivan focused on the ideals of discipline and institutional dignity. He may have been choosing to continue studying within the area of knowledge and practice that he had met with at MIT, through Ware and Eugène Letang, Ware's Parisian assistant. Perhaps his decision can be linked to the stern ideals of his maternal grandfather and his mother, who was born in Geneva and whose native language, after all, was French. In effect, his departure took him away from the lively figure of his father and, above all, from the competitive and fascinating company of his brother and his friends.

There is no reliable and thorough account in Sullivan's autobiography of the European exper-iences of this young American, endowed with insatiable curiosity and penetrating intelligence. Sullivan's recollections are few and far between, and

Aerial view of Chicago.

Ornamental design (dated Paris,
1 April 1875), ink on tracing paper
19.5 x 16 in.

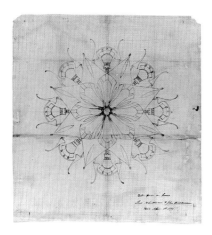

are all didactic in nature. It is impossible, however, to suppose that, upon his arrival in Paris, Sullivan failed to sense the tension of the major socio-political transition in the air, just three years after the historic events of the Paris Commune of 1870, and in the midst of the implementation of the *Grands Travaux* called for by Baron Georges Eugène Haussmann. Yet no mention of these events appears in the book. Indeed, all that we learn of his life in Paris is restricted to the new Beaux-Arts teachings and, even more surprising, the figure of a professor of mathematics: Monsieur Clopet. In Sullivan's depiction of Clopet, what emerges is the professor's determination to dissect reality with geometric precision, using a mental razor so sharp as to exclude all doubts. In Clopet's words, "Our demonstrations shall be so broad as to admit of *no exceptions!*"[2]

In essence, this rule accepted, with selective determination, a single truth excluding all else. And perhaps that is what Sullivan was seeking at this point in his life; a new weapon for achieving hegemony. The young Sullivan (as described by the old Sullivan) was struck by the seductive removal of all complexity that was promised by Clopet's mathematical method. As an old man, battered by the painful events of the last thirty years of his life, he subscribed fully to this idea of the mastery of complexity through the all-powerful exclusion of contradiction, despite three decades of failed hopes and ambitions methodically quashed by historical reality.

In architectural terms, Sullivan was learning from Emile Vaudremer, recipient of the Prix de Rome and an orthodox high priest of the Beaux-Arts credo. He was receiving an introduction to French standards of architecture, which the young man probably took at face value as an obligatory route to gain entry—as did Hunt and Richardson before him—to the inner circle of American architecture. This was a demanding apprenticeship, and perhaps neither enjoyable nor interesting. Nonetheless, it was a great privilege, considering the École's limited admission—just thirty students, varying in age from fifteen to twenty, selected through annual examinations. So great was this privilege (and historians have wondered who offered Sullivan the recommendation that helped him obtain it, with some

suggesting Letang) that it clearly persuaded Sullivan to accept the unstimulating studies, and even made him overestimate the results.

Sullivan left Chicago on 10 July 1874, spent a few days in England, and took the École's admission exams on 11 September.[3] These exams were notoriously difficult, and even Hunt and Richardson had barely passed them (both failed the first time). Sullivan passed them with flying colors. For the eighteen-year-old student, this brilliant success at the world's leading institution in the field was good reason to be proud. And this pride, which lasted through all the difficult experiences of Sullivan's life, explains the space devoted in his autobiography to his experiences at the French school, while the rest of his time in Europe is virtually ignored.

Sullivan's account is both inaccurate and incomplete. The first and most important discrepancy concerns the length of his stay, which actually lasted no more than ten months and was broken off by a hasty return to the United States. He landed in New York on 24 May 1875.[4] Sullivan must have considered this stay embarrassingly short, as he wrote that it lasted two years. Undoubtedly, he was torn by a yearning to return to the stimulating atmosphere of Chicago and to his new friends. One indication of his painful homesickness is found in the drawings he did in France; they are dedicated to John H. Edelmann.

Travels to Italy—and to Rome in particular—were a standard part of the Beaux-Arts approach to training, though Sullivan claimed he had been prompted to see the Vatican's *Last Judgment* after reading Hippolyte Taine. In any case, this trip served to interrupt the dull classwork and rigid classical discipline of school. The sight of Italy's incredible wealth of monuments—viewed, perhaps, with slight distraction—and, especially, the overwhelming effect of Michelangelo's work in the Sistine Chapel were liberating experiences for Sullivan: he hailed Michelangelo as a "Super-Man," a "great Free Spirit," the "first great Adventurer," and the "first mighty man of Courage."[5] The sight of this work rebelliously rekindled his childhood idea of "power," in the form of indomitable vitality, courage, and imagination.

Design for an ornamental ceiling frieze (dated Paris,
29 November 1874), ink on tracing paper, 10 x 16 in.

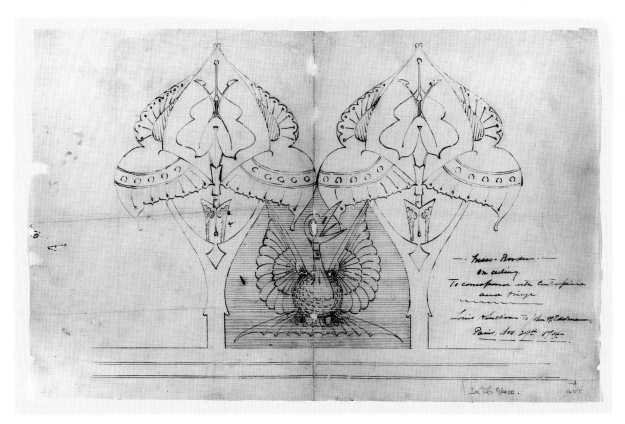

Perhaps Sullivan thought that he had finally found the synthesis of his contrasting aspirations in Michelangelo's massive nudes—aspirations for liberty as creative autonomy, and for security as firm authority. After this enlightenment, Florence held nothing for him; even Paris was no longer enough, signifying to him only the code of Beaux-Arts rules. The young man's inventiveness and curiosity had been reawakened. These were the same aspects of his personality that had been galvanized by Furness's unconventional determination and by his own cultural and corporeal fascination with Edelmann— the side of him that experienced powerful and sweeping emotions like those he had felt at the age of five when, led by the hand of his father, far from the Swiss discipline of the List family, he had first glimpsed the sea.

Upon his return to Chicago, Sullivan was full of enthusiasm. He was encouraged by Edelmann, who—according to Sullivan's autobiography—invited Sullivan to come work with him. It would be an error, however, to minimize the impact of Sullivan's time in France, and of the rationalist doctrine that he had absorbed while there. In 1904, Sullivan himself was to credit that doctrine, and, in particular the mathematician Clopet, with having allowed him to develop the idea of a dependence between form and function, later so crucial to Sullivan's reputation. Still, it is safe to venture that the development of this idea was particularly influenced by the reading that Sullivan did during this period of his life, under the guidance of Edelmann. Assuming it is true that he was not familiar with the works of Horatio Greenough, which were particularly enlightening on the subject of "organic thought,"[6] the works of Herbert Spencer and Charles Darwin must have pushed him toward functionalism. If "form followed function," it was also true that "function developed the body." Athletics became important to him again, as did the Apollonian athlete, Bill Curtis, and Sullivan's brother Albert, who was so good at sports (especially at the hundred-yard dash and greco-

*Preliminary study for decoration of
the Sinai Temple, 1876, and design
for a ceiling, May 1876, ink on paper,
15.5 x 29 in*

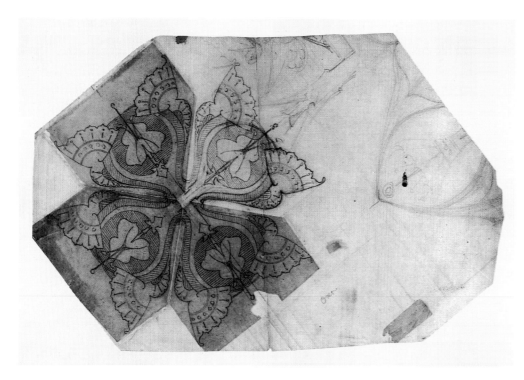

roman wrestling) and yet so unsuccessful in his professional pursuits. Albert left the railroad at about this time to become a draftsman, using his father's school of dance as a studio.

While Sullivan was away, Edelmann had left Jenney's firm and set up his own studio with colleague Joseph Johnston. His friendship with Sullivan remained close and friendly in the esoteric and slightly misogynistic atmosphere of the Lotus Club; the cultural debate between the two became richer and more interesting, as disagreements developed that Edelmann's greater maturity usually managed to keep under control. The older man was trying to restrain the individualistic pride of his youthful friend. When Sullivan declared, "Art is noble thought nobly expressed," Edelmann responded, "Ideas . . . give permanent value to an art production—Technical skill . . . is not art itself but merely [its] servant."[7] Or, in another instance, when Sullivan declared that the purpose of decoration was "to produce a combination of colors, which shall be harmonious in itself, and with its surroundings, forming a unity, of which the primary function is general effect," he replied, sharply undercutting Sullivan's definite emphasis, with a dry: "I believe the object of all *decoration* to be the pleasure to be derived from looking at it."[8]

Actually, Edelmann's Central European idealism, which brought him eventually "through socialism to anarchism," according to Twombly, tended to conflict with Sullivan's concrete approach to architecture, dampening the latter's messianic certainties and his individualistic pragmatism yet offering a classical ideal of beauty in exchange, one which was already contradicted by Sullivan's revivalistic designs.[9] For that matter, it was Louis's father, Patrick Sullivan, who gave Louis a copy of John W. Draper's book, *History of the Intellectual Development of Europe*;[10] the book provided a historical basis for Edelmann's theory that feudalism, by repressing man's spirit of individual initiative, discouraged free invention and forced art into traditional conventions, thus hindering the functional and creative development of architecture. This was clearly a negative conception of power, as feudal power was depicted in the form of obscurantist tyranny. Sullivan, who was

John Edelmann, sketches for the Bates House, by Burling & Adler.

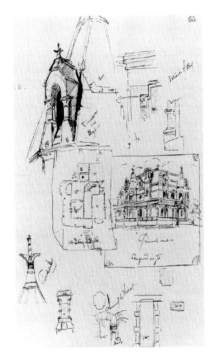

in no way interested in any real theoretical understanding, simply used this idea to attack the adversaries of his own idea of "power," which he saw as the greatest expression of creative freedom, to be attained in a climate of individualistic democracy.

The architectural work done by Edelmann during this period, in loose collaboration with Sullivan, survives in the drawings of the "Lotus Club Notebook," a series of sketches of buildings and details for Neo-Gothic buildings. These were, for the most part, sketches for projects that had not yet been awarded to the architects. They include the residences for E. Bates, the Sinai Temple, the Chicago City Hall, and the Cleveland Cathedral. In fact, Edelmann left Chicago to work on the Cleveland project, leaving Sullivan two other projects that were to constitute his first two professional assignments: the interior frescoes for the Sinai Temple and the Moody Tabernacle. These were non-architectural projects, but Sullivan attacked them with determination and courage and won an early measure of fame. All knowledge off them is derived from the daily press of the time: the newspapers were full of praise for all cultural events in the rough Midwestern city of Chicago. The *Chicago Times* praised the decoration on the interior of the synagogue for its beauty and harmony. The paper compared the ornamentation to Sullivan's work on the Moody Building, whose decorative themes were remarkably similar.[11]

Interest in the Moody Tabernacle was also spurred by the remarkable figure of Dwight Moody,

a flamboyant evangelist of considerable notoriety. Unfortunately, the public was disconcerted by the evangelist's colorful personality as well as by the remarkable decorations designed by Sullivan, rich in contrasting color and devoid of perspective. Nonetheless, the young artist was sufficiently confident to take immediate advantage of the uproar over his work, and he was so skillful a publicist that his fame soon outshone that of his friend Edelmann. And yet, for the period when Edelmann left Chicago for Cleveland in an attempt to get the commission for the cathedral, there is little information on Sullivan and his budding career. This lack of documentation lasts for a fairly long time, right up until 1880, leaving a gap of about four years. Historians have attempted to explain this without much success. Sullivan, in his autobiography, casts a positive light on this period: "Louis was satisfied with things as they were going. He was ambitious but cautious; he was waiting for the right man to show up. He did not remain too long in any one place, and each time increased his salary."[12] What we do know is that his brother Albert moved out of the family home in 1877, and that Louis followed him the following year, moving into a boarding house at 396 East Chicago Avenue, where he lived until 1883. We also know that the boys' father was in considerable financial difficulty; he had stopped working, and he was to die in 1884.

1. Robert Twombly, *Louis Sullivan: His Life and Work* (Chicago: University of Chicago Press, 1986), 52.

2. Ibid., 63.

3. "I am honored to present to the Director of the Select Imperial School of Fine Arts Mr. Louis Sullivan residing at 17 Rue Racine, an architecture student. I ask that the above cited student be admitted as a student and certify that he is willing and able to take his entrance examinations." This declaration was submitted by Vaudremer, quoted by Twombly, *Life and Work*, 64.

4. On 24 May 1875, the *New York Times* listed Louis H. Sullivan as one of the passengers arriving from Liverpool on board the *Britannic* (ibid., 73). Note that Lewis Mumford, *The Brown Decades: A Study of the Arts in America, 1965–95* (New York: Dover Publications, 1955) speaks of a four-year stay.

5. Louis H. Sullivan, *The Autobiography of an Idea* (American Institute of Architects, 1924; reprint, New York: Dover, 1956), 234.

6. Sherman Paul, *Louis Sullivan. An Architect in American Thought* (Englewood Cliffs, NJ: Prentice-Hall, 1962) maintains that Greenough

was not known in Chicago, and F. O. Mettienssen, *Rinascimento americano* (Turin: Einaudi, 1954) claims that Sullivan "unquestionably had never heard of Greenough's writings."

7. Twombly, *Life and Work*, 85.

8. Ibid., 84–85.

9. Ibid., 94.

10. Draper's book was given as a gift, supposedly, in 1876, the year it was published. Ibid., 79.

11. *Chicago Times*, 21 May 1876.

12. Sullivan, *Autobiography*, 253.

According to Sullivan's autobiography, John Edelmann returned to Chicago to join the studio of Burling & Adler following a "dull spell" spent in Iowa "trying to play the game of farming." This prodigal friend was no longer described as a mentor upon his return, but rather as an entertaining and agreeable nuisance. Nonetheless, Edelmann once again played a decisive role in Sullivan's career by introducing him to both Dankmar Adler and his partner, Edward Burling. The portrait that Sullivan later gives us of the two architects is so sharply drawn that it deserves to be quoted here at some length.

> Burling was slouched in a swivel chair, his long legs covering the desk top; he wiggled a chewed cigar as he talked to a caller, and spat into a square box. He was an incredible, long and bulky nosed Yankee, perceptibly aging fast, and of manifestly weakening will—one of the passing generation who had done a huge business after the fire but whom the panic had hit hard.
>
> Further away stood Adler at a draftsman's table, full front view, well lighted. He was a heavy-set short-nosed Jew, well bearded, with a magnificent domed forehead which stopped suddenly at a solid mass of black hair. He was a picture of sturdy strength, physical and mental.[1]

Later, at the beginning of 1880, Edelmann told Sullivan that he had left the firm of Burling & Adler, and that the practice was being dissolved. Edelmann urged Sullivan to contact Adler, who was already well known in Chicago, especially for his successful construction of the Central Music Hall, inaugurated in 1879; this new hall seated nineteen-hundred people, and the acoustics—one of Adler's specialties—were considered to be ideal. Sullivan's meeting with Adler went splendidly, at least according to Sullivan. As he tells it, the two architects, one thirty-six and the other twenty-four, hit off so famously that they came to an agreement whereby the younger partner was given a one-third share of the business, beginning 1 May 1880. There was also an understanding that, as early as the following year, Sullivan was to become an equal partner. That, however, was not

how things would work out. The ensuing events are rather unclear, at least as far as dates are concerned. Those that appear in Sullivan's autobiography—and Hugh Morrison is among those who accept his version of events—are gainsaid by the documents used by Twombly. Twombly maintains that a building permit was issued for the Borden Block only in September 1880; yet Sullivan states that the studio was based in the Borden Block at the beginning of 1880. In 1881, the firm of Louis H. Sullivan, Designer, appeared at 135 La Salle Street, next door to the studio that Adler had left; it is not until June 1882 that we find the name of Sullivan, in parentheses, next to that of Dankmar Adler & Company. Only in 1883 did the studio of Adler & Sullivan appear as such, emblazoned on the front page of the *Chicago Tribune*. The shaky chronology found in the autobiography, compounded by the unwillingness of historians, and especially hagiographers, to cast a critical eye on the issue of dates, makes it particularly hard, in this early stage of the successful partnership of Adler and Sullivan, to attribute proper credit for such projects as the Borden Block, as well as other work done during the period when Sullivan was still "in parentheses."

If the sequence of events that Twombly constructs from available documentation is accurate, then Sullivan could have worked as an outside designer, still in the early stages of his creative development, beginning at the end of 1879, and certainly in 1880, when the design phase of the Borden Block project was verging on completion. And yet, while this office building is certainly innovative, the features that make it so—the structural rationalism of the lightweight and light-permeable surrounding shell, and the elegant balance between load-bearing structure and the ornamentation (reliefs and coloring)—can be attributed quite plausibly to Adler's masterful style, which at this point was quite solid and self-assured. The entire matter of allowing for natural light, which was facilitated by the reduction of the façade to a skeleton of vertical and horizontal elements, as well as the objective of a continuous application of this grid, had been two of the principal goals pursued in the production of metal-framed

opposite: Dankmar Adler

below, left: Dankmar Adler &
Company, Borden Block, Chicago,
1880.

below, right: Dankmar Adler &
Company, Central Music Hall,
Chicago, 1879, section and floor plans.

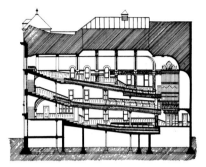

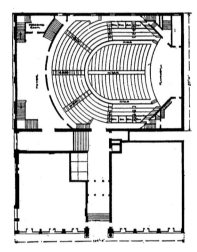

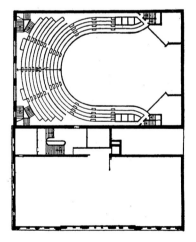

Sullivan's design for the door of the office of Adler & Sullivan, 1883.

View of the First Leiter Building, by William Le Baron Jenney, Chicago, 1870.

buildings, especially in downtown New York and in the projects done by Jenney in Chicago. Indeed, Jenney, with the all-metal structure of his First Leiter Building (1879), seems a proto-Rationalist whose work anticipated many of the later developments of the Chicago School. Before long, however, Jenney had returned to a muddled and heavy-handed style in his Home Insurance Building (1884–1885).

The Borden Block has been demolished, so it can be evaluated only from old photographs; nonetheless, its most striking aspect is the sense of measure and proportion that distinguishes the various architectural elements. Clearly, there was a master planner at work, tightly controlling both structural and aesthetic aspects of the building, allowing neither one to prevail over the other. Also held in tight rein were the assorted highly-colored features: the light, neutral-colored stone facing; the base, with emphatic colossal order; and the cornice, elegantly punctuated by a series of arches cut into the light-colored stone, under the shadow of a dark roof looming above on short pillars. Sullivan, a new arrival in the studio, may certainly have worked on this project, but his contribution cannot have amounted to much more than the design of the decorative reliefs, such as the lunettes under the arches, the panels beneath the windows, or the decorations on the interior. The roles of the two architects were probably no different in the design for the new residence of John Borden, built in the same period. The solid compactness of this building, which is so much more sheltered and thick-walled than the office building, seems clearly the work of Adler, as do the tall brick chimneys, the narrow windows, and the rigorous alternation of light-colored stone framing elements and fired brick infill. If Sullivan worked as a decorator, designing specific elements for precise locations, this need not be considered a limitation of his creative stature; rather, it was an obvious claiming of territory, allowing for a respectful acceptance of the style of the chief architect of the studio—a perfectly acceptable style, no less—in a compatible continuity. Implied autonomy, therefore, was exercised solely within the limits of Adler's overall structure; in exchange, Sullivan had full freedom of expression in a territory all his own.

The partnership between the two architects, then, while technically not an equal one at the beginning, seems to have been one of mutual respect from the outset, free of compromise in qualitative terms; it is, however, quite difficult to say, over time, just who did what and who held which title. The three buildings begun in 1881—the Revell Building, the Jeweler's Building, and the Rothschild Building—prompt a variety of interpretations. The first two are volumetrically staid, informed by a middle-class dignity; the latter is more daring and innovative, even in its ambiguous reinvention of past styles.

It seems reasonable to suppose that Sullivan played a larger role in the design of the Rothschild Building—which has sadly been demolished, as has the Revell Building—and that this role went perhaps far beyond the narrow limits of decoration; in the Rothschild Building, in fact, the decoration overflows into the load-bearing structure. The idea of recycling Gothic or Venetian architectural models in the decoration of a metal-structure façade with an ample array of windows was anything but new; recall the cast-iron structures of New York mentioned previously. Here, however, a number of noteworthy elements are visible: the repetition of triads that breaks up the façade, making it appear almost like a double tower; the system of fenestration that, in the top three floors, is crowned by increasingly arched plate glass windows; and the trusses that mark each floor, decorated with friezes that similarly become more vivid in style with each floor, up to the richly adorned attic. The entire decorative program, in short, displays a creative taste for revivalism that would be reminiscent of Furness if it were less rigorous and logical, as well as less aggressive. In any case, this revivalist taste hardly seems like the work of Adler. It may be interesting to note (in light of the successive development of events) that the appearance in the attic story of a floral decoration of repeating round modules—a brand-new theme—may hint at the oculi which later appeared in a number of skyscrapers designed by Sullivan, beginning with the Wainwright Building.

By this juncture, in the 1880s, construction in Chicago was booming; clearly this growth outpaced the concentration on quality that was the basis

Adler & Sullivan, Walker Warehouse, Chicago, 1889–90, exterior view and façade detail.

of Sullivan's work. This situation led the young architect, in his desire to make himself known one way or another, to attempt to harness the incredible potential of a city that was growing in so startling a manner. The metropolis was born of mud and built in open defiance of nature from the ground up, on land that was artificially raised and perfectly flat, in antagonistic proximity to the absolute horizontality of the lake. This was a setting that cried out for tall structures as a challenge to nature. In architectural terms, this vertical imperative translated into a challenge against accepted architectural traditions of style.

Referring back to this period, and speaking only of himself and in the third person, Sullivan was to write in his autobiography: "A series of important mercantile structures came into the office, each one of which he treated experimentally, feeling his way toward a basic process, a grammar of his own." In

the massive renewal of construction, problems of providing natural light and high-rise structure inexorably shifted design away from the work of Furness and Richardson, awakening new interest in that of Jenney at the First Leiter Building; the engineer's pride in advanced technology, in some cases, won out over every other consideration. The Borden Block won fame for its innovative foundation, the work of a German named Frederick Baumann;[2] the Revell Building can safely be called the first fireproof commercial building.[3] Indeed, the Revell Building persuaded Martin Ryerson—with George Pullman, Marshall Field, and Ferdinand Peck—to commission the firm to do six more buildings in the seven years that followed. The buildings commissioned by Martin Ryerson (and his son, also named Martin Ryerson) were: the Jeweler's Building (1881–82) and the Revell Building (1881–83); then the Ryerson Building (1884); the Ryerson Charities

Trust Building (1886); a third Ryerson Building (1887); the Walker Warehouse (1888–90); and lastly, the Ryerson Tomb (1887). Of these, the first Ryerson Building is certainly the most innovative, and here Adler was a follower rather than a leader. In this building, the interrupted transparent grid of the façade recomposes its image through the authority of three-fold vertical scansion, squared-off by tall pillars. These pillars, faced with a light-colored stone carved into bizarre totemic shapes on the ground floor. This sculptural reference, directly in contact with the street and its fervid vitality, draws the attention of the observer to the tall structure, which is overrun by an extravagant body of ornamentation—like that found, in more sober form, on the skyscrapers designed by Sullivan in later years—that surges beyond all traditional limits, blithely ignoring the utilitarian rules of production endemic to competitive capitalism.

The Troescher Building (1884) adhered to a far more moderate line of experimentation; this may have been the result of Adler's management. Once again we see the crown of the building featuring arches filled with decorative lunettes, as in the Borden Block. Here, however, there is a four-part scheme (A-B-B-A) isolating an unsuccessful, overstated decorative treatment at the center of the top floor. Moreover, the ground floor is problematized by a rusticated arch raised above all four vertical bays, clearly inspired by the work of Richardson. This is a respectful but unpersuasive reference to the brutalism of the master, and it reappears in the Dexter Building of 1887. Here, the rustication surrounds plate glass and is surmounted by regular fenestration set in a smooth wall dramatized by an enormous central panel, which is in turn punctuated by slender cast-iron columns.

What is astonishing—and certainly must have stood out from other structures of dull Yankee commerce—is the variety of what Sullivan rightly considered to be a series of hands-on experiments, building by building, a variety notable even in buildings that were virtually devoid of stylistic features. Among the lesser known buildings is the Knisely Building (1884; since demolished). This sober structure was articulated by a series of tall pilasters but

Ornamental design (dated 13 April 1885), pencil on paper, 10.8 x 6.9 in., and study of a nude (dated 17 November 1880), pencil on tracing paper, 13.3 x 8.3 in.

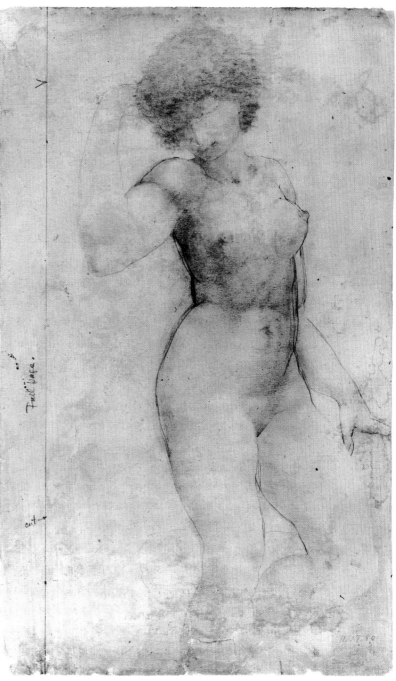

Dankmar Adler & Company (with Sullivan), John Borden Residence, Chicago, 1880, (since demolished).

Adler & Sullivan, Revell Building, Chicago, 1881–83 (demolished in 1968).

was nonetheless broken up by a subordinating ground-floor entrance and large fourth-floor arch. The Selz Schwab factory (1887), was designed with a series of broad, flat, brick pillars that endow it with a serene rhythm—surprisingly similar to the style of Peter Behrens—and an overall effect of great security and authority.

The firm's prestige, however, came not so much from the ardent production of tall commercial or office buildings, but from a specialization that Adler had already developed before Sullivan joined it—theater design. Insofar as Adler had already triumphed in this area with his design of the Central Music Hall, one could say that Sullivan had to take a back seat, at least initially. This fact is minimized in Sullivan's later writings, where he claims to have worked with Adler on that project; nevertheless, as Twombly notes—though Willard Connely and Sherman Paul accept the accuracy Sullivan's reminiscences—Sullivan did not enter the studio as a full-time employee until two years after the music hall opened. Adler wrote, "When I found myself so overcrowded with work as to be unable to discharge my duties to my clients . . . [I] began my business connection with Mr. Louis H. Sullivan."[1] And it was precisely the success that Adler enjoyed as a result of his work on the Central Music Hall and the Grand Opera House—the latter with Sullivan working at least as decorator—that brought the firm notoriety and, in particular, helped him get that first commission outside Chicago: the Academy of Music in Kalamazoo, Michigan.

If the dates that Twombly carefully provides for the Academy of Music project are indeed accurate, they provide a good illustration of just how fast decisions could be made and buildings designed and constructed. This rapidity, of course, should be taken into account when evaluating the quality of the architecture, and in particular the freshness, innocence, and daring that characterize the work of the Chicago School in this period. Note the following chronology: in June 1881, a small committee from Kalamazoo came to Chicago to choose an architect. They immediately offered the job to Adler, who accepted. From that time, only seven months passed

*Adler & Sullivan, John M.
Brunswick & Julius Balke Factory,
Chicago, 1881–83.*

*Kohn, Adler & Felsenthal Residences,
Chicago, 1885–86 (since demolished).*

before the first plans had been drawn up, the committee had given its approval, the blueprints completed, the construction contracts assigned, and the theater completed. In February 1882, the roof closed over a hall that could seat 1,250 people, and on 8 March it was inaugurated. It has since, regrettably, been demolished, and is now known only from a drawing—signed "Adler & Sullivan Architects"—of the front elevation, which was rigorously symmetrical. The building was made of red brick and light-colored stone, typical choices for Adler. Also typical of Adler's work—as seen in the Borden Block—were the crowning arches and decorative lunettes at the top of the structure, with pinnacles rising from a balustrade above the cornice. This last section—certainly the work of Sullivan's refined hand—was never built.

This episode clearly reveals the degree to which—given the pragmatic, functionalist urgency of the "provincials" from Kalamazoo—Sullivan's contribution, at least as far as the exterior of the building was concerned, was considered to be just so much "added value." Highlighted in promotional contexts—as the surviving drawing must have been—it was marginal to the actual operative strategy of the office.

The year was 1882, an important one for Sullivan, as it was the year in which he attained his first clear personal success, independent of Adler, though on a project they designed together. This event came in conjunction with another development that was crucial to Sullivan's career: the first publication of Sullivan's collaboration with Adler, in an interview in the *Daily Inter-Ocean*, on 12 August 1882. These two events, of course, are not independent of one another. Nonetheless, the conjunction of building and interview creates speculation as to Sullivan's role, since there is inadequate information concerning the actual construction; we have only descriptions, however enthusiastic, of the built work.

The text of the interview, however, shows a self-assured twenty-six-year-old Sullivan, who speaks of his work with great confidence, describing it as his own creation and showing no doubts as to its exceptional value. When asked by the reporter to

left: *Dankmar Adler & Company
(with Sullivan), Jeweler's Building,
Chicago, 1881–82.*

below: *Adler & Sullivan, Martin A.
Ryerson Building, Chicago, 1884
(since demolished).*

describe his work stylistically, "'I have no terms to characterize what you see,'" was his reply. The interview continued:

> 'I have not given study to the nomenclature of the peculiar art forms developed in these boxes or carried out in that proscenium crown,' indescribable anyway, he insisted, in 'stock' phrases. Then how do you define your work 'in words'? he was asked. 'I cannot,' he replied. 'I prefer that you speak of it as the successful solution of a problem. The vaguer you are in such matters the better I shall be pleased,' particularly since Chicago people 'are not prepared' for 'a discursive consideration of art in architecture,' partly because 'we have no appreciative art criticism here.'[5]

Sullivan continued, setting forth a number of concepts that, to his astonished interviewer, must have appeared to have very little to do with art criticism, citing the principles of Spencer and the doctrine of Darwin, and daringly relating them to his own design techniques. The perceptions that led Sullivan to make these critical observations, at any rate, were of considerable importance in the context of the prevailing culture of his time. He was one of the first intellectual architects capable of both understanding the innovative breadth of new concepts being developed in the field of scientific thought and applying those concepts to his own field of endeavor. He had perhaps been preceded, in the more general field of art, by Horatio Greenough, though it is unlikely that Sullivan was familiar with his writings. It is more plausible that Sullivan's mind had been opened to this body of thought by Frank Furness, the Philadelphian architect so familiar with the works of Emerson and Ruskin, an intellectual roundly opposed to the classicizing Beaux-Arts culture that then prevailed internationally, with its predilection for classifications and its reluctance to accept evolutionary theory.

It is certainly safe to say that Sullivan—and Edelmann played little part in this—had adopted the genuine vitality of American organic and transcendentalist thought developing from the ideas of Emerson (about whom Sullivan may have learned from Furness) and Whitman (whom Sullivan greatly admired), and powerfully expressed in the literature of Melville.

Sullivan, moreover, seems to have been perfectly aware of the denotative value of language; in rejecting classical nomenclature, he was clearly expressing his dislike of rigid categorization and the partition of discipline and style that, in his view, paralyzed progress and hindered free, creative thought.

But how could so revolutionary a body of concepts be infused into architectural production? This was certainly a great, if unconfessed, quandary for Sullivan. And it was this nagging conundrum that drove him, even in the face of countless professional necessities, the limited and limiting cultural demands of his clients, and the constraints of the society that received his architecture.

Things were different for Adler: accustomed to the iron-bound laws of commerce and competition, yet unhindered by any preconceived notions, he had little or no difficulty in accepting the technical and functional innovations made possible by engineering. If the face of the American city changed radically as a result of the great projects undertaken and completed by builders like Roebling and Jenney, Adler accepted as a natural development, however surprising or even shocking, society's incredible new capacity to transform its environment. In any case, this kind of growth could hardly be opposed on cultural or even aesthetic grounds. Yet criticism in this vein—insecurely grounded though it was on European models of classification—persisted, tending to object to buildings on the basis of "taste" or "school." Architects of the period were obliged to take into account objections of this sort.

Having accepted the imperative of innovation with respect to technical challenge, Adler encountered nothing but respect and appreciation. When it came to problems of structure and foundation design, he encountered no debate or polemic. Sullivan's work, on the other hand, was the subject of harsh debate, in that he was working in a field—aesthetics—far less open to innovation according to the prevailing view of the period. Having rejected the

29

Dankmar Adler & Company
(with Sullivan), Max M. Rothschild
Building, Chicago, 1880–81
(demolished in 1972).

facile loophole of an officially accredited body of stylistic reference in favor of an imperative for creative research, which he considered to be a fundamental value of freedom and democracy, Sullivan all the same found himself obliged to fit his work into communicable forms of architectural language. Other architects, including Frank Furness—who Sullivan mentions rarely, but who certainly remained in his mind as a successful, cultured model—communicated through a rich array of citations and references brought to life by fervent creativity. H. H. Richardson, on the other hand, advocated the acceptance of a model taken from the past, a far-reaching, Roman and Romanesque style charged with monumentality and a potential for the extreme simplification of design. And there was a middle road between the work of these two masters, that of Sullivan's colleague John Wellborn Root. Only six years older than Sullivan, Root—along with Daniel H. Burnham—had already displayed a great capacity for innovation along the same path that Sullivan was following.

Caught maneuvering in the narrow margin between popular taste and personal innovation, yet intolerant of that narrow space due to his powerful intellectual motivation, Sullivan took up the challenge of finding a field in which to apply his own creative and inventive capacities. He seems to have found it in the area of architectural ornamentation. This was a field largely free of economic and functional limitations, unhampered by codified models, and well suited, by its definition as "added value," to pure linguistic experimentation. It proved to be an excellent choice: the descriptions of his ornamental work tended to take up as much column space in the press as did descriptions of technical aspects like acoustics and structure, all the bailiwick of Adler. Note the attention lavished on the interior of the McVicker's Theater by C. H. Blackall, editorialist of the *American Architect and Building News*:

> The general effect of the color is salmon and dull bronze. The tones of the wall start from the bottom with a decided salmon tint as a ground, fading out as it rises, until in the center of the ceiling

Adler & Sullivan, A. F. Troescher Building, Chicago, 1884 (since demolished).

Morris Selz and Charles H. Schwab Residences, Chicago, 1883 (since demolished); view of a fireplace in the Selz Residence and detail of the façade.

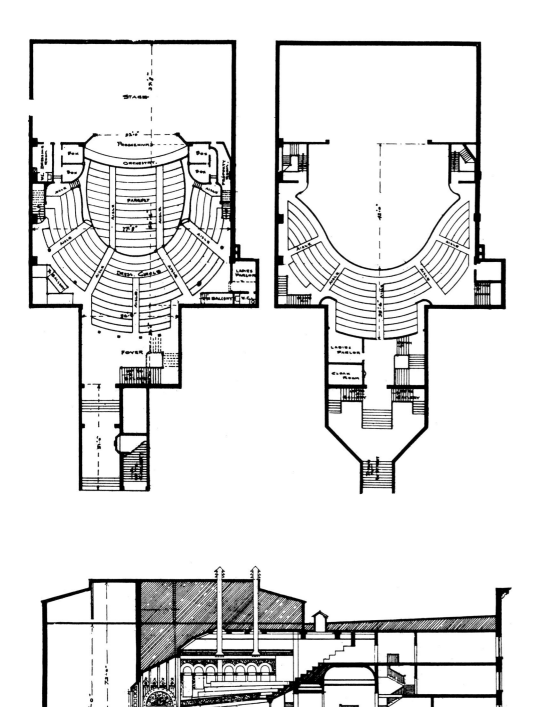

it becomes a delicate buff. Over this is a large pattern formed in relief with heavy rosettes like the centre [sic] of a sunflower, and lines of long, spiky leaves, touched up with strong, red bronze, the pale salmon, however, remaining the principal color. This decoration is carried over nearly all surfaces, no distinction being made between walls, beams and ceiling, except by accentuated lines, rosettes of varied ornament in relief, or by using slightly deeper tones of the general color.[6]

The construction of the McVicker's Theater, "the pride of Chicago" preceded the triumphant Auditorium Building project, though it was marked by a far more troubled and unfortunate history. The McVicker's project entailed the reconstruction of an old theater building originally erected in 1857, destroyed in the Great Fire of 1871, immediately rebuilt the following year, and rebuilt yet again—but apparently with unsatisfactory results—at the beginning of the 1880s. The dissatisfied client turned to Adler & Sullivan at the beginning of 1883. A project already underway was rejected and revised, with new construction set to begin in April 1885 and inauguration scheduled for 1 July of the same year. Even after its completion, however, this tormented project had not reached a final conclusion: further debate ensued in 1888, when a well-known specialist in architectural ornament named Twyman, who had worked on the interior decoration of the building, announced publicly that he had been responsible for the ornamentation of the entire structure, triggering an angry dispute that lasted for months. Finally, in the summer of 1890, arson triggered a disastrous blaze that definitively destroyed what had been considered the model theater of the nation.

The difficult history of this building—of which little more than an exterior drawing survives—seems to be expressed in the complex architectural result that emerged from repeated revisions of design. The organic harmony of the interior—made still more magnificent by 1,235 electric light bulbs, used for the first time as a decorative element—contrasts with a particularly distasteful and muddled exterior. Still, if there is one image that

Dankmar Adler & Company (with Sullivan), Academy of Music, Kalamazoo, Michigan, 1882 (since demolished).

Adler & Sullivan, J. H. McVicker's Theater, Chicago, 1883–1885 (demolished in 1925).

represents, with effective immediacy, the heroic period of Chicago in the 1880s—a raw and surprising, contrived and daring, paradoxical and spontaneous town—it must be the drawing, signed by Adler and Sullivan, of the McVicker's Theater towering over Madison Street. The front wing, which presented the theater to the city, was studded with broad windows, as if it were an office building. The structure as a whole had an ambiguous appearance; each floor having a slightly different plan. The box-like structure was reassuringly unified by a top story with rounded corners and cornice. Below, however, an undulating volume was carved by two deep recesses partially occupied by balconies. On the third through sixth floors, this created three octagonal towers cut off below by a two-story, arched portico, and above by the top story and cornice.

The heterogeneous whole suggests the fascination with the "ugly" that some have attributed to the architecture of Furness. Indeed, the depiction of the building's surroundings and rear wing in the sketch suggest the urban context that must have existed at the time of the theater's opening. Clearly, it stood in the heart of a tough city built in haste in a sea of mud. Every structure expresses both its determination to exist and its struggle for existence; perhaps, then, the building's interior was meant to charm the varied elite who attended the theater in their Sunday best, while the exterior was designed to meet the brutality of the street and the ruthless aggressiveness of its urban surroundings. The theater, then, in its expression of technological daring and mechanistic assemblage, was both uncompromising and surprising, a design that followers of the Beaux-Arts ideal would find verging on scandalous. Meanwhile, the great profusion of windows, arranged in a varied set of patterns and lit up at night, were a festive announcement—to one and all—of the wonders of color and acoustics contained inside that great shell.

This great machine of spectacle, music, light, and color, a magic treasure chest set in the heart of the crowded city, along with the other great theater project constructed in those same years (the Interstate Exposition Building, which had already been demolished by 1892, and about which very little is known) established the reputation of the firm by the end of 1885.

Along with the firm's new fame, Sullivan—closing in on thirty—had attained a public role of his own, one not yet in conflict with the office. Sullivan had become a mature man: he had read widely and well, and was an unusually articulate speaker. In his first public appearance, he would introduce a range of unusual and surprising concepts, concepts that he was able to put into a literary form well suited for his purpose. In October of 1885, at the Second Annual Convention of the Western Association of Architects in St. Louis, his speech, "Characteristics and Tendencies of American Architecture," was received as the avant-garde manifesto of a truly American architecture.

The paper that he read opened with a decidedly negative appraisal of the current architectural situation and a solemn promise. He referred to his outmoded dream of a "Minerva-like architectural splendor springing full-formed into being," before his search for "the early signs of a spontaneous architectural feeling arising in sympathy with the emotions latent or conspicuous in our people."[7] Although he did not say so explicitly, his references to the birth of a goddess without a mother is remarkable. As Sullivan went on to state that it was only in the individual that the architectural sensibility for which he was calling could be generated, it became clear to a careful reader or listener that Sullivan was comparing himself to no less a figure than the father of the gods, from whose forehead Minerva had sprung fully formed and clad in armor, bearing a spear. In the heated rush of this speech, however, his narcissism remained implicit.

In offering a diagnosis of the limitations of current architectural culture, Sullivan made use of a parallel with literary production: excessive attention to detail, timidity and awkwardness in tracing a general outline, mystification with regard to passion, the whole developed with patience, honest hard work, and diplomatic linguistic moderation—all that, he said, may be "exquisite but not virile."

As Sullivan was delivering this speech, Richardson's Marshall Field Wholesale Store was in the final stages of construction. Clearly, Sullivan

Adler & Sullivan, Leon Mannheimer
Residence, Chicago, 1884.

H. H. Richardson, Marshall Field
Wholesale Store, Chicago, 1885–87.

was not capable of teaching Richardson, the master of utterly masculine monumentalism, a lesson in virility. And yet he seemed to go well beyond Richardson in his criticism of so many architects' reliance upon the dead-weight of artistic tradition and his call for more brains and more soul in design. Sullivan, perhaps in reference to Furness and Root, wrote that even the receiving and assimilating of "fresh impressions, reaching new conclusions," was insufficient: "This romanticism is, in the main, also exquisite but not virile." What did Sullivan mean by virility? "Creative power." And so he returned to his childlike idea of power; but this time his idea, linked

to architectural language, took on a special significance. Now, he called for the development of "a plastic alphabet by means of which to identify our beliefs." This idea of an alphabet, which perhaps could be described as an architectural vocabulary, is particularly significant. He wrote: "The formation of an alphabet, and the simplest combinations of its terms, are matters of much importance" in which we are hindered only by excessively complex reasoning.

Sullivan acknowledged that the businessmen of the day knew perfectly well how tough and single-minded one needed to be in order to attain power, the paths to which were "crude and harsh as to be

*Adler & Sullivan, Solomon
Blumenfeld Flats, Chicago, 1884
(since demolished)*

*Ann Halsted Residence, Chicago,
1883*

*Max M. Rothschild Flats, Chicago,
1883 (since demolished).*

prophetic overtones, charged by the stunning and slightly obsessive flavor of his exquisite ornamental designs. In the throes of inspiration, Sullivan concluded:

> Then, in the affluence of time, when a rich burden of aspiring verdure may flourish in the undulating fields of thought, wrought into fertility through the bounty of nature and the energy of the race, the mellowed spontaneity of a national style reaching its full and perfect fruition shall have come from out the very treasury of nature.[8]

Is it possible to gain a clearer understanding of these words by comparing them with the architectural work he did at the same time?

We have already seen—in Sullivan's experimentation in the series of commercial buildings designed and built in the early 1880s—a vigorous body of work in which he incorporated and juxtaposed, in his buildings, elements that could be repeated with elements that were autonomous, often leading to surprising visual results. There was, however, another area of experimentation in which Sullivan expressed his intent to establish a vocabulary of architectural terms in a spontaneous and powerful language packed with deep meaning but also endowed with a great communicative immediacy. This area of endeavor concerned the residence, a field of design in which the studio had engaged right from the very start, but which began to take on particular importance—and that, to the best of our understanding, through the direct involvement of Sullivan—from 1884 on.

The Max Rothschild Flats of 1883 appear decidedly sober and regular, with a broad alternating rhythm of arches and windows, and a general solidity and unity typical of Adler. But the Leon Mannheimer Residence and the Solomon Blumenfeld Flats (1884) opened a whole new direction, perhaps the opposite direction, and marked the beginning of a new design program, long overlooked by architectural historians, to which close attention must be devoted. It should be stated that the two latter examples are small buildings: single-family dwellings—row houses—of the common

revolting to a refined taste . . . but once subtilized, flushed with emotion and guided by clear insight, it is a worker of miracles." Indeed, this talk should be taken as indicative of a well defined professional and cultural program whose aspects already appear in his design work.

He continued, "Ideal thought and effective action should so compose the vital substance of our works that they may live, with us and after us, as a record of our fitness, and a memorial of the good we may have done." The talk culminated in a finale with

Adler & Sullivan, Ann Halsted Flats,
Chicago, 1884–85, main elevation,
view of street façade, floor plans.

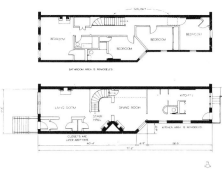

two-story typology, in which the narrow front corresponds to a deep residential section. In the small rectangle of these façades, we can see the articulated organism of dwellings of considerable prestige, greatly differentiated in use and in the hierarchy of the interior rooms. And it is natural to attribute to Sullivan's creativity so intense a concentration of compositional commitment to the narrow and limited spaces found in these two buildings.

The necessarily asymmetrical organization of the floor plan—arranged in consideration of whether rooms were to be used in day or night—results in an equally sharp differentiation in the elements and finishing materials. What emerges is a breakdown of the façade into four parts, differing in size and purpose, but also decidedly different in terms of formal typology: bay window for the living room, door with stoop for the entrance, a mullioned window for the bedroom, and so on, with the individ-

ualization of each element in an intentionally discontinuous yet rhythmic montage of different parts, each endowed with considerable autonomy.

This design approach—not found in the Ann Halsted Flats (1884–85), the only group in this series to have survived, but where Sullivan instead sought continuity—recalls a medievalist's approach to architectural research, and is in any case decidedly not classical. This method may be linked to the linguistic ferocity of Furness, but it must chiefly be assigned to Sullivan's programmatic commitment to invent a new theoretical vocabulary. One can clearly sense that Sullivan has set himself up, as an evidently enlightened individual, to serve as a trailblazer—in the name of "creative power"—on the road to the foundation of a masculine and authentically American architecture.

1. Louis H. Sullivan, *The Autobiography of an Idea* (American Institute of Architects, 1924; reprint, New York: Dover, 1956), 252.

2. Baumann was the author of *A Theory of Isolated Pier Foundation* (1873); see Robert Twombly, *Louis Sullivan: His Life and Work* (Chicago: University of Chicago Press, 1986), 93.

3. Louis H. Sullivan, "Development of Construction" (1916), in *Louis Sullivan: The Public Papers*, ed. Robert Twombly (Chicago: University of Chicago Press, 1988), 211ff.

4. Dankmar Adler, *Autobiography* (unpublished manuscript), see Robert Twombly, *Louis Sullivan: His Life and Work* (Chicago: University of Chicago Press, 1986), 141.

5. Louis H. Sullivan, as cited in Twombly, *Life and Work*, 145.

6. C. H. Blackall, as cited in Twombly, *Life and Work*, 151.

7. Louis H. Sullivan, "Characteristics and Tendencies of American Architecture" (1885), in *Public Papers*, 3.

8. Ibid., 6–8. "Then, in the affluence of time, when a rich burden of aspiring verdure may flourish in the undulating fields of thought, wrought into fertility through the bounty of nature and the energy of the race, the mellowed spontaneity of a national style reaching its full and perfect fruition shall have come from out of the very treasury of nature."

A notable group of Chicago tycoons, among them Ferdinand Peck, an illustrious philanthropist, Nathaniel Fairbank, a major pipe manufacturer, Richard T. Crane, and other leading businessmen of the city, needed a large building to house the Chicago Opera Festival. In late 1884 they had decided to renovate the Interstate Exposition Building, an immense structure that had been built on prestigious lakefront territory back in 1873, and had been pleased with the results of that commission, granted to the office of Adler & Sullivan. Thus when the same group of clients founded the Auditorium Association on 8 December 1886, with the stated purpose of constructing an immense $3.2 million building, Adler & Sullivan immediately offered its services. This, after all, promised to be the most noteworthy architectural project that was likely to materialize anywhere in the Midwest in the foreseeable future. The choice of architect was an interesting one, as one member of the committee of businessmen was none other than Martin Ryerson, already one of the firm's best clients. But the committee, chaired by Peck, also had as members figures like Marshall Field and George Pullman, each of whom had his own favorite architect; but Richardson, the personal architect of Marshall Field, happened to die that year, leaving only Solon Beman, who had built the Pullman Building three years previously. None of the competing architects, however, had a resume rich enough in the construction of theaters and multipurpose buildings to compete with that of the architects of the McVicker's Theater.

The proposed project was extraordinary: it was to endow Chicago with the most costly building in America, as well as the tallest (seventeen stories) and the heaviest (110,000 tons). The theater would seat 4,200 people, second only to La Scala in Milan; there would be a four-hundred-room hotel, and 136 offices and retail stores. The enormous obstacles in purchasing the vast lakefront lot needed—some of the most valuable real estate in the city—were overcome by dint of the power of the managing committee. The firm of Adler & Sullivan was immediately hired to provide a number of preliminary sketches, which Sullivan completed in December.

Concerning the quality of these drawings—which are known as two "preliminary schemes," and which apparently left the Board of Directors with some degree of skepticism, especially with respect to Sullivan's youth—historians have expressed implicit reservations, often without adequate arguments to support their disapproval. In general, the improvement in quality that unquestionably appeared between these "preliminary schemes" and the final construction is attributed to the decisive influence (even Hugh Morrison describes it as such) of the Marshall Field Wholesale Store, designed and built by Richardson. The store opened in early 1887, coinciding with the completion of the main blueprints for the Auditorium.

It would seem, however, that a more thorough scrutiny of the available documentation is required concerning the undoubtedly operative and significant relationship between Sullivan and the great architect from the East. Beginning in early 1885, Richardson was in Chicago for the construction of the major residences of John Glessner and Franklin MacVeagh, as well as for the construction of the Marshall Field building. Blueprints for this latter project were completed by the end of the year, and construction began immediately, finishing at the beginning of 1887; thus, at the end of 1886, when Sullivan presented his first two designs for the Auditorium, the store was almost completed. In any case, every architect in Chicago, and Sullivan in particular, had been familiar with the final plans for the store for a year; moreover, Richardson, who had been ill since March, died at the age of forty-eight in April, leaving others to finish the construction, which was faithful in every detail to his blueprints. Sullivan was certainly influenced by this project, but not, as some have said, in the period between the early, unsatisfactory designs and the final project. Rather, it would seem that the great model of the Marshall Field department store had already been weighing like a mighty boulder for some time on the intricate methodological fabric that Sullivan had been weaving, both experimentally in his practice and theoretically even in his early projects and essays. If this was in fact the case, then a radical revision of the influ-

Adler & Sullivan, partial renovation of the Interstate Exposition Building on behalf of the Chicago Opera Festival, Chicago, 1885 (since demolished), design sketch and view of the auditorium.

ence exerted by that project and of the quality of the final result is necessary.

In effect, the approach that Sullivan was developing was quite innovative, and not easily understood by his contemporaries. It pursued an unprecedented synthesis of daring research on architectural syntax—which bordered on the iconoclastic, as it did in the work of Furness—with an unqualified acceptance of the latest developments in production and technology. This was a combination that part of the establishment had difficulty understanding, and therefore found suspect—hence the skepticism of the Board of Directors. It was also a difficult combination to maintain in the context of the colossal Auditorium project, which was a tremendous professional opportunity and the challenge of a lifetime. It is therefore necessary to attempt to understand the effect and influence that Richardson's great project had on Sullivan's work by exploring the intellectual tension that engulfed Sullivan on the verge of this historic opportunity, which came at a crucial juncture in the development of his own explicit cultural program, incomprehensible though it was to most.

With Marshall Field, Richardson's work reached its own definitive culmination in the triumphal expression of a great sacrosanct commercial building. Roman classicism and a laissez-faire aesthetic were expertly counterposed, with classicism invoking the eternalizing aspect of ritual in which language, precisely because it is little diversified and strongly conventional, served as a sort of iron-clad rule, both defining and definitive. Marshall Field was thus a cumbersome model, one that could hardly fail to cast a mighty shadow over an ardent search for an indigenous architectural language—intentionally open and non-conformist—undertaken by Chicago architects, most of all by Sullivan himself. Moreover, Sullivan found himself answerable to a review committee made up of extremely powerful men who were equally unsure of themselves in this matter, and who were certainly not amenable to cultural adventures of any sort, since it was their own capital that was at risk.

The powerful programmatic statement embodied in the Marshall Field department store was

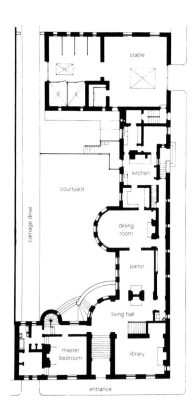

underscored by the triumphant reception it received upon its opening. This left very little space for either of the directions being pursued by Sullivan in his research: neither that of creative freedom inspired by the poets of the culture of the self—by the transcendentalists, by the audacious work done by Furness—nor that of total acceptance of new modes of production and technology, assimilated to the model of Darwinian evolution. As Sullivan sought out a middle ground between his own work and the great model that stood before him, which was surely recommended to him frequently by the entire Board of Directors (not only by Marshall Field), he discovered the work of Root. He had before his eyes such recently built projects as the Atkinson Topeka & Santa Fe General Office Building and, along La Salle Street, the Insurance Exchange Building, the Commerce Building, and, lastly, the huge Rookery, in which Burnham & Root had their studio. All of these buildings were excellent pieces of architecture, and the inspiration of Richardson—particularly evident

in the homes built by Root, such as the Edward E. Ayer House—can be seen clearly in the frequent use of large arches on buildings, mimicking Roman aqueducts and thus breaking up the monotony of the windows, as well as in the use of a central, arched portal framed by ashlar blocks, first used by Richardson in the North Easton Library of 1877–78.

It was these projects by Root—much more than Richardson's Marshall Field Store, which was further from his ambitious research—that Sullivan had in mind when he sat down to design the most important project of his life, in the space of a few days. Both sketches that he produced feature arches covering the body of the enormous structure; these arches were also clearly evident on the recently completed Studebaker Building on the lakefront. Also distinctive of the style of Root—and that of Richardson—was the attic with small, regularly-spaced rectangular windows; Sullivan had always opted for more elaborate formal inventions in the

Solon S. Beman, Pullman Building,
Chicago, 1880, courtyard detail, and
elevation.

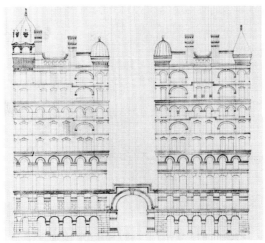

past. And the great street-level portal in the form of a large centered arch, which was quite common in the buildings designed by Root, was repeated over and over again in the two sketches by Sullivan, punctuating the base of the building.

The tower, which was to mark the entrance to the theater, rose only slightly in the first sketch, to a height of ten stories, and to a height of twelve stories in the second. The most evident difference between the two sketches, however, seems to be a matter of style: in the first version, there are steeply pitched roofs and mansards, both in the main block and in the tower, giving the building a distinctly Middle-European appearance, which would have been decidedly out of place in Chicago; in the second version, the roof has disappeared, and the tower—now taller and bolder, appearing as a smooth rectangular volume—is capped by a curious pyramidal top. Both versions of the tower—with mansard and pyramid tops—suggest it is reaching for maximum height.

A careful observation of the drawings reveals the presence of voids containing loggias with large architraves over the entry portals; as autonomous elements attached to the building, these constitute the only evidence of Sullivan's typical experimentation with building façades. The loggias are more pronounced in the second drawing; one extends over the three-arched entry that faces the street directly below the tower, and the other extends over the other three-arched entry (here the three apertures are much more widely spaced than they are under the tower) marking the center of the lakefront façade.

The Board of Directors decided to name an outside expert to judge the project; they settled on William R. Ware, who had been Sullivan's professor at MIT and was now the director of the Columbia University Department of Architecture. Was this just luck, or was the selection guided by a friendly hand? In any case, after looking over the drawings, Ware suggested a few minor modifications to simplify and unify the structure, and otherwise expressed great admiration for Sullivan's work. All the same, the Board of Directors remained uncertain, and—once Ware's modifications had been incorporated—

approved the project "in the main,"[1] still reserving the right to approve each step of the design.

Peck, who had actually instigated the project, was of the opinion that all future modifications in the plans should move "in the direction of severe treatment."[2] Twombly stresses that Adler himself expressed a certain disappointment regarding the austerity of the design of the exterior of the building; the directive for this severe style Twombly connected with the influence of Richardson's great department store building. It is particularly surprising that the most distinctly conservative and nineteenth-century aspect of the design of the Auditorium Building—the fact that the structure extends to the boundaries of its rectangular lot, its palatial appearance concealing the irregular shape of the theater within—has never been thoroughly studied by architectural critics or scholars. Certainly, there were economic reasons for choosing a traditional solution, as it took full advantage of the full length and height of the lot on all sides. And yet one would expect that an innovator like Sullivan, who

was a functionalist and saw every building as an organic whole, might have attempted to introduce on the exterior of the structure at least one element that interrupted the smooth continuity of the façades, as a reference to the complex spatial structure enclosed within. This sort of innovative approach can in fact be seen, if still in an embryonic form, in the earlier McVicker's Theater.

Yet neither Sullivan nor Adler seemed to consider this problem of the relationship between form and function in the Auditorium project. In terms of the function and concept of the theater, they limited themselves to developing, perhaps in an overstated way, the architecture of the interiors. This distinction between exterior and interior, which was perhaps unavoidable for a variety of reasons, can, for that matter, be found in the theaters that Adler and Sullivan had built previously, including the McVicker's Theater. The contrast reached a new level in the Auditorium—the difference between the austere gray exterior façade and the painstaking spatial and chromatic layout of the interior is so great

*Burnham & Root, Rookery Building,
Chicago, 1886–87, elevation, floor
plans, and exterior view.*

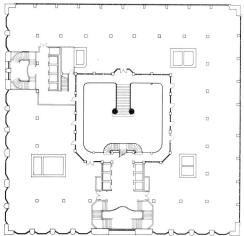

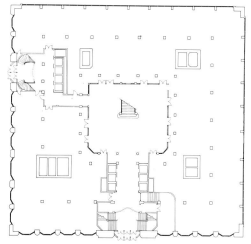

that it gives the impression of looking at two separate works of architecture, juxtaposed. It is hard to imagine how Sullivan reconciled this schizophrenic effect.

However, after decisions had been made and work was underway, all doubt was abandoned; minor reservations were set aside once the impressive efficiency of the builders became evident. The vast construction site began to require technological inventions, formal contrivances, and human energies to cope with difficulties such as a challenging set of problems with the foundations, the daring and intricate floor framing system, the completion of the interior spaces, and the exceedingly painstaking array of finishes on both interior and exterior.

Most of the construction was finished over the course of the year 1887, and by Christmas, it was announced that the great auditorium would be open in time for the national conventions of the Democratic and Republican parties, to be held the following summer. This was a promise that had to be kept, as it placed the Auditorium Building in the spotlight of national attention as a symbol of municipal progress.

The incredible push to complete the building, which drew on all the resources of a city experiencing enormous growth, can be compared with a great project completed in New York just five years prior—the Brooklyn Bridge—not to mention the Eiffel Tower, being built in Paris at almost the same time. As was the case in these vast collective endeavors (and as is always the case in major urban constructions), this effort had its costs. Among them was a high number of deaths, a fact usually kept as quiet as possible. Public notice was drawn to this statistic, however, by a bad accident that occurred at the end of March 1888; as a result, measures were taken to introduce a form of workman's compensation, intended to cushion the fear of on-the-job hazards.[3]

The office of Adler & Sullivan also had to achieve a major increase in productivity; accordingly, the staff rose to thirty. For the entire initial phase of the project, the two chief architects had an equal amount of work, as each had his own responsibilities. When the finishings were being applied in the final phase of construction, however, the incredible

45

quantity of decorative detail and interior fittings forced Sullivan to work long, intense hours. It was during this phase of work that the twenty-year-old Frank Lloyd Wright first made his appearance, coming from the office of Joseph Silsbee. Because of Wright's ready and flexible creativity, he was soon made Sullivan's direct assistant in the preparation of the building's ornamentation.

Thus a complex relationship began in the Borden Block studio—and soon continued in the tower of the Auditorium Building—between two major figures in the history of architecture. Just what their working relationship consisted of, at the start, is impossible to say; for an understanding of their rapport, it is necessary to rely on the later writings of Frank Lloyd Wright. In his vast literary production Sullivan mentioned his young associate infrequently. Wright's job upon entry into the studio was limited to developing the sketches that Sullivan produced for decorative finishings. Wright later wrote that, when asked by Sullivan to develop a detail, he would insert a geometric design that was more architectural and less sentimental than his master's floral style.[4] The objectivity of his recollection is unreliable, however, as it was surely affected by the gradual deterioration of their relationship. Even the difference in age between Wright and his *"Lieber Meister,"* which Wright gave as fifteen years, was inflated by four years. And yet Wright unquestionably had an influence upon his employer, given the mighty personality of the former and the emotional sensitivity of the latter. That influence can be best evaluated in the work that followed the design of the Auditorium.

In June of 1888, the Auditorium Building hosted the Republican National Convention, as planned; the Democrats, however, had chosen to hold their convention in St. Louis. The success of the Republican event made up for any regrets about the failure of hosting twin conventions. The building, however, was still not quite finished; indeed, final construction went on through the first few months of 1889, and other work had to be done the following year as well. The tower, in particular, was a source of problems, largely due to the courageous but slightly irresponsible decision made by the Board of Directors, and encouraged by Sullivan, to make it seventeen stories

Auditorium Building: east elevation,
angled view of elevation with tower,
and view from the south.

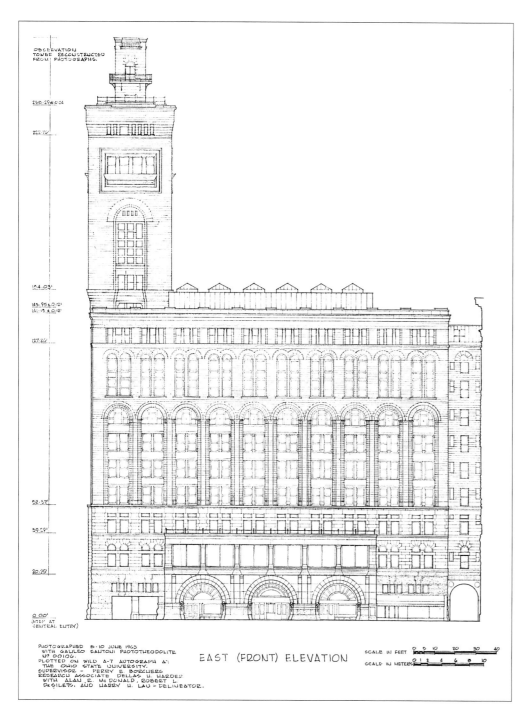

EAST (FRONT) ELEVATION

tall. When Adler returned from Europe, where he had spent the summer of 1888 touring large theaters and auditoriums, he was confronted by a virtually insoluble problem of static engineering—an extra 1,200 tons bearing down upon his carefully calculated foundations.

The difficulty of situating the tower on the unsteady soil of Chicago had, in fact, been the focus of Adler's attention from the beginning. The chief problem, even in the original project, had been the increase in weight that would bear down on the structural block from the tower that loomed above it. The added load, thrusting down upon the finished structure, would produce dangerous differentiated stresses in what had been a stable static equation. To prevent this, Adler hit upon the ingenious solution of adding an artificial preliminary load made of brick and iron upon the foundation; this load corresponded, in weight and bearing, to the load that would be produced by the raised section of the tower. This extra load would, of course, be removed gradually and progressively as the tower rose above the building.

Thus the decision to add an extra story to the tower—a source of pride for the clients and an opportunity for Sullivan to endow the building with greater formal independence and representative power—became, for a refined and conscientious structural engineer like Adler, a sort of betrayal: it was a tremendous problem, which produced a series of difficulties over the years, and was a trying experience for Adler's personality. It is not unlikely that the differences between the two architects, which had always existed, became an increasing motive for separation from this point forward.

All that, however, came later; in the meanwhile, success was ensured. Adler himself was triumphant, universally recognized as a genius of acoustical engineering for his structural and spatial solutions to the theater. There, he had designed the ceiling with a series of cross arches, emulating a model that had already been tested in the Interstate Exposition Building. The hall was thus transformed into something similar to a giant sounding instrument, comparable to the natural structure of a seashell or a human throat. Sullivan had also succeeded: he was

Floor plan and longitudinal section of the auditorium.

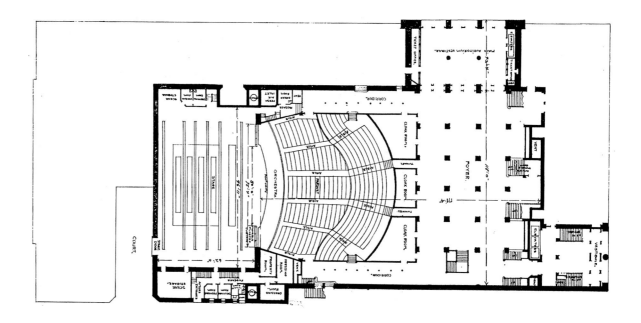

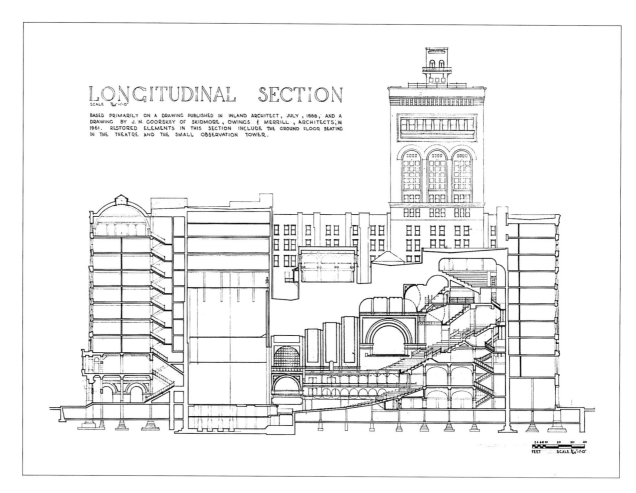

LONGITUDINAL SECTION
SCALE 1/32"=1'-0"

BASED PRIMARILY ON A DRAWING PUBLISHED IN INLAND ARCHITECT, JULY, 1888, AND A
DRAWING BY J. N. GOORSKEY OF SKIDMORE, OWINGS & MERRILL, ARCHITECTS, IN
1961. RESTORED ELEMENTS IN THIS SECTION INCLUDE THE GROUND FLOOR SEATING
IN THE THEATRE AND THE SMALL OBSERVATION TOWER.

shown to be a true master of ornamental and chromatic design, providing an unexpected and deeply moving aesthetic spectacle for the building's visitors. And precisely midway between the virtuoso engineering and the artistic conception was the electric lighting system, which made use of a vast number of low-voltage light bulbs.

The descriptions of the interiors are diverse and detailed, and are generally extremely positive. One novelty was the polychrome flooring: 250 square meters of marble mosaic that was the painstaking work of Italian craftsmen. The faux-marble columns in the lobby were also the product of Italian masters. The reception desk of the hotel was particularly impressive, with its dominant green and gold color scheme; the bar on the Congress Street side, too, was striking, as it was decorated in brown tones, ranging from the light hues of beer to the dark hues of cognac, and rich bronze friezes. Lastly, a generous array of elevators allowed people to move around the building quickly, and also made it possible to place the main dining room on the tenth floor, where a roof garden overlooked a panoramic view of the lake.

Such opulent hedonism was not in keeping, however, with the deep theoretical concerns that emerged in all of Sullivan's public speeches. These speeches became more frequent in the first few months of 1887, a time of intense work on the drawings for the Auditorium, which was already under construction. Before proceeding to a comparative analysis of the building itself and Sullivan's writings from the same period, however, it is important to examine the often-overlooked issue of the building's exterior, as its architectonic identity (as already noted) appears so at odds with the effect produced on the interior.

This stone colossus, when casually viewed as part of the sequence of prestigious façades lining the lakefront, or as a massive presence overlooking Congress Street, presents itself as gray, composed, and monumental. When observed more carefully, however, the building shows surprising harmonies of proportion and measure; a more penetrating critical analysis reveals refined and subtle ambiguities that convey an understated complexity. The motif of

Ornamental detail designed by Frank Lloyd Wright for the uprights of the railings of the hotel and theater of the Auditorium Building, pencil on paper, 9.6 x 8 in.; view of the main entrance.

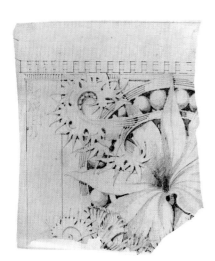

*Drawing of detail (1963 reconstruc-
tion) and view of the stairway of the
hotel.*

HOTEL LOBBY

repeating flattened arches dominates the middle section, from the fourth to the seventh floors; the height of this zone is precisely equal to that of the bottom three floors. Although this central band is unified, the three levels of the base are distinguished by three separate vocabularies and three shades of gray. Further up, the top section is divided into two zones: the lower, comprising the eighth and ninth floors (corresponding to one-half the height of the middle section) features a continuous motif of double openings in the form of simple double-hung windows. The attic, on the other hand, features small rectangular windows in groups of three, aligning with the pattern of the arches below. There is no mighty cornice above this; only an unadorned parapet, which serves, much as in the Marshall Field Building, as a frieze under the building roof.

The structure is, however, substantially different from Richardson's work, in a way that is only subconsciously evident unless it is specifically sought out. There is a rejection of symmetry in the clearly conscious decision to break up the lakefront façade into ten modules—that is to say, into an even number of apertures. This approach, which Vitruvius would have rejected, is repeated on the Congress Street façade, but with twenty modules. Richardson, with his groupings of thirteen and seven arches, kept the main opening on the central axis on both sides, thus conforming with traditional precedent and with established cultural norms.

Sullivan, instead, was looking for that slight margin of ambiguity that might pass unobserved by most people, but that engenders a subtle kind of disorientation through the emergence of almost imperceptible contradictions. In fact, the solid structure on the central axis dominates the entire building, except at street level where the three portals occupy six modules. This places the main arch in a central position, consistent with tradition but in contrast with the overall architectural pattern. This arch, like the other two, is topped by a pilaster above the keystone.

Such an observation should not be considered purely the product of an excessively attentive critical analysis. Due to his compositional approach, in fact, Sullivan was able to endow the triple-arched entry (a fairly cumbersome piece of architecture) with a distinct autonomy from the rest of the elevation and the structure. In this manner, he created the effect of montage on the juxtaposition between portal and building proper. As was already visible in his smaller projects, this was one of the most positive goals of his design research; the first two preparatory drawings featured even more pronounced versions of this juxtaposition.

On the façade overlooking Congress Street, it is the tower itself that confounds all efforts to attain symmetry. Looming over the mass of the structure, the tower stands atop the entrance to the theater, attaching itself to the façade of the building by means of two broad pilaster strips that break up the regular rhythm of the façade. This tower—which underwent a restoration of its exterior after World War II—is fascinating due to its severity, which is anti-classical but also anti-Romantic due to its the total absence of medieval motifs. This severity is made elegant by the slight tapering of the highest portion of the shaft, which is set directly above the deep indentations of the window openings, punctuated by short columns on all four sides. It provided an eminent platform from which the firm of Adler & Sullivan could metaphorically dominate the city and the region; the firm's offices were installed on the highest floor of the tower even before final work on the building was complete.

The overall result of Sullivan's work on the Auditorium Building could no longer be considered in any manner Richardsonian. Nor did the similarities to Root's work, found in the two initial designs, survive in the finished building in any recognizable form, save perhaps in the system of archways, which were, however, not splayed in Root's creations of the time (though we do find a certain similarity in the Burlington & Quincy General Office Building of 1882–83). Sullivan seemed to be attempting to establish a certain distance from Root in this period. He had an opportunity to do so at a meeting of the Illinois State Association of Architects, in March 1887; the subject was "What Are the Present Tendencies of Architectural Design in America?" Sullivan responded harshly to the position, expressed by Root

Drawing of detail (1963 reconstruction) and view of an entrance hall of the Auditorium Building.

THEATRE LOBBY

Drawing for a modillion of the Auditorium Building, pencil, 7.8 x 4 in., interior view.

and others, that architectural style was the product of an adaptation of historical tradition to contemporary situations, saying, "I do not believe the origin of style is outside, but within ourselves, and the man who has not the impulse within him will not have the style."[5]

This was the theoretical point of view that Sullivan was to express with increasing frequency and peremptory style from this period on. This idea of architectural style was reiterated and further developed at a symposium held by the same association, in an essay entitled, "What is the Just Subordination, in Architectural Design, of Details to Mass?"[6] Sullivan did so, moreover, with a notable display of erudition, which may best serve as a measure of the critical depth of his thought. Despite limitations imposed by his socio-cultural context, he explored the problem of architectural design, beginning with a critique of the dry ingenuity of the title of the symposium. He stated that an answer to such a poorly-conceived question could not be formulated in abstract terms, but would at the very least require some additional context, "today and here in Chicago." He rejected, moreover, the word "subordination," preferring the term "differentiation," "because this word symbolizes to my mind an idea which is very congenial to it, namely, that of an expansive and rhythmic growth, in a building, of a single, germinal impulse or idea, which shall permeate the mass and its every detail with the same spirit . . ." He further illustrated this

*View of the columns and drawing of
the capital, frieze, and elevation of the
hotel dining room.*

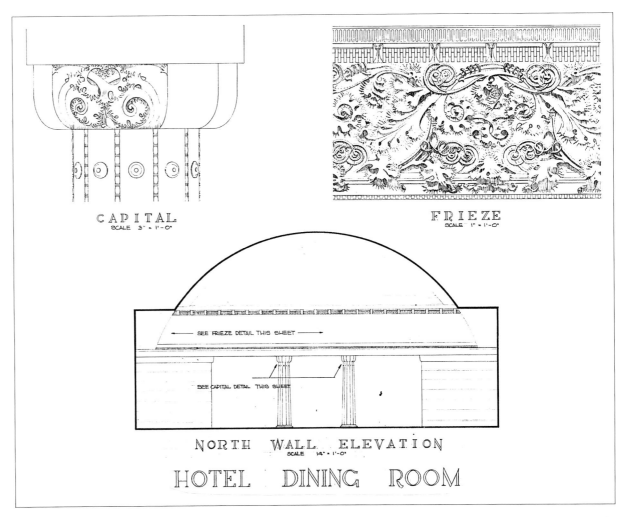

concept, which proved to be quite similar to organic thought, through the metaphor of the relationship between a tree and its leaves.

From this point, Sullivan pretentiously continued, airing increasingly lofty platitudes, with which he was certainly able to impress an audience more naive than he. "I value spiritual results only. I say spiritual results precede all other results, and indicate them. . . . I say present theories of art are vani-ty. I say all past and future theories of art were and will be vanity. . . . The soul [is] the only permanent link between the finite and the infinite. On this rock I would stand. . . ."[7] His mind had taken flight; his tone was now messianic. Upon this rock, he seems to be saying, I will build my Church: "This is why I say that contemplation of nature and humanity is the only source of inspiration."

1. Robert Twombly, *Louis Sullivan: His Life and Work* (Chicago: University of Chicago Press, 1986), 167.
2. Ibid., 168.
3. Ibid., 174.
4. Cited in Italian edition of Sullivan's autobiography, *Autobiografia di un'idea* (Rome: Officina, 1970), 41, note 58.
5. Louis H. Sullivan, "What are the Present Tendencies of Architectural Design in America?" *Inland Architect and News Record*, 9 March 1887; reprinted in Louis H. Sullivan, *Louis Sullivan: The Public Papers*, ed. Robert Twombly (Chicago: University of Chicago Press, 1988), 28ff.
6. Louis H. Sullivan, "What is the Just Subordination, in Architectural Design, of Details to Mass?" (1887); reprinted in Sullivan, *Public Papers*, 29ff.
7. Ibid., 33–34.

Hésler, Chicago

It is possible to understand Sullivan's precise intentions at this time through a comparative analysis of his projects and writings, especially the writings done prior to his formulation of the famous slogan, "form follows function" in 1896. Sullivan, now in his thirties and enjoying some professional success, was given the role of trailblazer on the unexplored frontiers of a new architecture by a young and impetuous American society. Indeed, he seemed to stop searching the intellectual world for a model, or a series of models, to follow and began instead an attempt to establish himself in this position. His primary objective, especially from the Auditorium Building onward, increasingly became that of imposing his own uniqueness, of distinguishing himself—often polemically—from all others.

In the decoration of the McVicker's Theater, Sullivan was seeking a design as free as possible from the invasive pragmatism that so dominated the American marketplace, specifically in American construction and manufacturing. Design was, moreover, the field that best lent itself to a search for an architectural language unhampered by practical demands; that was best suited to an expression of the deepest and most personal values of the ego.

"Ah, that supreme erotic adventure of the mind that was his fascinating ornament," wrote Wright, with a hint of sarcasm, in his autobiography.[1] Referring to Sullivan's demanding essay on inspiration, Wright spoke of "howling at the moon." Twombly himself admits that when, in November 1886, Sullivan read this dull but somehow inspired essay before the third convention of the Western Association of Architects, the response must have been fairly discouraging; indeed, from that day on, Sullivan was never asked to address the association again.[2] Sullivan held fast, however, to his hard-won independence. "The sensations of a true artist are always complex," he wrote in "The Artistic Use of the Imagination" (1889), "for to susceptibility of the senses, he adds susceptibility of the heart. Every object, therefore, that he regards, will give him a double sensation, specifically the sensual and the emotional."[3] He seems to have been indifferent to or even gratified by the hail of criticism that was raining down upon him; he was even censured (either

explicitly or implicitly) by those who were close to him—Adler, that is, since Wright did not yet dare to enter the debate.

The accusation was probably always the same: that Sullivan was fleeing reality, floating among the clouds of emotion and feeling. Being isolated and misunderstood, however, did not frighten him: his thoughts, translated into verbal and graphic terms in his writings and ornamentation, expressed a great determination toward limitless exploration. This undoubtedly fascinated those who wished to follow safer and faster paths, but at the same time it appeared to them to be excessive. One of those who found this to be the case was Wright, who boasted that he had introduced into sketches by Sullivan that he felt were too sensuous a number of geometric features, features that were "more architectonic"—that is, more constructively defined.

"But, lest you should tend to consider this sort of writing too metaphysical, too fine-spun, too unpractical—ornamental rather than useful...Do I understand that my poetic web has caught your practical fly?"[4] Perhaps here Sullivan was only putting on a display of self-confidence. This loudly-proclaimed diversity began to offend his peers and generated a certain indifference and even suspicion. More explicit suspicions begin to appear in the writings of more recent historians, who do not hesitate to allude to a latent homosexuality[5] or a tendency toward autoeroticism.[6] These, are, however, merely interpretative shortcuts. They simply gloss over—with gross simplification—a long, arduous, and important period, leaving many of its most interesting aspects unexamined. And they ultimately reject the acceptance of complexity that Sullivan used as his own personal foundation.

Far more subtle and complex critical tools are needed to analyze Sullivan's writings and work. In particular, we should consider his essay entitled "Style," read to the Chicago Architectural Sketch Club in April 1888, and published in May in *Inland Architect and News Record.*[7] This essay should be reconsidered, in particular, with an eye to the way in which Sullivan seems to explore with considerable sophistication what were then only partially understood linguistic mechanisms.

opposite: Sullivan in 1890

below: Adler & Sullivan, second remodeling of the J. H.
McVicker's Theater, Chicago, 1890–91 (demolished in
1925), longitudinal section, detail of the auditorium hall,
and drawing of the foyer.

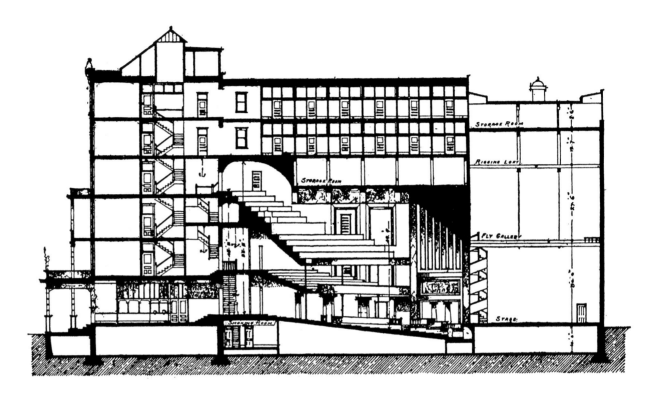

*Adler & Sullivan, second renovation
of the J. H. McVicker's Theater,
Chicago, 1890–91, ornamental design
for the molding (dated 27 January
1891), pencil, 10 x 8.5 in.*

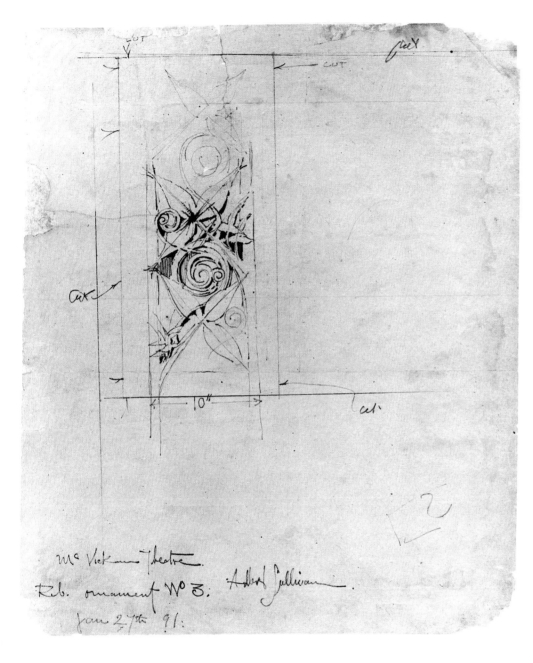

That which we call style, or rather, the word style itself, is as dubious in meaning as is any word in common use. The fact that a word is, and has been for generations, in common use, signifies that it has gathered to itself the multiple experiences of the race, and has become thereby thoroughly vitalized. Now note that the greater number of such experiences are largely independent of words, and the more subtle ones almost absolutely so, and this will suffice to indicate how true it is that one's capacity to interpret the meaning of a word, to perceive its obscure but real significance, is dependent upon the richness of his life experience within the domain of feeling that the word has come to symbolize.[8]

Having thus broken down all established cultural conventions for his listeners, Sullivan went on to postulate his admittedly vague prescription:

> Therefore, I counsel you, if you would seek to acquire a style that shall be individual to you, banish from your thought the word style; note closely and keenly the thing style, wherever found; and open your hearts to the essence style at all times and in all places. This is the germ. . . .
> The style is ever thus the response of the organism to the surroundings. How simple are the surroundings and experiences of a tree. How multiple are the surroundings of a man. When his eyes are opened to them, how complex become his experiences.[9]

Sullivan finally felt that he could forcefully oppose the solidity of Adler, who perfectly mirrored the existing socio-cultural environment. Any criticism thrown at his work, moreover, simply bounced harmlessly off Sullivan's theory of complexity. In a certain sense, he used this idea of complexity as a "mantle of fog," as Perseus did to fight off monsters. And yet one might also refer to a "magic cap . . . [drawn] over our own eyes and ears," to quote Karl Marx, "so as to deny that there are any monsters."[10]

During the period in which he wrote "Style," and in which he was working hard on the interior

Adler & Sullivan, Victor Falkenau Flats, Chicago, 1888 (since demolished).

finishings of the Auditorium, Sullivan may well have thought that the worst was over. He had recovered from the period of the early 1880s, when life had been difficult in Chicago, a city on the economic frontier of a West that was finally and definitively being won. The city had undergone chaotic growth, and was a place that only a reckless and stubborn youth like Sullivan could have adopted as his home ("*This is the place for me!*"). Also over was the period of great unrest in the middle of the decade, which had been marked by the frightening and (for him) uninspiring social turmoil of the Gould Strike (1885) and the Haymarket Riot (1 May 1886). The city had subsequently experienced a phase of capitalist organization (1886–1892), which had also been difficult because it had been enforced by a harsh repression of all social conflict. For all its cruelty, this was a vital phase, one that was particularly positive for Chicago's group of major architects. Sullivan himself, for that matter, had only a partial understanding of politics, and he made no mention of any of this in his autobiography. Edelmann, with his revolutionary ideas, had a very different belief system than Sullivan; at this point Sullivan viewed labor unions as feudal organizations that distracted workers from productive activity.

The situation in Chicago at this time was far from stable, with no real balance or equilibrium between East and West, between labor and capital, or between culture and production. Contradictions were particularly evident in the building trades; Sullivan, as a member of one of the leading professional design firms, was necessarily preoccupied. And in the area of design, which he saw as architectural and thereby artistic, the passive-aggressive use of complexity, which he brandished as a privileged tool in intellectual debate, was particularly ineffectual. His problem was not so much that of dealing, in qualitative terms, with such rivals as Furness, Richardson, Root, and (soon) Wright; rather, it was a matter of dealing with such matters as labor and the organization of production.

Sullivan was not shy about assuming a prominent role in contemporary debate. In 1888, many of his public speeches had to do with the economics of the field and other purely professional matters, in

right: Adler & Sullivan, Opera House
Block, Pueblo, Colorado, 1889–90
(demolished in 1922), exterior view
and longitudinal section.

below: Design for the Opera House
Block, Seattle, Washington, 1890.

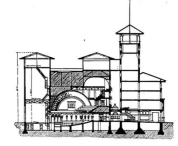

which he was clearly in favor of defending the privileges of his profession. He participated enthusiastically in the promotion of a national association,
clearly meant to function like a professional guild. In
the summer of 1888, every architect in the United
States received a letter from the executive committee
of the Illinois State Association of Architects. The
letter had been drawn up with Sullivan's help, placing him at the forefront of the formulation of a
national code of ethics designed to preserve the
independence of the profession of architecture.
From the opening statement, the letter clearly shows
that the association's central concern had to do with
the architect's financial responsibility toward various suppliers and workers in the construction trades.
Another big problem was the architect's relationship
with the client; in the general absence or ambiguous
wording of a legal document, and as a result of the
growing tension stemming from financial difficulties, clients would often sue their architects. Besides
these issues, there was the problem of difficult relationships with skilled craftsmen, with suppliers, and
with tax collectors, all of which placed architects
and designers in a constant state of risk, accompanied, of course, by a state of anxiety.

In February of 1890, Sullivan spoke up during
a highly technical discussion at the annual meeting
of the National Association of Builders.[11] He proposed drawing up contracts between architects and
specialized suppliers, and envisioned the complete
elimination of general contractors.

By the summer of 1889, the brutal pace
required to complete the details of the Auditorium
(which was finished by the beginning of 1890) as
well as various professional worries caused Sullivan
to undergo a slight nervous breakdown; he rested for
several weeks and in early 1890 decided to take a
vacation. In the same period, Adler continued to
work, though, as Sullivan himself was to note, problems with the tower were clearly causing him stress
and ultimately shortened his life.

This pause hardly seemed to slow Sullivan's
creative drive; indeed, his best work was still to
come, and can be dated to the period between his
return to work in 1890 and the great depression of

1893. One project that began before his vacation in
January 1890 should be mentioned, in particular, it
was an unusual building that the studio was working
on at the same time as the Auditorium tower: the
Opera House in Pueblo, Colorado, designed in the
summer of 1888. This building is known only from
drawings, plans, and descriptions, as it was entirely
destroyed by fire in 1922. There is a particularly
sharp division between the interior and the exterior.
From the external appearance of the building it is
impossible to predict the remarkable spaciousness of
the interior auditorium. The hall, which seated
twelve-hundred people, was notably rounded in
form, and was covered by a remarkable system of
intensely decorated vaults. It had a noteworthy balcony, the first in America to span an auditorium
without intermediate buttressing.

Attention should be directed to the exterior,
where a feature new in Sullivan's work might point
to a decisive contribution from Wright: the broad
projecting roof. This architectural element gave a
strong symbolic identity to the project, and does not
appear in Sullivan's previous works, yet it became a
standard feature in later works, often in the form of
a simplified geometric projection. The first major
project on which such a projection appears is the
Wainwright Building. Yet this characteristic element
was already used in the Pueblo Opera House, resting
atop a simple square block, sufficiently powerful to
disguise the variety in Sullivan's various round-arch
portals.

Discussing Wright's influence on the work of
Sullivan, and vice versa, or discussing the interplay
between their roles during the period of collaboration from 1888 to 1893, means confronting rather
delicate questions, ones that have been discussed
extensively and repeatedly by critics and historians,
yet have never been answered to complete satisfaction. One can either accept the version of events
offered in the autobiographies—in Wright's autobiography, primarily, as Sullivan chose to leave Wright
out of his autobiography entirely—or else be satisfied with the various conjectures that can be based
on a purely formal analysis. But restricting understanding to this latter view is a waste, given

Sullivan's superior writing skills, especially in the use of analogy and quotation (though Wright holds his own in this field as well).

According to Wright, during the period in which he worked in the studio of Adler & Sullivan, they attempted to avoid working on residences entirely, and the few houses that they were required to design fell to Wright himself. In fact, he actually did the work outside of the office. Beginning with the Victor Falkenau Flats, the very first residential structure designed after Wright joined the firm in early 1888, the roughly fifteen residential designs—including two houses for Sullivan himself, one in Chicago and one in Ocean Springs, and two for James Charnley, in the same locations—were supposedly done solely and entirely by Wright. There seems to be good reason to doubt this, as is the case with many statements in Wright's autobiography, both because of the reasons given by Twombly concerning Sullivan's explicit statement in 1890 that he himself had designed Ocean Springs College,[12] and because of the clear stylistic kinship to Richardson, rather than Wright, visible in the Falkenau Flats. There is also an obvious continuity visible in the residences produced prior to 1887—Twombly tells us that there were no fewer than forty-four of these projects[13]—as well as the similarities among the Mannheimer and Blumenfeld residences of 1884, the Halsted and Lindauer residences of 1885, and the residences designed after Wright's arrival in the studio.

Admittedly, the Falkenau Flats were presented to the client in a drawing signed by Wright, but this—as Twombly correctly points out—hardly amounts to proof of authorship. Rather, this drawing may simply add validity to Wright's admission that he habitually rendered Sullivan's sketches in a more architectural manner. The appearance of two unusual windows, whose style is rather cold and severe in comparison with the familiar traditionalism of the rest of the façade, may hint at the hand of the brilliant young apprentice, although Wright was still too young to impose his characteristic projecting roof, which was the legacy of his teacher, Joseph Silsbee. This element did appear, at later date and in

below: Floor plans for the studio of Adler & Sullivan in the tower of the Auditorium Building.

below: Adler & Sullivan, Chicago Cold Storage Warehouse, 1890, partially built

opposite: Kehilath Anshe Ma'ariv Synagogue, Chicago, 1889–90.

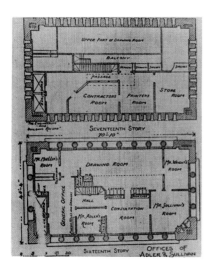

a more modern version, on the most Wrightian house produced by the studio—the James Charnley Residence (1891).

There is one interesting building, however, that displays two different formal directions typical of each of the two architects, who by this point were virtually rivals: the Seattle Opera House. Unfortunately, this design was never completed, due to financial problems that brought construction to a halt in the summer of 1890, canceling what had been slated to become the most important architectural structure in the West. The sudden collapse of this project had negative ramifications, both psychological and financial, for the studio of Adler & Sullivan.

Unlike the Pueblo Opera House, the multipurpose theater complex designed for Seattle was planned as a building with an intricately articulated exterior, which is perhaps the most important single piece of experimentation that we can attribute to Sullivan. Because all that survives is a view of the building from the square, it is difficult to speak of the relationship between exterior and interior, or of whether the theater found on the interior is evident on the exterior. What is visible from this document, however, is sufficient to judge that this was a remarkable building, lively and eclectic. The struc-

ture combined, in an adventuresome and interesting paratactic montage, the heterogeneous syntactic elements of a daring set of juxtaposed citations.

The building is dominated by its tower, which does not resemble the tower of the Auditorium in any way; as the latter was set off to one side of the underlying structural block, in a volumetrically arbitrary location. In this building the tower is instead set firmly in the heart of the lower building, interrupting its façade with determination and iconic force. Yet it is not placed in the center, where it might have hypotactically unified the overall image of the building. Rather, it demonstrates a finely calibrated asymmetry, at the center of a structure that is clearly composite in nature. The parts of the building that overlook the street are also differentiated, as they are covered partly with a steep-pitched roof, and partly with a flat roof. The same holds true for the motifs on the façade: a regular progression of rectangular windows punctuates the wings of the building that are covered with pitched roofs, while the wing that has a flat roof marked by narrow vertical loopholes.

Still, the tower is the element with the most distinct identity. It too is composite in nature, rising from a broad doorway containing three openings with archivolts; this portal rises two stories and is

extensively decorated. The central part of the tower's shaft, which cuts through the façade and rises above the eaves, is distinguished by a bay window motif. The upper shaft is, conversely, marked by a very tall tripartite mullioned window, which accentuates the tower's verticality. Finally, a massive crowning element with a loggia projecting on all four sides tops the thrusting structure, covered by a broad pitched roof that rises like a pyramidal spire.

In this strange design, the stylistic references and citations are deliberately jumbled together. References to the work of Richardson can be seen in the rough stone and in the wall pediments of the lower wings, which close off pitched roofs without eaves. A hint of the Chicago School office block can be seen in the bay windows. The tower block, with its vertical slot windows is possibly a reference to Adler's Chicago Cold Storage Exchange Warehouse. The sharply projecting roof on the tower may have been an idea of Wright. The graduated small turret in the English vernacular style contrasts sharply with the French-style classicism evident in the triumphal arch of the entrance. And the large plate glass windows on the ground floor are in an unabashedly modern style.

If this building had ever been constructed, the unusual mix of different architectural elements would probably have been toned down to some extent. Or perhaps it would have been a remarkable document revealing a crisis of architectural language, expressed in the most immediate of terms—almost a lively debate, carved in stone—and seemingly bent on demolishing all that remained of the old in order to pave the way for the new. Instead, the debate took place—in the panoramic offices installed in the highest tower in Chicago—in silent tension between the protagonists of an important chapter in the history of American architecture.

A plan of the office, drawn in 1890, shows the workspaces and thus the roles of the various staff members. Sullivan had the largest and nicest room—it was square, with a large fireplace in the corner and a row of windows overlooking Congress Street and the melancholy immensity of the lake. This room was in direct contact with the draftsmen's room, the meeting room, and Wright's studio, which

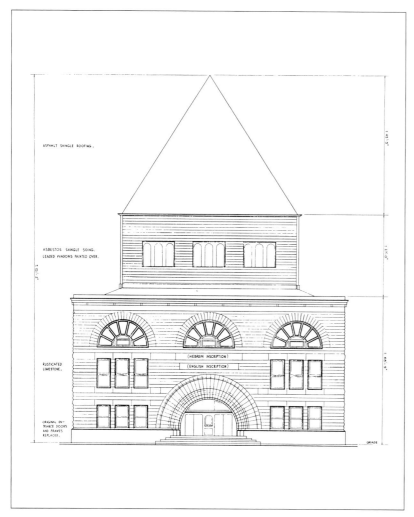

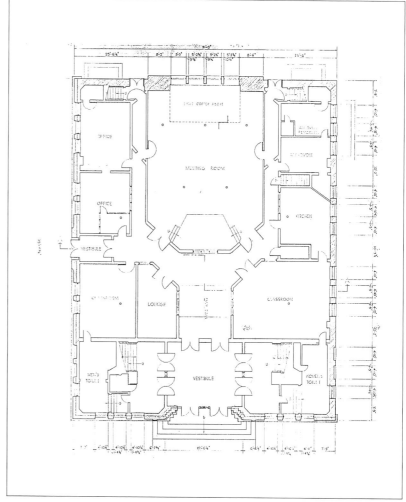

71

below: *Adler & Sullivan, Martin A. Ryerson Tomb, Chicago, 1887.*

opposite: *Carrie Elisabeth Getty Tomb, Chicago, 1890; ornamental design for the cornice (dated 16 October 1890), pencil on paper, 8.3 x 17 in., and view.*

stood at the other corner of the short side of the tower. Wright's room was smaller than Sullivan's, but it also had windows on two sides, one set overlooking the lake, and—besides being linked with the room of the chief architect—it was directly connected to the draftsmen's room. The meeting room was large, and was located on the long side of the tower, facing south, between Sullivan's and Adler's offices. Adler's office was smaller than Sullivan's, but it was close to the hall and the elevators. It was linked to the meeting room as well as the general office. The drafting room occupied the entire north side of the tower, and was twice the height of the other rooms. Above were areas for contractors, printers, and storage.

Sullivan's standing in the office was, of course, high, but the professional contacts seemed to be in Adler's hands. Relations with Wright were still quite close, but were about to deteriorate irreparably. Sullivan no longer sought compromise—at the age of thirty-four, he seemed to feel that any further discussion was useless, at least any discussion concerning who held the position of command. After the conflict over the construction of the Auditorium and the exhausting tension of the previous two years, in his projects from 1889—which seem to show some general confusion—he was able to come up with the two most impressive designs of his whole production: the Getty Tomb and the Wainwright Building.

Before discussing these two projects, however, which seemed to mark the beginning of a short period of stylistic leadership in the circle of the Chicago School, it is important to introduce another building, as it has the unique position of being the only synagogue designed by Sullivan's office. The Kehilath Anshe Ma'ariv Synagogue, a project beyond the usual interests of the office, was designed in 1889 and built in 1890. In this case, the client was Adler himself, or rather, the congregation to which Adler's family belonged. Indeed, Adler's taste is evident in the massive structure with its geometrically simple and symmetrical floor plan. The walls are punctuated by plain apertures, either repeated rectangles or semicircular arches. Both architects were probably responsible for the strongly secular character of

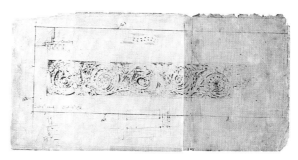

the building, which triggered some surprise and dis-agreement. In an interview, Sullivan reacted in his usual manner, rejecting all affiliations with architectural schools. He claimed the building had no historical styles, that it was the present. Sullivan's hand can be seen in the broad semicircular portal, already considered to be a Richardsonian element in Root's work; here, for the first time, it is distinctively flat-tened. There is nothing else of particular note on the exterior, save for the stone facing, elegantly joined at the corners, and the narrow, tripartite windows rising above the hall of worship.

These tripartite windows are similar to those seen in the Seattle Opera project, although in that building they were far narrower and used in the tower. But the three-fold pattern of apertures on a raised set-back block refers to another exquisitely Sullivanesque structure: the Martin Ryerson Tomb of 1887, a remarkably creative piece of work. In a certain sense, the synagogue recycles the image of that tomb on a larger scale and in a more severely geometric fashion. In this remarkable building, which paved the way for other projects by Sullivan that point in the direction of a religious definition of unity, it is possible to see a sign of the architect's emotional yearning for an identity that—as theorized in his essay "Inspiration"—did not exclude death as a vital part of life.

Sullivan's first tomb, in fact, seems to express an attempt at synthesis that is entirely lacking in his other projects. In fact, many of his other works have the opposite aim: the emphasis of contrasts. In this project, the weighty calm of the horizontal lines, repeated in broad rows across the entire structure, along with the dark construction material—finely worked gray granite from Quincy and blue marble from Bedford—are resolved and unified in the angular lines of the volume that converges dynamically at the top of the structure. All this affirms Sullivan's synthesis of opposites in a formal structure devoid of stylistic references, in a newly invented structure that is, however, rich with references to sacred and funerary architecture from every place and time.

1. Frank Lloyd Wright, *An Autobiography* (New York: Horizon Press, 1932), 271.
2. Louis H. Sullivan, *Louis Sullivan: The Public Papers*, ed. Robert Twombly (Chicago: University of Chicago Press, 1988), 10ff.
3. Ibid., 65.
4. Ibid., 67.
5. In particular, see Robert Twombly, *Louis Sullivan: His Life and Work* (Chicago: University of Chicago Press, 1986), chapter 12, esp. 402.
6. See David S. Andrew, *Louis Sullivan and the Polemics of Modern Architecture* (Urbana: University of Illinois Press, 1985), 13.
7. Reprinted in Sullivan, *Public Papers*, 45.
8. Ibid., 47.
9. Ibid., 48–50.
10. Karl Marx, *Capital* (1867; reprint, New York: Vintage Books, 1977), 91.
11. Sullivan, *Public Papers*, 67.
12. Twombly, *Life and Work*, 231.
13. Ibid., 229.

When a major industrialist turned to the studio of Adler & Sullivan for the construction of a high-profile building in the center of St. Louis, Chicago's rival city, Sullivan probably sensed that this was his opportunity to hit a high note in the context of the then unformed typology of the skyscraper. The client was the influential and culturally ambitious brewer Ellis Wainwright, with whom Sullivan had a solid friendship. Wainwright set forth a specific agenda for his building, aimed at synthesizing the most advanced technology with sophisticated design, thus imposing a new vision on a city that had demonstrated little concern over aesthetic matters.

The production of tall urban office buildings was a significant new field that had developed in the 1870s with the innovation of new elevator technologies. From that time, major architects of the East and West competed for leadership; those on the East Coast—Richard Morris Hunt foremost among them—practiced a style of design that hearkened back to European models, employing the architectural language of the Beaux-Arts; those in the West, on the other hand, sought solutions less constrained by historical precedent, while accepting the seriality suggested by new technologies and imposed by production methods. These two approaches were divergent, but there were points of contact, resulting in the creation, in the late 1880s, of buildings such as the Union Trust Building of New York, by George B. Post, and the Tacoma Building of Chicago, by Holabird & Roche.

Production, in short, wavered for a few years between a confusing array of building types and technologies, construction techniques, and cultural directions, a mix that expressed the tensions—delightfully, when considered without prejudice from the vantage point of the present—of the American city and the vital anarchy of free-market competition. Sullivan's critical approach, however, reflected a master's demand for order and intellectual hegemony. Indeed, Sullivan casts the design of the Wainwright as a sudden epiphany, an event so unexpected and triumphant that it ended—in a single stroke—the chaotic search for a formal identity for the skyscraper. And it is difficult to withstand the

temptation—to which so many have succumbed—to accept this version, considering that, for once, the two direct witnesses of this "magic moment" (Sullivan himself and Wright) agree on both the immediacy of the conception and the primary importance of the "birth of the skyscraper."[1] This phrase, so often repeated, might bring a smile to the lips of anyone who has seen the building in St. Louis—certainly a handsome structure, but hardly a soaring one, even in comparison with other buildings of its type from the same period.

The enthusiasm displayed by the architects of this project and its historians—the latter having certainly been influenced by the assuredness of the former—requires some explanation. According to Sullivan's account, which was actually written ten years after the events in question, it was a sort of mental explosion that led him—after inspecting the site and then hurrying back to his studio—to trace out "literally in three minutes" the sketch "that broke" with all precedent and quickly blossomed into a recognizable model.[2] In turn, this model marked "the beginning of a logical and poetic expression of the metallic frame construction."[3] Wright wrote about this incident even later, describing the way in which Sullivan burst into his room with sketch in hand, thrusting it under Wright's nose: "I was perfectly aware of what had happened. This was Louis Sullivan's greatest moment—his greatest effort. The 'skyscraper' as a new thing under the sun."[4] Both Wright and Sullivan, evidently, were working from memory and, at least in part, from imagination. Indeed, Wright's recollection is laced with a subtle condescension, describing the sketch or ideogram as the "greatest" that his master was ever to achieve. Missing, in any case, is the account of George Elmslie, another talented assistant, who may also have contributed significantly to the project, though we cannot reconstruct with any certainty to what degree.

At this juncture, Sullivan's design work seemed to be heading in two different directions, quite diverse in theme. This diversity is best illustrated by the drawing for the complex of the Pueblo Opera House, on the one hand, and by Sullivan's first burial

structure, the Ryerson Tomb, on the other. In looking at the essays written in this same period, however, this odd two-fold set of interests and approaches does not appear. Sullivan's theoretical thrust, then, appears to have been toward a deeper understanding and an explication (to an audience that did not wish to listen) of the multivalent nature of any artwork. In this phase, Sullivan was clearly showing his awareness of semantic stratification and the indirect relationship between meaning and language. But while he may have understood this relationship in theory, he failed to present it in practice. Once Sullivan had taken on the daunting and ambitious role of messiah of a new architecture—an architecture that synthesized production and technology with an American aesthetic of "the new"—he had the option of swinging between two opposed extremes: the hypotactic consolidation of a blend of differences and opposites, versus the graphic, manifest impossibility of such a blend. The result was an endless pursuit of paratactic assemblages.

Of these two general lines of work, the first is best expressed in the Wainwright Building in St. Louis. The courage behind this choice can be seen precisely in Sullivan's awareness of the arbitrariness, or fungibility, of the final outcome. This is quite the opposite of what Sullivan had later tried to set forth when he wrote of his product with a vaunted certainty, despite Wright's later attempts to identify him with that momentary and transitory work. And that work, incidentally, was an architectural object that must have been particularly pleasing to Wright, since it bears a number of unmistakable, Wrightian features.

What the Wainwright Building declared, in the most assertive manner imaginable, is the definibility of form, even though it is set within the context of an evolving process; likewise, one should note the striving for quality, though this takes place within a context of strictly quantitative values. Thus, the metal structure—which Sullivan boasted had attained logical expression—is revealed on the exterior solely by its corollary of repetition. Yet this repetition is contradicted twice: first because it is doubled in its rhythm; second, because it varies in width in the corner module, which is broader and

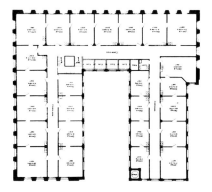

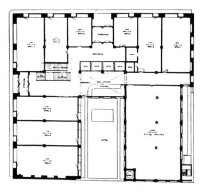

which concludes the motif. And if the two-fold rhythm of the architectural uprights, as opposed to the structural uprights, had the purpose of accentuating the verticality of the building, this verticality is, in turn, decidedly negated by the proportions of the volume and by the static thrust of the horizontal elements—the base, and the attic. The horizontality of the attic is accentuated by the sharp, flat projection of the roof, in harmony with a poetics used by Sullivan only after Wright's arrival in the studio.

What more fully reveals the unitary and stabilizing intent of the design are the corner pilaster strips, nearly two meters across and perfectly marked all the way up to the frieze of the attic. These pilasters elegantly absorb the greater breadth of the last bay, and, ending the intense vertical rhythm in a smooth stone terminal, they solidly link, in a reiterated trilith motif, the two stabilizing horizontal elements of the base and the attic.

Towering over the corner pilasters, the uninterrupted frieze of the attic completes the cubic mass (or apparently cubic; it is a U-shaped plan) with a horizontal projection, topping the building like an immense Doric abacus. Thus, Wright's poetic of the projecting roof was accepted here, but it was devoid of the heritage of the old shingle style; the flat roof would only later be recovered and relaunched by Wright himself.

The stolidity of the Wainwright's façade, augmented by the strong reddish tint of the Missouri granite, was imposed upon it at the cost of any consistency between interior and exterior in terms of functional correspondence. Conversely, this unity succeeds in completely disguising the asymmetrical, open form of the block, no doubt intentionally. In the context of a cityscape whose frenzied vitality generated a confused set of heterogeneous, conflicting messages in a continual process of metamorphosis, such a monument would inevitably draw attention. The idea was to block the psychological mechanism of perceptual distraction.

This project—clearly a cultural statement—is diametrically opposed to what we can deduce from the coeval drawing for the Seattle Opera House,

taken here as a sample of the opposite, paratactic line of endeavor. This opposition (hypotactic vs. paratactic) seems worthy of particular attention, given that architectural historians—adopting the opposed positions of the protagonists themselves—have generally defended only one of the two approaches, in the process misunderstanding the other. As a result, they are generally caught at a loss in their understanding of successive developments from the Schiller Building on.

The history of the Schiller Building, at first called the German Theater or the German Opera House, is radically different from that of the Wainwright. Each and every project, in the end, became an experiment all its own, with every situation influencing the initial intentions of the design studio. If the Wainwright Building was born suddenly, growing in a rush and all in one piece, the Schiller Building developed slowly, and was constructed in fits and starts. Design and planning began in March 1890; the final version was approved—according to Twombly—in February 1891;[5] the building itself was not inaugurated until September 1892. Moreover, the Schiller was to be a multipurpose building, with an auditorium on the interior, much like other projects done by the firm. This fact certainly affected the building's increasingly complex appearance, as well as its discontinuous construction process. Lastly, there were also a number of problems with the site, which had a very restricted frontage on Randolph Street next to the old Borden Block, and an exceedingly long lot, which required the considerable extension of the building.

The resulting structure is of great interest, although it is now known only from photographs, as it was demolished in the early 1960s in what must be characterized as a piece of rank vandalism. In any case, what is known of it does seem to bear out the interpretation that there were two different and divergent impulses in Sullivan's design for the building: the affirmation of unity, and the display of plurality. In the Schiller Building, in fact, there is an attempt to establish a balance between two hermeneutic lines, and this is the first time we see such a determined effort in Sullivan's work. It was a difficult approach, which perhaps failed to yield the results expected by American architectural critics; on the whole, the building is not thought to be one of Sullivan's finest, ranked somewhere below the Wainwright and Guaranty buildings. Twombly cautiously describes it as "one of Adler and Sullivan's best if not most exquisite" works.[6] In this context, it remains difficult to understand the enthusiasm of the English architectural historian Banister Fletcher, who considered it the finest building ever erected in the United States, going so far as to say that it bore "the same relationship to the new style of tall buildings as the Parthenon bears to the architecture of Greece."[7]

The façade of this building—the underlying conception of which should be analyzed with some thoroughness—forms part of a haphazard sequence of fronts lining the street; it stands out for its aggressive appearance and its unified personality. Particularly notable is the building's tower, with its straight and slender shaft, massive base, elegant top, and turret towering above the eighteenth floor. There are two smaller wings on either side of the tower, symmetrically flanking it like two shoulders, and thereby enhancing the hypotactic character of the whole formal structure.

Unlike the Wainwright Building, however, the Schiller Building clearly announces itself as an assembly of autonomous parts, and the architectural language seems designed to emphasize that autonomy. The central tower is the dominant feature, and it takes the form of the archetypal fluted pilaster, with base, shaft, and capital. The capital is a projecting square abacus, as in the Wainwright Building, but it is even more intricately decorated in its projecting cornice and collar of small windows. Deeply etched flutes running continuously from base to capital divide the windows of the tower's shaft into vertical bays, with three bays on each façade. The base, however, is inherently in conflict with the cohesive force of the pillar, extending as it does beyond the bounds of the shaft of the tower in order to encompass the side wings of the building and incorporate them into the shaft. These two side wings, though they are small and clearly subordinate in terms of design, are

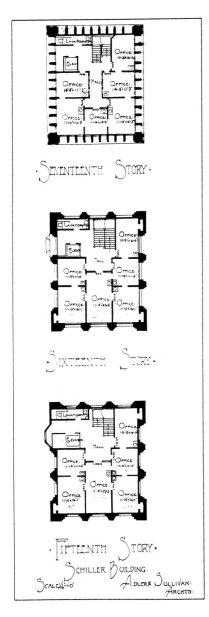

81

Interior of the tower of the Schiller Building. Floor plans of the theater and detail of the proscenium.

clearly distinct architectural forms. They establish a formal autonomy all their own, emphasized by their central bay windows and the flat roofs that turn each of the two into smaller towers. The base itself is broken into two horizontal components, with the stark color and relief of a richly decorated loggia jutting continuously across the full length of the façade above the entry level. Completing the assemblage are a series of vitrines and portals on the street level, and a small lantern/observatory on the roof that unfortunately diminishes the dramatic effect of the cornice.

In the comparison of the Schiller Building with the Seattle Opera House, an unbuilt project that serves as an ideal foil to the Wainwright Building, a number of singular and insistent references come to light. These include the deep, tripartite division of the towers, and the use of vertical bay windows that in the former served to mark and differentiate the lower shaft of the tower and in the latter served the same function for the smaller flanking towers. Additionally, if one eliminates the enormous pitched roof of the Opera House, leaving only the balcony, the crowns of the two structures become virtually identical. Likewise, there is a close relationship between the tower and the base, each building having a decorated loggia over a row of portals.

Unity and plurality, assertiveness and a problematized approach, synthesis and—at the same time—a declaration of the impossibility of synthesis. Just how deliberate can Sullivan's pursuit of a cultural project of such complexity and cognitive depth have been in Chicago in 1891? And, at this stage in Sullivan's career, what role can be assigned to the other members of the firm, beginning with the staunch Adler? What were the contributions of Wright (who would open his first studio in the Schiller Building) and Elmslie, who had both already begun to display interesting architectural personalities in their own rights? And, finally, to what degree do the poetics of montage, which reappears in this project following the hiatus of the Wainwright Building, depend on the fact that Sullivan chose to delegate the task of drafting blueprints, a standard procedure in his studio, thus giving partial independence to the members of his staff?

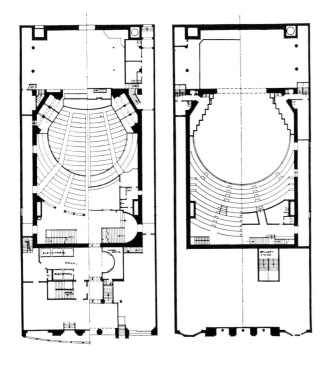

Schiller Building, section and partial elevation of the loggia (1964 reconstruction).

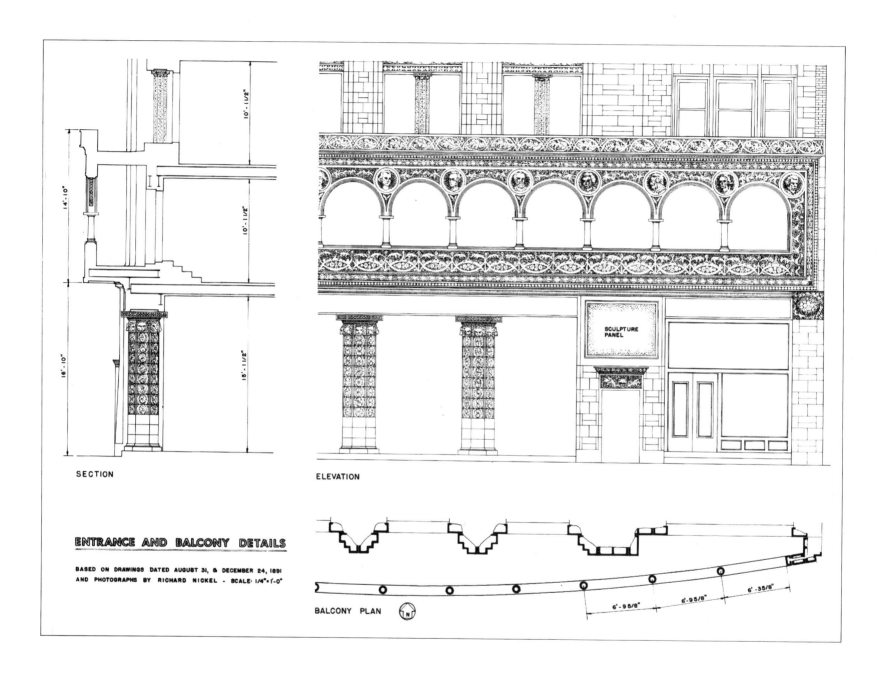

SECTION

ELEVATION

SCULPTURE PANEL

ENTRANCE AND BALCONY DETAILS

BASED ON DRAWINGS DATED AUGUST 31, & DECEMBER 24, 1891
AND PHOTOGRAPHS BY RICHARD NICKEL · SCALE· 1/4"·1'-0"

BALCONY PLAN

6'- 9 5/8"   6'- 9 5/8"   6'- 3 5/8"

Schiller Building, longitudinal section
and detail of the interior of the auditorium.

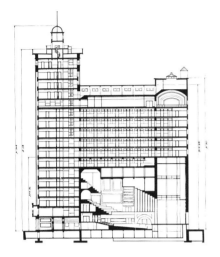

*Schiller Building, mosaic for the land-
ing of the stairway leading to the
gallery and view of the interior of the
German Club Room.*

At the time, the division of different architectural responsibilities was not only an accepted practice, but an admired one. Certainly, it was common to
treat the interior and the exterior of a building as
two separate projects, as has been demonstrated in
the theater projects. Here, the skill with which the
theater is inserted into the narrow, deep building is
masterful. Adler's remarkable parabolic cross-arch-
es—wedged into the block structure but glittering
with Sullivan's gold, green, and red coloration, and
studded with Elmslie's dense and elegantly geometric decorations—create the effect of a grotto or a
narrow canyon while producing excellent acoustics.

By shifting attention to the other building
designed in 1891 for St. Louis—immediately following the Wainwright Building in that city—
it becomes clear that Sullivan's experimentation
resumes in full force. In the massive, sunlit block
of the Mercantile Club Building, all of the elements
that had predominated in Sullivan's earlier work
reappear now composed in a slightly different manner. The building's tower, with its massive crowning
element covered by a steep, pitched roof, is distinctly
reminiscent of the unbuilt tower of the Seattle
Opera House. The same is true of the bay windows,
set against an unadorned wall punctuated with rectangular windows, and likewise the base, which
is pierced by broad, square windows. Here, however,
the composition is clearly intended to reinforce the
unity of the building's overall design, which shines
through despite the variety of linguistic elements.
At the same time, there is an accentuation of the
contrast and interplay between the vertical elements—a sign of the structural efficacy and technological efficiency of the bay window motif—and
the horizontal features, including the broad loggias
and long, lavishly adorned balconies that reiterate
the stability and opulence of the building.

The Mercantile Club Building can be considered yet another highly questionable compendium of
previously used architectural elements; one might
even brand it as the product of a recidivistic weak-
ness for eclecticism. It seems that the architects set
out not so much to recover styles of architecture
from the past, as to cite them as parts of a new architectural language, obtained through a process of

Adler & Sullivan, design for the Mercantile Club Building, St. Louis, Missouri, 1891.

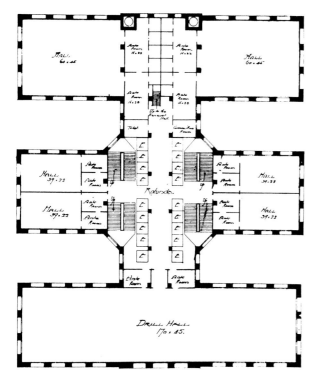

Adler & Sullivan, design for the Odd Fellows Fraternity Temple Building, Chicago, 1891, floor plan for the tenth floor and rendering.

*Burnham & Root, Monadnock
Building, Chicago, 1890–91.*

research. It was, in short, a somewhat bombastic mark of the all-powerful versatility of this Chicago firm, an effort somewhat worn-out and unpersuasive. Not surprisingly, the city of St. Louis decided not to construct the building.

Even as this project was dying on the vine, however, a new line of research was already being pursued in Sullivan's office. This new area of investigation viewed skyscrapers not as monuments but as large-scale urban structures designed to meet a series of specifications and functions, chiefly technical in nature. This was a radical new development in Sullivan's design work, and it has not been adequately explored or understood. Its origins rest in the atmosphere of fierce competition between design firms battling to ride the still-cresting wave of the American economy, which was about to plunge into the trough of the 1893 depression.

Looking around at the city of Chicago, Adler and Sullivan could hardly help but be impressed by the changes taking place. In the Loop in particular, there was a frenzy of construction. Burnham & Root, the firm of Sullivan's rival John Wellborn Root, produced dozens of buildings in a year. That office—unlike Sullivan's, which was based on the complementary areas of expertise of its two chief architects—was directed by a pair of architects who unquestionably differed from one another, but who were first and foremost great designers. Capable of a wide range of tasks, it was often difficult to tell the work of one from that of the other. Their partnership came to an unfortunate end with the premature death of Root in 1891.

The firm of Burnham & Root represented the principal challenge to Sullivan & Adler in the race for leadership in the design of tall buildings. In 1890, that office designed the Masonic Temple, the tallest building in the city. Constructed in 1891, at the corner of Randolph and State Streets, the building was inaugurated in 1892. An immense, twenty-story block commissioned by the Masonic Lodge of Chicago, the Temple's vast expanse of wall was perforated by an array of windows organized into a cohesive design that summoned up an oddly traditional image.

If the Masonic Temple was a dauntingly massive structure with an overgrown palatial silhouette, the Monadnock Building—constructed between 1889 and 1892, and chiefly designed by Daniel H. Burnham[5]—may well be the most beautiful building erected by the Chicago School. Its sixteen identical floors are punctuated vertically by an elegant succession of bay windows cut and shaped into a perfect weave of colored brickwork, shaded from dark purple on bottom, to red, and then yellow on top.

In the face of such daunting competition—exacerbated by the 1890 assignment of the Columbian Exposition to Burnham—the office of Adler & Sullivan found itself in turn forced to develop ideas that were more forceful than the refined, experimental studies in visual language that Sullivan had been producing. It was Sullivan himself who set out to theorize a rational new approach to the field, elevating the skyscraper from the scale of a building to that of a city. In so doing, his work anticipated the ideas of European rationalism. It is remarkable to note that this giant step forward evolved from a two-phase process; the design of a large building—meant to be the largest building in the world—leading to a great theoretical development.

While Burnham & Root's Masonic Temple rose to a height of twenty stories, Adler & Sullivan developed a project that was truly meant to touch the sky: the Odd Fellows Fraternity Temple Building, which was to rise thirty-six stories into the air. The office had found a client willing to challenge the Masonic Temple with a temple of its own, at a cost of $3.5 million. Designed to reach a height of nearly 460 feet, the building was a challenge to which Sullivan responded with a skillful shift in methodology; by using well-tested typological and stylistic concepts, he could reach skyward practically without limitation.

This project, designed in the last few months of 1891, was concentrated around a giant volume broken up into a largely symmetrical series of blocks, culminating in a central tower. The ground plan, composite in nature, comprises an overlay of a cross upon an extended H-plan. The rectangular blocks rose to three different heights, the four shortest

"The High Building Question,"
drawing published in the Graphic,
1891.

being the furthest from the central tower, the tallest. Each of the blocks, which all were to have square plans, was modeled after the Wainwright Building: the same set of motifs appear, to scale, in the four lowest blocks; in the four intermediate blocks, these motifs were elongated and a double-height crowning frieze was added. High above, the central tower was crowned with a projecting decorated loggia surmounted by a small cusped turret. It was to be a tall structure paratactically assembled out of separate parts united into a single composition. Centrally planned in the classical manner, it was designed as a single formal type. To complete and reiterate the hypotactic nature of the layout, four entries were aligned symmetrically at street level, emphasized by broad, semicircular splayed arches. This major component of the design was not culled from the model of the Wainwright Building.

As early as December 1891, it had become clear that this project would never escape the drawing board. According to Montgomery Schuyler, three factors prevented construction: lack of money, the absence of an appropriate site in the downtown area, and a city ordinance that limited building height.[9] It was at this point that Sullivan proposed to rationalize the city's building regulations in an article published in the *Graphic* entitled "The High Building Question" that was accompanied by mediocre but suggestive drawings.[10] The proposal—a forerunner of New York's 1916 zoning code—called for setback buildings: "What more simple solution can there be than this—that the individual be allowed to continue the further erection of his building above the prescribed limits provided that, in so continuing, the area of the building as it emerges from the limit shall occupy not more than, say, fifty percent of his land. Let him so continue until he has reached, say, twice the height of the original limit." And as for the risk, not insubstantial given business practice in Chicago, that the higher section of the building, though set back, might be moved forward to loom over the street, Sullivan suggested that special taxes or tariffs could be applied to force the setback toward the center of the lot.

The drawing, possibly supplied by the magazine—certainly not by Sullivan or any of his more talented assistants—offers a view of the city as it would appear under the recommended regulations. Anything but reassuring, it is chilly and unpleasant—despite the presence of two copies of the tower of the Auditorium Building—a nightmarish cityscape softened only by a few eclectic rooftop affectations in poor taste. Nonetheless, the quality of production in the office was by no means on the decline. Indeed, several of the firm's most successful projects came in the last few years of Adler and Sullivan's partnership, between 1892 and 1895.

1. On this subject, there is a vast body of writing, of little conceptual: see David S. Andrew, *Louis Sullivan and the Polemics of Modern Architecture* (Urbana: University of Illinois Press, 1985), chapter 5.

2. Louis H. Sullivan, *Kindergarten Chats and Other Writings* (1918; reprint, New York: George Wittenborn, 1947), chapter 22.

3. Ibid.

4. Frank Lloyd Wright, "Louis H. Sullivan—His Work," *Architectural Record* 56 (July 1924): 29.

5. Robert Twombly, *Louis Sullivan: His Life and Work* (Chicago: University of Chicago Press, 1986), 293.

6. Twombly in any case describes this as "the first true set-back skyscraper," see Twombly, *Life and Work*, page 294.

7. Ibid., 298.

8. I insisted upon Burnham's authorship of the Monadnock Building in my essay, "Per una città imperiale, D. H. Burnham e il movimento City Beautiful," in *La città americana dalla guerra civile al "New Deal"* (Rome: Laterza, 1973), 14ff.

9. Twombly, *Life and Work*, 304.

10. Louis H. Sullivan, *Louis Sullivan: The Public Papers*, ed. Robert Twombly (Chicago: University of Chicago Press, 1988), 76ff.

In the time that elapsed between the triumphant completion of the Wainwright Building in 1890, and the construction of what may well be considered the two most successful tall buildings designed by Sullivan (the Union Trust Building in St. Louis and the Chicago Stock Exchange), a great international event was held on the shores of Lake Michigan. This event, the World's Columbian Exposition, would dominate the history of American architecture for decades to come, virtually obliterating the so-called Chicago School and influencing design methods, particularly urban design methods, everywhere. It was an event, in brief, that shifted all reference points in architecture, imposing—throughout the western United States—a specific cultural conditioning on the very same field of intellectual endeavor that Sullivan was attempting to control and move in a sharply different direction.

Sullivan's office was still at work on the schematic design of the Schiller Building, one of the most assertive, programmatically challenging projects undertaken, when what Sullivan later described as the "small white cloud" began extending its shadow—a blighting shadow, in Sullivan's view—over the cultural landscape of Chicago.[1] The Fraternity Temple project, which was the manifesto of an original, forward-looking, urban design method, coincided—though no one has yet fully taken note of this fact—with one of the most demanding phases in Sullivan's battle against the great event.

The account of this fair, in the biased version given by Sullivan thirty years later in his autobiography, is so powerful and convincing, and so tinged by the author's desperate rage, that it has become difficult to offer a less polarized view of the facts in a less livid light. Sullivan's opinion, which was so heavily vested in a particular cause, must be questioned. In a sense, Sullivan played only a minor part in the fair, at least from the point of view of its chief actor, Daniel H. Burnham, who succeeded in winning a place for himself in architectural history only after the death of his partner, John Wellborn Root.[2] But to Sullivan, Burnham appeared as a threat to Sullivan's own vital intellectual and artistic effort. Sullivan immediately took steps to contest Burnham's image, at first in veiled terms, and, much later in life, in a furious and effectively violent manner.

Burnham was too different from Sullivan for the latter not to perceive the former's work as an insupportable attack upon the credibility of his own production. Burnham was a few years older than Sullivan, and he had experienced a series of difficulties and failures in the course of his life; this string of problems, however, was not enough to dim his lucid determination to pursue large-scale projects. He attempted—before Sullivan—to work in architectural offices, and worked briefly for Jenney. But Burnham had higher ambitions, and soon chose another path—he went to work in the mines of Nevada. The endeavor failed, and he entered politics, and fared no better. Soon he was back in Chicago, trying his hand at architecture once again. In 1871, the Great Fire destroyed Burnham's office. In 1873 he founded another office, this time with William Holabird, and Clinton Warren. When this enterprise took off, Burnham was thirty years old and was about to taste success for the first time. His marriage to the daughter of the great financier John Sherman got him off to a good start in business.

Burnham's approach to life was received with great immediacy by Sullivan, who, with his complex sensibility, seems at times to have been intimidated by his rival's aggressive determination, even while disapproving of Burnham's ways. Recalling the Burnham of 1874, Sullivan describes in his autobiography his rival's swaggering speech, "'But I'm not going to stay satisfied with houses; my idea is to work up a big business, to handle big things, deal with big business men, and to build up a big organization.'"[3]

Sullivan described Burnham himself, many years later, as a "big business man." But how did Sullivan feel about Burnham in 1890, when the situation was far different? Sullivan was still unmarried; he had attained considerable fame in his own city and in much of the United States; and the economy was still doing well, though growth seemed to be faltering here and there. Sullivan seemed unaware of any gathering clouds. He accelerated his efforts to establish cultural hegemony, taking—with his work on the Wainwright Building—the high road of quality, while putting himself forward—with the Fraternity Temple—as a first-rate architect in the production of large urban buildings.

In the year 1890, the United States began to prepare to celebrate the four hundredth anniversary of Columbus's discovery of America. Two years is not a long time in which to prepare a world-class event. There was a long and hard-fought battle among various large cities for the honor, but in the end Chicago prevailed, in April 1890. Burnham had a head start on the other architects. He was the first to perceive the great opportunity, and he set out to select the proper site even before Chicago had been officially chosen. This, however, was an international event, and the powerful group of eastern architects, Richard Morris Hunt leading the charge, was not about to be pushed aside without a struggle. The fair's commission, in fact, assigned the task of selecting a site to Frederick Law Olmsted, who chose Grant Park, a section of the lakefront for which the great landscaper with Calvert Vaux had designed an unexecuted park in 1871.

In September, the government policy of supporting an international event with an anti-local, international character began to emerge; indeed, an event was to be perfectly balanced between east and west. This balance was evident from the choice of Burnham and Olmsted, who were immediately joined by Root and Harry S. Codman, selected by the first two architects as a way of maintaining equilibrium. The government's internationalizing intentions were evident from the choice of architectural style for the great event—French classical, with a predominance of white. Thus, if Chicago was chosen as the site of the exposition, it was, however, forced to yield to East-Coast architectural mores for the prevailing style of the event. After this negotiated settlement, Sullivan had no chance to influence the course of events. Burnham had become the great mediator of this historic transaction. With this compromise (which some ideologically minded historians have described as a betrayal), Burnham, the Chicago architect, was undermining the foundation of Chicago's glorious architectural school.

Still, the great conflict was not so much a struggle between schools as it was a struggle between two different cultural strategies: on the one hand, an approach that boasted proud independence from Europe, with a staunch adherence to the values of American individualism, bolstered by the economic protectionism of the preceding decades; on the other hand, an attitude of anti-localism and anti-provincialism, reaching out for the international and intercontinental contacts that had become historically necessary, even at the risk of cultural dependency upon the Old World. The opposition between these two approaches, therefore, was only partly architectural in nature.

It should also be pointed out, in connection with this ideological split, that neither Burnham's nor Sullivan's ideas can be reduced to the two models described here. The complexity of Sullivan's attitudes toward artistic production and visual language have already been noted here—it would be reductive to interpret his theoretical positions and his architectural work in terms of protectionism against a feared Beaux-Arts takeover. And Burnham's world view, which led him to become a guarantor, as it were, of a consolidated and even conventional architectural style, cannot be reduced to a merely instrumental stance, even though it did in fact win him the reins of cultural power.

According to Burnham's account, expressed in a 1913 interview, he was the promoter and mediator of the exposition. In December of 1890, Burnham was impatient and insisted that the committee take action and begin work. By January 5, 1991 he had received orders to select ten firms, five from Chicago and five from elsewhere. He then made his selections and presented them to the committee, some of whom were politicians. Burnham insisted that the committee did not come to an agreement because the politicians did not want to give him the power of selecting the firms. Finally, Gage put forward a motion in his favor; the committee finally voted in favor of Burnham by a margin of four to three. [4]

In reality, it is known from surviving documents that Burnham had already been acting as coordinator before January and had clearly been

Adler & Sullivan, Transportation Building, Chicago, 1891–93, general view and detail of the Golden Doorway.

forming a preliminary understanding with eastern architects.[5] On 12 December 1890, in fact, Burnham sent out five letters, with his signature, addressed to the five firms not based in Chicago; in these letters he specified that the commission under consideration was for the artistic design of the largest group of buildings in the fair. It was not until later that Burnham assigned the commissions instead to the Chicago-based firms: Adler & Sullivan, William Le Baron Jenney, Henry Ives Cobb, Charles S. Frost, and Burling & Whitehouse.

For Burling & Whitehouse, and even more so for Adler & Sullivan, the situation quickly turned bad. There was some discussion of assigning the designers of the Auditorium, who were specialists in the area of theater design, to do the small, outlying Music Hall. That assignment was greeted less than enthusiastically; in part, Adler & Sullivan's reluctance stemmed from the fact that this, like most of the buildings for the exposition, was to be a temporary construction. The proposed assignment of the Art Building—planned as a permanent structure—

was also met with hesitation. This was, however, no time for uncertainty, and the Art Building was awarded to the young architect Charles B. Atwood of Boston.

By mid-January 1891, nearly all of the buildings had been assigned; only the idea of separating the Transportation Building from Machinery Hall, supposedly Sullivan's idea, resolved the problem of assigning Adler & Sullivan a project.[6] Still, the working conditions were fairly humiliating: the ground plan of the building was determined by the commission, and the height of all the buildings was to be the same, sixty-five feet. All that the designers were asked to do was to prepare the design drawings: floor plans, cross-sections, elevations, and decorative details; the working drawings were to be drawn up by the Department of Construction, under the direction of Burnham.

According to Sullivan, writing in 1924, Burnham's role was destructive to the dignity of Chicago architects, and his posture was close to pandering and prostitution. In Sullivan's words, "Burnham had

Renderings of several pavilions for the Columbian Exposition: Transportation Building, Adler & Sullivan; Horticultural Building, William Le Baron Jenney; Fine Arts Building, Charles B. Atwood; Machinery Building, Peabody & Stearns.

believed that he might best serve his country by placing all of the work exclusively with Eastern architects; solely, he averred, on account of their surpassing culture."[7] It had been Edward T. Jefferey himself, the powerful chairman of the Committee on Buildings and Grounds, who had asked that the western architects be allowed to take part. Sullivan offers an eye-witness account of the uproar that ensued in the first meeting of the committee, in Chicago on 10 January: "The meeting came to order. Richard Hunt, acknowledged dean of his profession, in the chair, Louis Sullivan acting as secretary. Burnham arose to make his address of welcome. He was not facile on his feet, but it soon became noticeable that he was progressively and grossly apologizing to the Eastern men for the presence of their benighted brethren of the West.

"Dick Hunt interrupted: 'Hell, we haven't come out here on a missionary expedition. Let's get to work.' "[8]

The powerful alliance between the architects of the East and Daniel Burnham—who became their trusted delegate—took control of the enormous project of the World's Columbian Exposition. These architects, especially Burnham himself, had fully grasped the historic moment that coincided with the beginning of a major shift in the American system of production. Indeed, the exposition was a dress rehearsal, and a bellwether, of the new direction in economic policy that was to be known as the "open door policy."

In this context, the office of Adler & Sullivan found itself in a strictly marginalized position. Adler, with all of his technical expertise, was completely shut out, as has been noted. Sullivan—at this point enjoying his success with the Wainwright Building and cherishing his great ambition of founding a new, authentically American culture— found himself faced with a difficult challenge: despite a late start and, so to speak, an outside track in architectural circles, he was being called upon to produce better work than ever before in a context that basically hobbled his creativity.

Sullivan's Western pride and cultural background that prevented him from envisioning the inevitable development away from laissez-faire capitalism. The world was increasingly dominated by an impersonal form of production; it had begun to reach a scale too large to be managed by the old, individualistic form of simple competition. This was a new world that, with "its tendency toward bigness, organization, delegation," seemed to have been created for the mind of someone like Burnham. Even Sullivan himself admitted this; he described Burnham as "the only architect in Chicago to catch the significance of this movement." Sullivan referred to this historic shift toward a world dominated by corporations, in a vague description of the "formation of mergers, combinations and trusts in the industrial world."[9] There was an overall commitment to coordination that prompted Charles Zueblin to write that the White City was a socialist achievement, the product of many minds inspired with a shared goal, working for the common good.[10]

An essential new objective—coordination in the service of unity—was set up as a model for competitive development, not in the narrow sense of free-market competition within national boundaries, but, rather, on a worldwide scale. This objective brought together all of the intellectual forces that were inspired by a collective ideal—an ideal that had been expressed a few years previously in the book *Looking Backward* by Edward Bellamy. This novel, a utopian depiction of the year 2000, was published two years after the Haymarket Riot and sold widely. In the book, society was run by a military regime; all social conflict had been eliminated, as had all classes; and life was run by a single universal corporation, planned and organized in accordance with a classical ideal.

In 1890 the architectural culture of the East and its representative in the West, Daniel Burnham, were already oriented to this ideal and its concept of production. It was this architectural elite, by no accident, that was assigned the task of defining the most important section of the fair, the triumphal zone of the Court of Honor, which was accessible both from the lake, via a monumental landing dock designed by Charles Atwood, and by land, from a railroad terminus with a dozen lines. These tracks led to the most eminent building, the Administration Building; its temple form, with centralized plan and cupola, was

designed by the eastern patriarch Hunt, president of the American Institute of Architects. This building stood at the focal point of the entire complex. The other major buildings—those that overlooked the court—were all assigned to the leading members of the New York "family," McKim, Mead & White and George B. Post, who designed the largest building of the fair, the Manufacturers Building. Only one Chicago-based architect, Solon S. Beman, was able to intrude on the immense, formal space of the Court; his Mines Building was sited in a subordinate location. Among the various Chicago architects, Root (at Burnham's side) seemed to have been given a major role in architectural coordination. And yet it was Burnham who, in the commissioning letter dated 12 December, limited his partner's power. Burnham wrote that Root, as consulting architect, would act as an intermediary and would not allow his personal taste to interfere with the work.[11] Root's eclectic taste, clearly present in several of his drawings from 1890, must, understandably enough, have done little to impress the architects from the East. Root, a quarrelsome, sensitive Irishman, could not stand for a situation of this sort, but the matter was soon to become moot, as he would die in January of 1891.

In the areas further removed from the lakefront—the strip of the Midway Plaisance and the vast rectangular area of Washington Park—stood the foreign pavilions, distinctive but of decidedly lesser importance. The hierarchy of buildings only reinforced the great allegory underlying the fair: the American zone overlooking the lake referred to orderly, grandiose efficiency and a colossal, formal representation of value; and the pavilions of the Old World scattered among the inland parks, amidst a series of oddities and amusements, were certainly not adequate models of a developing society.

And Sullivan? The Transportation Building was included in the area known as Lagoon Park, separated from the inland parks and behind the major buildings that overlooked the Court of Honor. It consisted of a giant roof over a vast and rhythmic interior that housed the various exhibit stands. In his initial proposal, Sullivan suggested two monumental entrances on the long side of the building, facing Post's enormous Manufacturers and Liberal Arts Building. Burnham, however, was concerned with the overall effect these entrances would make—he had an unshakable belief in the greater validity of the classical approach and the academic style of the great white buildings lining the Court of Honor and feared that Sullivan's project might disturb the overall harmony. He must have felt that, by limiting the stylistic and chromatic interference to just one doorway, he could fit Sullivan's unique work in with the stylistically uniform context of the whole.

Sullivan fancifully expressed his own opposition to the overall homogenization of architectural expression at the fair with the famous golden doorway. Surprisingly, it is shown in a letter that Burnham sent Sullivan on 11 February 1891, that this doorway, which was to enjoy pride of place in the pages of every history of American architecture, was actually a direct consequence, at least in its colossal size and its location, of insistent recommendations by the "big business man."

"The best possible method for handling the axis trouble we discovered the other day," he wrote, "will be for you to have one grand entrance toward the east . . . much richer than either of the others you had proposed . . . on the axis running through the center of the Manufacturers Building. It's the natural place for an entrance anyway. . . . I am sure . . . that the effect of your building will be much finer than by the old method of two entrances."[12]

Sullivan responded by placing upon that single entry—which was off-center with his own building but in line with the largest mastodon of the fair, the Manufacturers Building—a phantasmagorical doorway, glittering with gold, reliefs, and colors—the brightest triumphal arch of all time. For the triumph of whom? That of the indomitable artist, capable of illuminating the world with his intellectual labor. The splendid semicircle is a rising sun, or perhaps a radiant sunset. Sullivan was incapable of entertaining such a symbolic meaning at the time. His individual triumphs were too recent; too distant from his mind was the viewpoint found in *Looking Backward.* Indeed, Sullivan's rebellion against the rules of Burnham's overall coordination—based on the elementary regulation of eaves, the classical idiom of the Beaux-Arts style, and the prevailing color

*Main elevation, schematic floor plan,
and view of the interior of the
Transportation Building.*

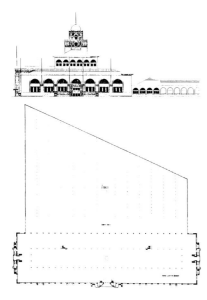

white—were clearly expressed in his building, where he respected only the dictates on eaves' height. Sullivan later wrote:

The Transportation Building is simple in architectural treatment, although it is intended to make it very rich and elaborate in detail. In style it is somewhat Romanesque, although to the initiated the manner in which it is designed on axial lines, and the solicitude shown for good proportions and subtle relation of parts to each other, will at once suggest the methods of composition followed at the École des Beaux Arts.... The main entrance to the Transportation Building consists of an immense single arch enriched with carvings, bas-reliefs, and mural paintings; the entire feature forms a rich and beautiful yet quiet color climax, for it is treated entirely in gold-leaf and called the golden door. The remainder of the architectural composition falls into a just relation of contrast with the highly wrought entrance, and is duly quiet and modest, though very broad in treatment. It consists of a continuous arcade with subordinated colonnade and entablature. Numerous minor entrances are from time to time pierced in the walls, and with them are grouped terraces, seats, drinking-fountains, and statues.

The interior of the building is treated much after the manner of a Roman basilica, with broad nave and aisles. The roof is therefore in three divisions. The middle one rises much higher than the others, and its walls are pierced to form a beautiful arcaded clear-story. The cupola, placed exactly at the center of the building, and rising 165 feet above the ground, is reached by eight elevators....

Not the least interesting feature of the Transportation Building is the beautiful scheme of polychrome decoration to be applied to its exterior. To treat the building externally in many colors was the original thought of the architects in the first conception of their design. The architecture of the building, therefore, has been carefully prepared throughout with reference to the ultimate application of color, and many large plain surfaces have been left to receive the final polychrome treatment. The ornamental designs for this work in color are of great and intricate delicacy; the patterns, interweaving with each other, produce an effect almost as fine as that of embroidery. As regards the colors themselves, they comprise nearly the whole galaxy, there being not less than thirty different shades of color employed. These, however, are so delicately and softly blended and so nicely balanced against each other that the final effect suggests not so much many colors as a single beautiful painting....

The color scheme of the building as a whole, of course, culminates in the great golden doorway. This entire entrance, 100 feet wide and 70 feet high, which is encrusted over its entire surface with delicate designs in relief, is covered throughout its entire extent with gold, and colors in small quantifies are worked in between the designs and reliefs so as to give the whole a wonderfully effective aspect.[13]

In this report, which was presented on 25 February and signed by Adler and Sullivan, the latter allowed none of his unease or protest to show through, despite his feelings about the Coordinating Committee. Yet his opposition persisted and was expressed in the insistent use of color and decoration unfettered by the classical canon. The outrage of the off-axis position of the great but unprecedented portal was brilliantly resolved to appear perfectly symmetrical, through the creation of thirteen similar bays on both sides of the golden doorway, which were, however, slightly different in width. At first, it seemed that Sullivan's opposition to the norms of the Columbian World's Exposition was technical in nature. It had not yet developed into a rift between him and the architectural community that was making a bid for continental hegemony in the context of the exposition, much less into the gulf that would find such daunting, and historiographically fertile, expression in his autobiography.

According to Frank Lloyd Wright, the construction of the Transportation Building (between July 1891 and October 1892) absorbed Sullivan completely.[14] What particularly exhausted the architect

was not so much the matter of the golden doorway—which actually posed few if any problems for Sullivan and his highly skilled craftsmen—but rather the endless array of technical and functional concerns raised by the organizing committee of the exposition. The real criticisms, however, had to do with Sullivan's failure to accept the directives issued by the committee. Sullivan's friend Montgomery Schuyler expressed himself cautiously, admiring Sullivan's consistency in his interpretation of the formal and expressive modes of a "plaster architecture," while noting his failure to comply with the dominant stylistic context.[15]

Criticism of the finished building, however, was rampant. It can be detected in the exasperation expressed by a part of the press. One Australian critic went so far as to write in the *Melbourne Argus*, "I have never met anybody who could explain what it all means, or how such a sanguinary-looking blot was allowed to be placed in the White City."[16] In effect, the Transportation Building was the one contradictory element in an event of vast importance for America, which greeted the exposition with a virtually unanimous chorus of ecstatic enthusiasm.[17]

Those who were not in agreement with the chorus of approval found a useful—and clearly outnumbered—point of reference in the work of Sullivan. This, for instance, was the position of the French, important and respected cultural arbiters, even if (in this case) their contemporary culture was distant from the Beaux-Arts majority in the United States. The most important and most appreciated recognition of Sullivan's work in the exposition, in fact, came from the *Revue des Arts Décoratifs*, the official journal of the Union Centrale des Arts Décoratifs, whose president, André Bouilhet, praised virtually nothing in the fair but the golden doorway. He requested an interview with Sullivan, went to see his various projects and buildings in Chicago, and invited him to send his drawings and models to Paris's Musée des Arts Décoratifs. Sullivan was proud to comply; he sent casts of the decorations of the Transportation Building and models of the portal of the Wainwright Building and the Getty Tomb. In short, Sullivan emerged from the experience of the Columbian Exposition with some benefits; yet there was considerable controversy, and not for Sullivan alone, concerning the historic significance and value of the White City.

Claude Bragdon later wrote that the fair was a sham filled with plaster buildings, students acting as policemen, and crowds interested only in crass commercialism.[18] If, however, this was largely true, what sense was there in the oppositional participation of a proud and individualistic intellectual in such a chauvinistic and populist brand of kitsch, an intellectual who was to offer the stunned populace a refined, golden triumphal arch, dedicated in the final analysis to himself?

1. Louis H. Sullivan, *The Autobiography of an Idea* (American Institute of Architects, 1924; reprint, New York: Dover, 1956), 314ff.
2. This historiographic revision of Burnham and the events of the World's Columbian Exposition and the City Beautiful movement were furthered in my essay, "Per una città imperiale, D. H. Burnham e il movimento City Beautiful," in *La città americana dalla guerra civile al "New Deal"* (Rome: Laterza, 1973).
3. Sullivan, *Autobiography*, 285.
4. See C. Moore, *Daniel H. Burnham, Architect Planner of Cities* (Boston and New York: 1921), 37ff.

5. Ibid.
6. Robert Twombly, *Louis Sullivan: His Life and Work* (Chicago: University of Chicago Press, 1986), 260.
7. Sullivan, *Autobiography*, 319–20.
8. Ibid., 320.
9. Ibid., 314.
10. Charles Zueblin, *A Decade of Civic Development* (Chicago: University of Chicago Press, 1905), 61.
11. Letter dated 12 December 1890, addressed to the Grounds and Buildings Committee, signed by Burnham, Root, Olmsted, and Gottlieb.
12. Twombly, *Life and Work*, 262.

13. Louis H. Sullivan, *Louis Sullivan: The Public Papers*, ed. Robert Twombly (Chicago: University of Chicago Press, 1988), 85–87.
14. Frank Lloyd Wright, *An Autobiography* (New York: Horizon Press, 1932), 265, note 31.
15. Twombly, *Life and Work*, 265, note 32.
16. Ibid., 266, note 34.
17. See Elia, "Per una città imperiale," 42ff.
18. Ibid., 46.

The trying experience of the Columbian Exposition was not enough to discourage Sullivan; he was in fact experiencing one of the most successful periods of his life. The opening of his 1892 essay, "Ornament in Architecture," which has not to-date been properly appreciated, has an unmistakably Jeffersonian tone: "I take it as self-evident that a building, quite devoid of ornament, may convey a noble and dignified sentiment by virtue of mass and proportion." Then why employ ornament, if it is merely "mentally a luxury"? Sullivan seems to imply that simple dignity is sufficient, praising, "the great value of unadorned masses."[1] Despite these words, by this point in his career, Sullivan had gained a reputation as a "premier architectural ornamentalist." He was even awarded a medal by the Union Centrale des Arts Décoratifs, placing a clear emphasis upon the ornamental aspect of his work. While this medal was indeed an honor, Sullivan strongly felt the need to direct his efforts toward organically integrating two aspects of architecture that had been arbitrarily separated: the structural and the decorative.

It is clear then that the opening questions of the aforementioned essay were entirely rhetorical in nature: the Jeffersonian self-evidence of the opening statement, indeed, does not have the single-minded ideological value that gives such power to the preamble to the American Declaration of Independence. On the contrary, it simply served as a springboard for one of Sullivan's most elaborate musings on the complex meaning of the coexistence of structure and ornamentation in his architecture; it served, therefore, as an introduction to a statement that actually diametrically opposed the idea initially presented as self-evident. And this occurred at a time when, in Chicago, this sense of symbiosis—the powerful, organic inherence of ornament in the architectural worth of a building—was laid open to question by the classicist and internationalist crusade led by Burnham. It was clearly too complex to be understood within the accepted schematic theories of the period.

"We feel intuitively," Sullivan wrote in "Ornament in Architecture," "that our strong, athletic and simple forms will carry with natural ease the rai-

ment of which we dream, and that our buildings thus clad in a garment of poetic imagery…will appeal with redoubled power, like a sonorous melody overlaid with harmonious voices."[2] He continued, in reference to himself:

> I conceive that a true artist will reason substantially in this way; and that, at the culmination of his powers, he may realize this ideal. I believe that architectural ornament brought forth in this spirit is desirable, because beautiful and inspiring; that ornament brought forth in any other spirit is lacking in the higher possibilities.
>
> That is to say, a building which is truly a work of art (and I consider none other) is in its nature, essence and physical being an emotional expression. This being so, and I feel deeply that it is so, it must have, almost literally, a life. It follows from this living principle that an ornamented structure should be characterized by this quality, namely, that the same emotional impulse shall flow throughout harmoniously into its varied forms of expression—of which, while the mass-composition is the more profound, the decorative ornamentation is the more intense. Yet must both spring from the same source of feeling.

Later in this essay, after stating that "the mass-composition and the decorative system of a structure such as I have hinted at should be separable from each other only in theory," Sullivan coined the expression, "organic system of ornamentation" and declared that in such a system, there was a "sympathy" between structure and ornament, which was to the benefit of both aspects, "each enhancing the value of the other." To explain this concept, he compared the value of certain leaves to the tree as a whole. If we consider the condemnation proffered five years later by Adolf Loos, who wrote that there was an inversely proportional relationship between the quantity of ornamentation and the cultural level of a country, it seems clear that Loos was driven by an ideological preconception.[3] We should recognize in Sullivan, on the other hand, a deeper theoretical complexity, one that was misunderstood by the his-

Adler & Sullivan, Chicago Stock Exchange Building, Chicago, 1892–93, general view and floor plans of the second floor and of a typical floor.

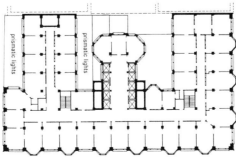

torians of the modern movement, who took only part of his message and cast it in a functionalist light.[4]

The great creative energy that Sullivan spent on ornamenting his buildings makes obvious the fact that he had a very clear sense of the direction of his work: decoration had been an area in which to experiment from the very beginning. Largely free from the harsh demands of production in a free-market economy, the realm of ornament was an area in which he could expand the emotional component of artistic expression. And yet the true interest of what Sullivan was trying to do with ornament lay in creating an organic link between this emotional component and the structure of the building. Of course, structure was the true determinant of function and cost, but he saw structure as a profoundly emotional component to design. Thus, Sullivan counted upon structure to act as locomotive to decoration; moreover, structure was necessary in the interplay between the two factors; it gave substance to the vitality of art. "We shall know," he concluded, "that the fragrance of a living art shall float again in the garden of our world."[5]

Was he thinking of the plaster colossus of the Transportation Building in this context, with its emphatic, overexposed, and humorless golden doorway, surrounded by angels, so many melancholy symbols of the American system of transportation? It seems more likely that he was thinking of the Wainwright Building, or perhaps he had in mind the tall buildings he was designing that very year, 1892: the Union Trust Building in St. Louis, and the Stock Exchange in Chicago.

St. Louis had proved to be a good market for Adler & Sullivan. They had been introduced to the town by the Wainwright family, and in the early 1890s they had opened an office with a local engineer named Charles K. Ramsey, who acted as general contractor and maintained links with local authorities. The booming city wanted to compete with Chicago and already featured a masterpiece of modern architecture: the Wainwright Building. By this point the office had designed other buildings, such as the Wainwright Tomb (1892) and the St.

Image that appeared in Harper's
Weekly *on 12 January 1895, and
views of the trading room of the
Chicago Stock Exchange.*

Nicholas Hotel (1892–93) in the city, and still others were on the horizon, beginning with the important Union Trust Building. Indeed, in 1895, a local exhibition was organized, featuring seven projects designed by the office.[6]

As had been the case with the Wainwright Building, Sullivan again felt that with the Union Trust Building a great opportunity had presented itself in St. Louis: a centrally located lot on the corner of Olive and Seventh Streets, and a powerful, wealthy patron. He could very easily have returned to the successful model of the Wainwright Building—only two years had passed, and the site would have been perfectly suited for a building of the same sort. Instead, however, the plan that was approved in the spring of 1892 was quite different, and in a certain sense, diametrically opposed. Considering the spectacular success that the Wainwright Building had enjoyed, it is surprising that Sullivan would have chosen such a different design scheme. However, the decision seems perfectly clear when understood in the context of his efforts toward integrating ornament and structure.

Sullivan adopted the same U-shaped plan with a similar layout and distribution of offices; here, however, he rotated it by 180 degrees. In this way, the block—which in the case of the Wainwright Building appeared as a large, unitary mass with the two separate arms of a great U-shape remaining hidden in the back—presented the arms of the U extending peremptorily toward the street, on either side of the entrance. While the Wainwright Building's dominant theme is that of unity, here—through a simple reversal of ground plan—Sullivan achieved the opposite effect: multiplicity. That multiplicity took the ambiguous form of a doubling: enough to undercut and oppose the idea of unity, but not sufficiently repetitive to establish a rhythm. Indeed, that very duplication, quite evident when viewing the elevation at an angle or from a distance, is neutralized in two ways: first, because the two tower-like structures, when seen from straight on, reveal their linkage as the arms of a U-shape, and second, because they are powerfully unified at the base of the building, where the two lower floors clearly join the bifurcated structure into a single unit. This impression is

further reinforced by the prominent central entrance, which emulates the well-known image of the exposition building that was at that time still in existence: the Transportation Building.

This great portal, then, was another "Golden Doorway," more unsettling than the gigantic but ephemeral version in the Columbian Exposition, in that it opens onto an axis leading into a void: a courtyard framed by two towers. It is an ostentatious entrance to an excessively ornate portion of the building. The entire second story is girded by a large and fabulous frieze of glazed terra-cotta. This frieze is punctuated by large round oculi similar to those that, on a decidedly smaller scale, were already present in the Wainwright Building and in the Fraternity Temple, set in the frieze tucked under the eaves.

Upon this lavish and surprising base, the two false towers rise up like fluted pillars, in the manner of the Schiller Building or the Seattle Opera House, with windows set in exceedingly tall insets, terminating at the top of the building in arches. Lastly, as if to accentuate the relationship to pillars, the top two stories are treated as a unit, with dense colonnades, taking on the guise of capitals.

The Union Trust Building is a truly excellent example of Sullivan's architecture, bent on emphasizing the cumulative juxtaposition of independent, diverse features with a single base unit. Added to the apparent division of the building into two parts is its classical articulation into architectural subcategories—base, shaft, crown—with a further, aggressive touch of montage in the typologically codified portal.

What relationship is there between this effort to create a paratactic composition and the role played by decoration? The ornamentation is without a doubt quite exuberant—more so than in other buildings—and on the façade, at the second-floor level, seven enormous lions, standing 8½ feet tall on their hind legs, herald the entry. These were largely attacked by architectural critics. Nevertheless, Twombly was later to write, without a hint of concern in regard to this disapproval, "the oversize portholes and lions, but especially the colonnade, comprised the coherence of Union Trust."[7] What is perhaps more surprising is that, at the time, there

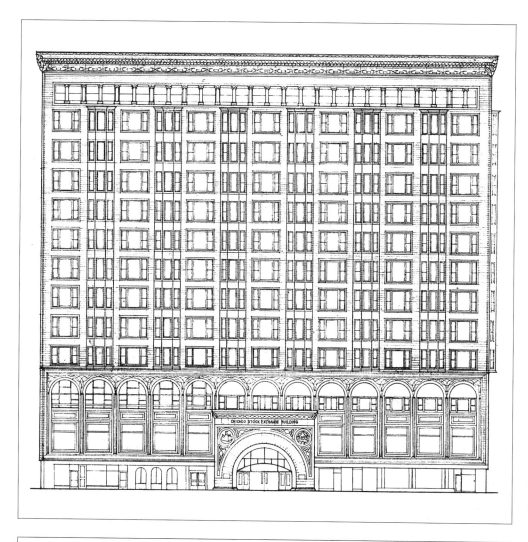

Chicago Stock Exchange, main elevation, detail design of the entrance, and detail.

were already a few who were capable of grasping the building's importance on a cognitive level—that this creation of Sullivan's could be perceived at two different levels. Clearly, the building was meant to interrupt the typically metropolitan state of distraction in the perception of passersby—from close-up, the overloaded ornamentation peremptorily demanded attention; from a distance, the building conveyed a singular overall image.

"Those who pass near the building will be attracted by the richness of the doorway and by the unique ornamentation of the second story. Those who will see the building from a distance will note the boldness and originality of the treatment of the two upper stories and the richness of effect of the main cornice and will be impressed by the twin tower effect . . . "[8] This latter ambiguous aspect is comparable, though unintentionally, to the symbolism of the columns of Hercules, placed seventy-five years later in a gigantic version overlooking New York Harbor in the World Trade Center of Minoru Yamasaki.

One of the most venturesome attempts to provide a critical analysis of Sullivan's ornamentation comes from D. S. Andrew, who, in writing about the Wainwright Building, spoke of "intricate geometric botanical abstractions," which, perhaps, "intend to say something about the process of biological evolution."[9] Andrew questions the relationship between this evolutionary reference and the economic situation in St. Louis in 1892. It seems reasonable to suppose—especially considering Sullivan's deep and abiding interest in evolutionary theory[10]—that he wished to convey the idea of an organic vitality in the growth of business-driven American capitalism.

Andrew further developed, in the same context, the idea that the ornamental elements and panels—"that seem reminiscent of primordial fauna and flora"—were a sort of defiance of the predominant role of technology, expressed metaphorically through architectural framing structures. Thus we can glimpse here an allegory of the subjugation of nature by rough industrial construction processes.[11] This interpretation can easily be inverted; like the analogous references to nature in Gian Lorenzo Bernini's works, such as the Montecitorio Palazzo,

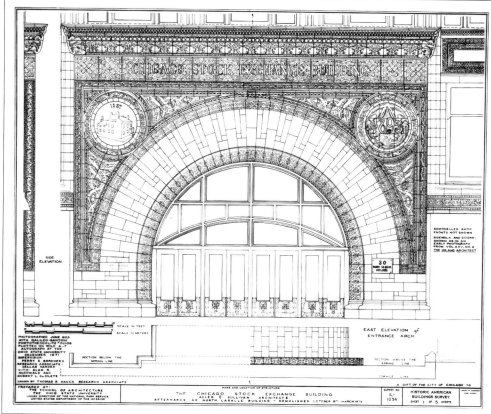

Adler & Sullivan (with C. K. Ramsey), Union Trust Building, St. Louis, Missouri, 1892–93, exterior views.

where the rustication of the building progressively transforms itself into natural rock. Is it the classicizing order of the palazzo that loftily dominates over primordial disorder? Or is it the unsettling depiction of the roots of rational human construction, of the irrepressible anarchic vitality of nature? Clearly, these two aspects were, for both Sullivan and Bernini, two faces of the artist's personality, the two sources of inspiration that fed all efforts at self-expression and the manifold results of those efforts, in an endlessly shifting, precarious equilibrium.

Sullivan's proposed methodology, set forth in his essay, "Ornament in Architecture," had by this time found perfect application in both the unitary Wainwright Building and in the Union Trust Building (designed while Sullivan was writing the essay in question). The choice of formal typology, then, was not determined by methodology. Sullivan was to continue to choose, as the occasion presented itself, between one or the other design approach, harboring differing sympathies in his heart.

What was emerging in his work at this time, then, is a fundamental feature—too little noticed by subsequent critics—consisting of an architecture that involved the assembly of distinct component parts, each with its own formal and typological autonomy, in accordance with a shifting array of compositional hierarchies. And this was the case in his use of both parataxis (coordinate order) and hypotaxis (subordinate order), in accordance with an overall design approach that made use of a constantly shifting set of compositional hierarchies among the component parts. It is certainly fair to describe that approach as anticlassical; a compositional strategy that was to find its most successful and exemplary expression in the Chicago Stock Exchange.

But before examining this latter project, however—which should be recognized as the finest product of American architecture of the nineteenth century—let us focus our attention on Sullivan's relationship with his former pupil Frank Lloyd Wright. That relationship was as strained as could be in this period, and it finally broke down in May of 1893. Indeed, the relationship collapsed during the long process of designing the Stock Exchange. The

Adler & Sullivan, Charlotte Dickson Wainwright Tomb, St. Louis, Missouri, 1892, view and ornamental design for the bronze door, ink on linen paper, 27.5 x 24 in.

fact that the breakdown of the relationship coincided with this project has never really been noted by architectural historians, who instead have focused on Wright's Charnley House (1891) and on the general area of home design, where in fact Wright tended to dominate.

It is the purity of line—predominantly horizontal—in the Charnley House that suggests a modernity attributed to the young Wright, viewed as a vanguard of rationalism. Twombly, too, accepted this thesis, and suggested that from this first independent success of the pupil grew the roots of the split with the master.[12] It was therefore natural for Wright to begin designing independently in Oak Park. Wright himself, in his autobiography, admitted that he had produced only three projects "outside of office hours" while he was under contract in the office of Adler & Sullivan.[13]

It is difficult to explain the harshness and intransigence with which Sullivan reacted to what he considered to be the breaking of a contract—Wright's five-year commitment to work for the firm. Wright was actually forced to leave the office a few months prior to the expiration of the agreement, probably in May of 1893, and there were threats to repossess the house that Wright had purchased with a loan from the studio; Adler, however, dissuaded Sullivan from this attempt.[14]

Sullivan's fury should be understood in the light of the fact that this episode came in the midst of Sullivan's greatest level of creativity and work pace. Worshippers of Wright tend to present the episode—based on Wright's memoirs—as part of a sequence of events that read as follows: Sullivan has a depressing experience with the Columbian Exposition; he quarrels with Wright; he quarrels with Adler, leading to the dissolution of the firm. Moreover, these hagiographers of Wright consider the Wainwright Building to be the finest and most "Wrightian" of Sullivan's projects; they link the subsequent decline to the break between the two and the sudden success of the younger architect. And, in their view, Sullivan's harshness, inevitably, is portrayed in the unpleasant tones of insecurity and envy.

And yet there is another interpretation that can be offered for these events, beginning with a proper recognition of the presence of Sullivan's hand in the design of the Charnley House. It might be considered, at the outset, as the product of a close collaboration between the two architects, each bringing something of his own to the project. This interpretation would then continue with a recognition that the years between the Auditorium and the Guaranty Building can fairly be considered to be a fertile period, indeed a time of increasingly fine creativity, a time of growing theoretical depth and design talent on the part of Sullivan. If this interpretation is accurate, then we can view Sullivan's wrath as that of a chief architect firmly in control, confident in the continued recognition of the excellence of his work, and proud of his own authentically personal creations. Thus, Sullivan was a leader, by this point (and for the moment) without rivals, who therefore could not and would not put up with the growing insubordination of his employee and pupil, who was wrongfully claiming credit—whether consciously or not—for work done together, until Wright finally came to consider himself Sullivan's equal and competitor in terms of creativity and productivity.

While questions remain over the authorship of the Charnley House and the Wainwright Building, the Stock Exchange was entirely Sullivan's work, and spectacularly so. In this building, the four-square, noble, and static structure of the Wainwright Building survived only in the elegant treatment of the corner, with a clear reference to pilasters evident in the upper section of the building, under an Italian cornice very different from the bare, flat projection—Wrightian in style—of the Wainwright Building or the Schiller Building. And yet, directly under the cornice, exquisitely carved, the façades were deeply cut by a sharp horizontal indentation running from one corner "pilaster" to the other, punctuated on all elevations by a row of low columns with lavish capitals. These were reminiscent of both Richardson and Root, yet they became perfectly typical of Sullivan in this straightforward contextual montage, and also typical of Sullivan as references to his earlier works, such as the Union

*Adler & Sullivan, James Charnley
Residence, Chicago, 1891–92, exterior
view, floor plans of the ground floor
and second floor, and view of the loggia.*

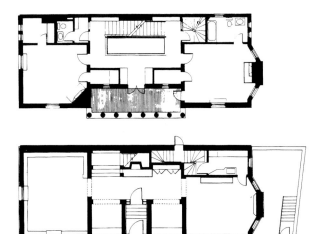

Trust Building of Buffalo, with the remarkable colonnaded heads of its pseudo-towers.

At street level, on the other hand, the Stock Exchange featured long lines of modern, functionalist display windows; above these stood a broad cornice and then a series of two-story, terra-cotta arches. The proportions of these arches and their unprecedented plastic treatment marked the high point of American architecture prior to the New Deal.

Lastly, between the three-story base of the building and the crowning element, which ran from the thirteenth story to the roof, stood the tall, substantial office block. Here, in a repetitive typology, ran an endless series of windows, punctuated by the alternating rhythm of three-part bay windows and flat walls with standard Chicago windows. Between the false arched portico of the base and the false colonnaded loggia of the attic—between these two precious, autonomous segments of a single block— the rhythmic typology of the repeating façade extended without syntactic mediation, in a purely paratactic relationship. This treatment was a typical feature of the Chicago School, which had already been explored authoritatively by Burnham and Root, but never by Sullivan. In the past, Sullivan had always used the bay window as an isolated decorative element, or had used it to punctuate a façade only sparingly, in the complex composition of architectural volumes. He had never repeated these forms in a continuous pattern, because of his long-standing hostility to any repeating form that was not directly linked to the model of the colonnade or a of series of arches.

In the poetics of assemblage, however, which Sullivan had constantly pursued and now mastered, the contrast between variously characterized linguistic components provided opportunities. And the stamp of that poetics, so exquisitely Sullivanesque, was immediately recognizable in the powerful independence of the deep, semicircular golden doorway, set in a finely carved rectangular shape, which displayed the elegantly geometric decorative style of George Elmslie. It was practically a triumphal arch which—in the style of the Transportation Building

of the same period—stood at the base of the building, interrupting any reiterative function in a peremptory style. That would apply first and foremost to the display windows, but also to the three arches, cut deliberately to declare the triumphal hegemony of the subject, which also dominated over an ennobled urban collective. Sullivan, then, insisted on his own architectural values in the face of classical homogeneity, which was represented in the United States by the architects of the White City and soon emphatically brought back by Burnham as a productive leap in planning on an urban scale. Sullivan was not afraid to set himself up as the champion of Emersonian ideals, well-worn thought they may have been, because of the authority that he felt he could represent in American culture, and because

of his awareness of being at the prime of his design capacity and theoretical prowess.

During this period he wrote "Emotional Architecture as Compared with Intellectual: A Study in Subjective and Objective," his first well thought-out tirade against the standardization that Burnham was now successfully propagating, in the wake of the great triumph of the Columbian Exposition. And it was in New York that Sullivan came into the open, on the home turf of leading White City architects and adversaries of his way of thinking and design. It was as if Sullivan were attempting to deny Burnham the authority of leadership of the school that he, Sullivan, so strenuously opposed. And Burnham—gifted architectural manager that he was, even better town designer, which he would soon show himself to be—was behaving like the head of the school. As such, in fact, he spoke authoritatively to Wright, who had left his *"Lieber Meister,"* and who must have seemed to Burnham like a loose cannon, loaded with explosive talent, but pointing in the wrong direction. According to Wright's autobiography, dated 1931, Burnham attempted to dampen Wright's powder, pushing him toward the standardized Beaux-Arts style. Burnham had summoned Wright to come see him in the offices of a capitalist named Waller, offering him a specific assignment with the businessman's support. Burnham offered to send Wright to France for four years, to recover, in the cradle of classicism, from the training of bad Chicago masters—Root and Sullivan, first and foremost—and to truly learn town planning. This was an apprenticeship that was considered strictly necessary, and would be followed by full-time employment for a lifetime. Reconstructing his thoughts on the matter nearly four decades later, Wright wrote that Burnham's offer would have made his life too easy and too dull. He considered it as an escape or a betrayal.

According to Wright, he could not betray Sullivan. But hadn't he already done so? His rigorously classical design for the Milwaukee Library, which seems like a creation of Charles Atwood, the most Hellenistic of the masters of the White City, dated from late 1893 or 1894. His negative reply to Burnham was, rather, the latest in a long series of indications of Wright's self-confidence and certainty of his own genius, already unrivaled at age twenty-seven. After having broken free of Sullivan's tutelage, he could not accept a four-year apprenticeship under masters that even Sullivan was unable to stomach for one year. Wright had even broken free of Sullivan's tutelage.

Remarkably enough, then, in 1894 the three points of the triangle said to represent the avant-garde of American architecture found themselves in direct contact: Sullivan, Wright, and Burnham. All three were at the apex of their faith in themselves and in the possibilities granted by the current cultural circumstances. And this was true, significantly enough, precisely at the time in which one of the worst economic and productive crises in American history was brewing, bringing a sea-change that was to favor of the three—and this was no accident—the very one who has been least praised by later critics: Burnham. Over the long run, it was to spell disaster for Sullivan.

1. Louis H. Sullivan, *Louis Sullivan: The Public Papers*, ed. Robert Twombly (Chicago: University of Chicago Press, 1988), 80.

2. Ibid., 80–81.

3. See Adolf Loos, *Trotzdem, 1900–1930* (Innsbruck: 1931). Cited by Nikolaus Pevsner, *Pioneers of Modern Design from William Morris to Walter Gropius* (Baltimore: Penguin, 1964).

4. Beginning with Montgomery Schuyler, who published *American Architecture* in the same year, 1892, and Russel Sturgis, a member of the same group, who wrote about it in *Architectural Record* 8 (1898–99).

5. Sullivan, *Public Papers*, 85.

6. Robert Twombly, *Louis Sullivan: His Life and Work* (Chicago: University of Chicago Press, 1986), 310.

7. Ibid., 308.

8. "The Union Trust Building," *Saint Louis Post-Dispatch*, 8 July 1892. Cited in ibid.

9. David S. Andrew, *Louis Sullivan and the Polemics of Modern Architecture* (Urbana: University of Illinois Press, 1985), 100ff.

10. See ibid., 38ff.

11. Ibid., 101.

12. Twombly, *Life and Work*, 233.

13. Frank Lloyd Wright, *Io e l'architettura*, (Milano: Mondadori, 1955), 233ff.

14. Twombly, *Life and Work*, 235.

For those who study the reasons for the rapid down-ward turn of Sullivan's professional career, the first signs of a coming decline are often glimpsed in two painful separations: first from Wright in 1893, and then from Adler in 1895. This leads to a tendency to limit the investigation of his decline to the areas of design and architecture. Many aspects of Sullivan's decline in fortune thus prove mystifying and are often laid on a mysteriously adverse series of events or on the tireless and subtle hostility of Sullivan's adversaries, first and foremost Daniel H. Burnham.

Such a reading of events is typical of the vast majority of the accounts written under the influence of Sullivan's autobiography, and of later accounts as well, right up to fairly recent times. These interpre-tations consider the professional decline of the young architect, not yet forty in 1895, as an unjust quirk of history, a fluke that can only be vindicated by historiography. But the establishment of a neme-sis, of course, is of no particular help in the writing of historiography. This demonstrates, once again, the validity of the cognitive principle whereby a phenomenon will appear to be inexplicable to those who fail to extend their field of observation to a suf-ficiently broad extent, one that contextually consid-ers the phenomenon in question.[1]

Those, on the other hand, who extend their observations slightly, so as to incorporate the histor-ical situation during Sullivan's career, have immedi-ately been impressed by the way in which the decline of his professional status came to coincide with the larger American economic and social crisis that began in 1893, causing particularly sharp turmoil and tension in Chicago in 1894. Sullivan, as was nat-ural for a man of his background, experienced this decline with a total absence of critical detachment. Tumultuous events surrounded a strike that began in the Chicago suburb of Pullman in the spring of 1894: a financial panic, mass unemployment, wide-spread hunger afflicting many immigrants, and the calling in of the army by President Cleveland. It is unacceptable to restrict these events of such tragic drama from the purview of architectural history. If these are sad chapters of social history, and if they must be regarded with fatalistic resignation, their influence, whether exerted directly or indirectly upon the construction of buildings and, still more indirectly, upon the culture of design, must be taken into consideration.

The office of Adler & Sullivan certainly felt the effects of the depression. In the years 1894 and 1895, the Guaranty Building in Buffalo, though a major work, was virtually the only new project com-pleted by the firm. And things were looking bad as early as 1893, when Chicago had tried to stave off the depression with the great exposition. The fact that the young and impatient Frank Lloyd Wright chose to leave the office at this time, becoming a canny and adventurous freelancer, must be linked to this looming disaster. In 1896, in a slightly different manner, Dankmar Adler jumped ship as well.[2]

Adler, then fifty-one and a skilled engineer, was exhausted by the trying experience of constructing the Auditorium tower, still slowly collapsing under the unexpected increase in height so glibly approved by Sullivan. No matter how fabulous the view from their offices high atop that very same tower, he could no longer work as Sullivan's partner, especially in an increasingly depressed office. Married with three children to support, he accepted the offer of his friend and former client Richard T. Crane, who hired him as consulting architect to his elevator company; in short, Adler became a salesman.

George Elmslie remained with Sullivan, trying to fill the vacuum left by Frank Lloyd Wright's departure. Elmslie continued to pursue Wright's goal of making Sullivan's entrancing decorative sketches "more architectural" as he developed them into blueprints. These drawings can soon be seen emerging in the production of the studio: the fresh-ness of his style, tending toward geometric repeti-tion, makes them far better suited to the serial repetition necessary for standardized terra-cotta decorative elements. Elmslie's designs for interior ornamentation were exceedingly elegant, especially in their rhythmic and luxuriant patterning. A good example of this was the Trading Room of the Union Trust Building of St. Louis, where a dense welter of geometric inventions had very little in common with H. H. Richardson's "animalistic Romanesque" decorations still present on the exteri-or of the building.

115

*Guaranty Building, typical floor plan
and views of the open courtyard and
the entrance portal.*

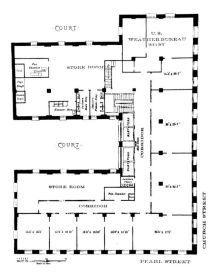

The presence of Elmslie alongside Sullivan was to be particularly evident in the Guaranty Building, a skyscraper that was initially called the Prudential Building, which was adorned with a decorative facing done entirely in terra-cotta. This was an approach that Wright had sharply opposed, as he failed to share Sullivan's enthusiasm for naturalistic and gestural flamboyance. "All materials were only one material to him in which to weave the stuff of his dreams. Terra-cotta was that one material. Terra-cotta was *his* material, the one he loved most and served best," he was to write, with ill-concealed condescension.[3] Elmslie, on the other hand, complied with Sullivan's style, and even expressed considerable enthusiasm in applying it. Many critics feel that the Guaranty was Sullivan's greatest skyscraper, and it can certainly be said to have been the work that hewed closest to his theoretical text, "Ornament in Architecture." Adler was also still working with Sullivan—in order to resolve the great technical problems of the foundation and the metal frame—between the beginning of design in late 1894 and the inauguration of the building in March 1896.

The architectural theme of the Buffalo building seems almost naturally to have assumed a similar configuration to that found in the Wainwright Building in St. Louis: a rectangular structural block, slightly more upward-thrusting in this case, with a similar U-shaped ground plan articulated in an absolutely regular and dignified symmetrical structure. Is there an explanation for the return to the static monumentality of the Wainwright Building following the more complex and interesting—but perhaps more troublesome and problematic—experiments of 1892 and 1893? Within this architectural context, the influence of the enormously volatile social situation can be of only relative importance. And yet the fact remains that the Guaranty Building was commissioned, developed, and designed in the midst of exceedingly serious tension and strife following the great financial panic of 1894 and the subsequent crackdown on social conflict.

The image of the White City, a general return to massive walls, and a classical-style architecture—championed by Burnham and the architects of the East—constituted the cultural face of deflationary Republican policies. The Republicans emphasized the widespread employment of unskilled (and therefore unorganized) labor. But the high-technology architecture of skyscrapers demanded a highly industrialized construction process and specialized types of labor generally organized into unions. This constituency tended to be supportive of the Democratic Party and its economic platform, which called for inflation in the economic sphere. Is there a parallel between this association and the confident and elegant tower of the Guaranty Building?

If so, the haughty, studied bulk of the skyscraper in Buffalo—with its remarkable continuous cladding extending over all of its architectural surfaces, and its refined, exquisitely shaped and finished hieroglyphics in terra-cotta—can be understood as a direct expression of the most advanced entrepreneurial aristocracy. That elite, buttressed by specialized technology and the privileged labor relations that accompanied that technology, withstood the economic depression and established a new, if insecure, leadership. This new hegemony was threatened by contemporary Republican deflationary policy, and it appeared that the Republicans were about to win at the polls again in 1896. As is always the case in architectural history, lack of security tends to be concealed behind the most assertive forms. This might serve to explain the return—amidst the tension of an economic crisis—to the most affirmative model of Sullivan's entire career: that of the Wainwright Building. This progressive urban architectural style was clearly opposed to the return to a classical town design of the European variety; no accident, considering that precisely this town design, which fit in well with the ideological shift that came with the new Republican administration, soon had as its protagonist none other than Burnham, with the city plans of Cleveland and Washington, D. C., and later, San Francisco and Chicago, in his hands.

If, however, the Guaranty Building can be considered as an expression of the theoretical program set forth by Sullivan in his 1892 essay, "Ornament in Architecture," it is doubtful that there was any such connection in the programmatic text mentioned in

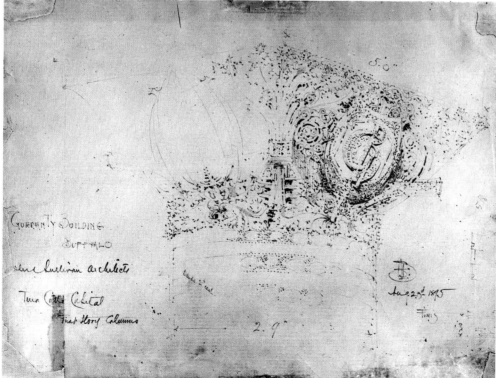

Wim de Wit's recent book. The text in question was
a letter written by Sullivan to Burnham, in response
to Burnham's query, as coordinating architect of the
Columbian Exposition, about the way in which Sullivan's design related to the general theme of transportation. Sullivan defended and justified his design
with these words:

> The thought we sought to express in the
> Transportation Building was this: An architec-
> tural exhibit. This thought subdivided itself as
> follows:
> 1. A natural, not historical, exhibit.
> 2. To be expressed by elementary masses carry-
>   ing elaborate decoration.
> 3. All architectural masses and subdivisions to be
>   bounded by straight lines or semi-circles, or
>   both in combination, to illustrate the possibili-
>   ties of very simple elements when in effective
>   combination.
> 4. The decorations to be of a very elaborate
>   nature and chiefly in color.
> 5. The combination of 3 and 4 to show how easily
>   and quietly large and simple masses carry elab-
>   orately and minutely worked out "ornamenta-
>   tion."
> 6. The chief object of 4 being to show that the
>   farther the process of systematic subdivision
>   be carried the quieter and more dignified
>   becomes the structure as a whole.
> 7. The use of colored decorations to show the
>   possibility of sequence combination, and repe-
>   tition when a great many colors are used: hence
>   the true nature of polychrome.
> 8. The use of a symbolical human figure in color
>   to show its great value in architectural decora-
>   tion.
> 9. A long series of minor considerations, entering
>   too minutely into detail to be here enumerated.
> 10. The summarizing thought, that all this should
>   be done in a natural and easy way,—as willing
>   to teach while searching for beauty.[1]

This letter, clearly written in a spirit of impatience with the interference of the coordinating
architect, sanctions a new direction for architecture,

Daniel H. Burnham and Charles B. Atwood, Reliance Building, Chicago, 1895.

yet elegant presence of a steel structure, although that structure was completely sheathed in a blanket of terra-cotta—a presence, evoked by the thin skeleton, that expressed a solid calculation of "maximum yield." The second aspect involves the use of a qualitatively and quantitatively "ornamental system," which was proposed as a comfort and a luxury within society's reach.

These two aspects—already present in the Wainwright Building but here brought to a higher level of expression—take differing paths toward the same end: highly specialized production in the areas of structure and ornament. These were precisely the two aspects that Sullivan had focused on in his essay on ornament in 1892, indicating that they were the two areas upon which the creative energy of the designer should be lavished, with a view toward their "organic" and vital harmonization. This is a radically different program from the merely polemic one found in the letter to Burnham, concerning the Transportation Building.

The Guaranty Building, then—unlike Burnham & Atwood's 1895 Reliance Building in Chicago, a skyscraper that looks to the future uncompromisingly—can be considered the "swan song" of the Chicago school in its previous, culturally more ambitious phase, exemplified in the work of Root. Now, however, only Sullivan was striving to recover the values of this period, a period whose entrepreneurial avant-garde was linked to a rapidly declining protectionist economic cycle.

Thus we find the remarkable power of the Guaranty Building underscored by the emphasis given to the softened, rounded projection of its crown. This element hearkened back to the extreme elegance of Burnham's Monadnock Building, and was organically linked to the ornate *trompe-l'oeil* decoration of the frieze, with its round oculi more pronounced than those found on the Wainwright Building. Unlike previous work by Sullivan, this incredible decorative array spills over and out of the panels and friezes to which it was supposedly confined, covering the entire architectural surface. Here, especially in the lower areas where the ornamentation is more geometric in nature, the skillful technique of Elmslie becomes apparent.

one in direct opposition to the American productivist phase of Beaux-Arts doctrine that Burnham supported following the death of Root in 1892. This new direction, which had been pursued by Sullivan only in the enormous temporary structure of the Transportation Building for the Columbian Exposition, was implicitly criticized by Wright, as evident when he accused Sullivan of conceiving buildings as if they were molded from a single material—terracotta. In fact, the theoretical significance of Sullivan's completed buildings is quite different. Wright's accusation does not even apply to the Guaranty Building, which is, however, faced entirely with terra-cotta.

There are actually two remarkable aspects to this project, rightly touted in art history books. The first has to do with defining an image capable of evoking, within the metropolitan grid, the powerful

Higher up, on the other hand, where the decoration is more naturalistic—particularly on the cornice, where it actually frees itself from the bounds of the building volume, spilling into the corners in free strands of vines—it is the work of Sullivan that evokes admiration. If one ventures to recognize, in the Wainwright, the iconic assertiveness of an Apollonian equilibrium, in the Guaranty Building it is the Dionysian aspect, always implicit in Sullivan's work, that indicates a new direction for a modern monumentality. Yet the death of Root left Sullivan to work in splendid isolation in this vein after the completion of the Guaranty Building, his "swan song". The collaboration with Elmslie was important, but it served only to sustain him in his aloneness.

It was at this point that he and Adler broke. The letter in which the older man announced to Sullivan that he would be changing profession, "trusting sincerely in the possibility that our pleasant relations will continue," is dated 11 July 1895. What determined the definitive break was the Guaranty Building. In the Guaranty Construction Company's rental prospectus, dated March 1896, the name of Adler appears only in the title, while the text excludes him entirely, insisting that the building was the "masterpiece of Louis H. Sullivan, who is famous in two continents for the beauty, originality, and refinement of his conceptions."[5] The partnership, based upon the complementary gifts of the two masters was worn out. Adler made the decision to go work for Crane, but, just six months later, reversed this decision, creating an atmosphere of confusion. Wright's efforts to put the two back together were destined to fail, however, and Adler's decline continued, rapid and irreversible. Sullivan still had plenty of wind in his sails, though; in 1896 he was just forty years old and America was making a decisive shift in economic policy. William McKinley had soundly trounced William Jennings Bryan in the presidential election, and following this historic victory the Republicans laid a firm grip on power right up to the outbreak of the First World War, launching an anti-protectionistic and imperialistic policy on a worldwide scale. Thomas Mann, in his *Betrachtungen eines Unpolitischen* (or *Reflections of Nonpolitical Man*) was to make it quite clear how important it was for a man to turn forty at a time of political and historic change.

Sullivan took the credit for the Guaranty Building—the perfect skyscraper that put its seal on an era—all to himself, excluding his collaborator, partner, and friend, Adler. Now he was alone, appropriately enough for someone who promoted himself as the leader of a new and alternative direction in architecture, a direction in opposition to that advocated by Burnham and founded upon the delegation of responsibility and the impersonal repetition of the urban models of the old world.

The power of Sullivan's theoretical approach was reinforced by the reintroduction of the ideas put forth in his writings from as early as 1885. Here, Sullivan navigated between the individualistic vitality of American transcendentalism, especially that of Whitman, and the Spencerian evolutionary organicism of Greenough, with allusions to Nietzschean heroism and romanticism. This philosophy could be repackaged in a productivistic guise in order to pro-

vide a new beginning for America's cultural identity, then at the risk of thorough European contamination. Aggressive and ambitious, this profoundly natural identity, could not help but find a metaphor for itself in the form of the skyscraper.

And so Sullivan published, in the March issue of *Lippincott's Magazine*, the essay for which he was to earn lasting fame, "The Tall Office Building Artistically Considered," with its famous maxim that "form follows function."[6] Yet this slogan was apparently intended solely to confer cultural dignity upon tall buildings, to refound the culture of design upon Sullivan's own philosophy: "The architects of this land and generation are now brought face to face with something new under the sun—namely, that evolution and integration of social conditions, that special grouping of them, that results in the erection of tall office buildings." Sullivan was not interested in discussing the social conditions leading to this phenomenon, considering it as he did the expression of a "vital problem" to be resolved. Sullivan proceeded to set forth the material ramifications at stake: offices were needed to do business; the elevator made "vertical travel" easy and comfortable; steel technology made it possible to erect inexpensive, solid, and very tall buildings; the rise in property values stimulated the increase in the number of stories, making the land more valuable and spurring more growth. Thus, purely material drives led to the birth of the skyscraper as the "product of the joint energies of the speculator, the engineer, [and] the builder."

Sullivan proceeds to state the problem represented by the tall building, at the same time laying down a challenge for the architect:

> How shall we impart to this sterile pile, this crude, harsh, brutal agglomeration, this stark staring exclamation of eternal strife, the graciousness of those higher forms of sensibility and culture that rest on the lower and fiercer passions? How shall we proclaim from the dizzy height of this strange, weird, modern housetop the peaceful evangel of sentiment, of beauty, the cult of a higher life?

The architect's role, then, is defined—given certain unquestionable technical necessities—as the nearly mystical redemption of beauty to a structure's formal appearance. It would seem, then, something quite different than "form follows function," something more akin to the pursuit of elegance exemplified in Sullivan's own Guaranty Building.

Now, however, Sullivan's discourse looked to the future, acquiring new and greater articulation.

The breakdown of the simple block structure—put forward as a design method—referred back to a technique of assemblage employed at the Chicago Stock Exchange.

Beginning with the first story, we give this a main entrance that attracts the eye to its location, and the remainder of the story we treat in a more or less liberal, expansive, sumptuous way—a way

based exactly on the practical necessities, but expressed with a sentiment of largeness and freedom. The second story we treat in a similar way, but usually with milder pretension. Above this, throughout the indefinite number of typical office tiers, we take our cue from the individual cell, which requires a window with its separating pier, its sill and lintel, and we, without more ado, make them look all alike because they are all alike. This brings us to the attic, which, having no division into office-cells, and no special requirement for lighting, gives us the power to show by means of broad expanse of wall, and its dominating weight and character, that which is the fact—namely, that the series of office tiers has come to an end.

This may perhaps seem a bald result and a heartless, pessimistic way of stating it, but even so we certainly have advanced a most characteristic stage beyond the imagined sinister building of the speculator-engineer-builder combination.

Sullivan proceeds to note that the essential quality of a skyscraper is its height, a characteristic that should stimulate the architect to communicates the forces of exaltation and pride of sovereignty. The skyscraper, in brief, proves to be "one of the most stupendous, one of the most magnificent opportunities that the Lord of Nature in His beneficence has ever offered to the proud spirit of man."

At this point, Sullivan returns to the idea of the "dizzy height" of the "cult of a higher life," calling on architects to push the limits of the skyscraper toward its most essential and vital meaning. He proceeds to make reference to the various programmatic means available for the pursuit of an adequate formal symbolism: the image of the column, with base, shaft, and capital; the anthropomorphic image, likewise tripartite (limbs, thorax, and head); the botanical model, based on the three parts of a tree (roots, trunk, leaves). These references, in rhetorical terms, were useful only in making themselves obsolete. They were ideas that concerned the "non-essential"—they did not focus upon the "vital" point. Was there such a thing as a "final, comprehensive formula?" There certainly was, and Sullivan went on to describe it:

All things in nature have a shape, that is to say, a form, an outward semblance, that tells us what they are, . . . Unfailingly, in nature these shapes express their inner life, the native quality, of the animal, trees, birds, fish, that they present to us; they are so characteristic, so recognizable, that we say, simply, it is 'natural' it should be so.

We must recognize that life and form are "absolutely one and inseparable," and that where "function does not change form does not change. . . . It is the pervading law of all things organic." And if this is law, then can art possibly violate that law? "Are we so decadent, so imbecile, so utterly week of eyesight that we cannot perceive this truth so simple, so very simple?" Here, Sullivan launched the formula "form ever follows function."[7] Clearly, its original connotation struck far deeper and far more complex values than the cold, reductive interpretation conferred upon it by the modern movement. Perhaps it was intrinsic to the formulation itself, in the evolutionary terms in which it was proposed, that it should have found the minimalist hermeneutic destiny that made its fortune and rendered it so exceedingly versatile. Sullivan must have guessed that he had a winning card to play.

Sullivan made the maxim a banner of his own resistance, staunchly avoiding its use as a measure of his own previous production. In all likelihood, he was well aware that its force lay in being only apparently clear and unequivocal. Indeed, Sullivan had been quite explicit about the existence of a plurality of meaning in all of his previous writings and lectures. It was therefore quite clear to him that the terms "form" and "function" referred back to many possible meanings that could be used on different occasions, thus confirming the constant validity of an aphorism that would otherwise be applicable only in a biological and evolutionary context. This was not mere craftiness, but the result of a desperate need for assertion and self-affirmation in order not to succumb to the pragmatic, schematic, and merely quantitative architectural solutions of the dominant culture represented by Burnham. Sullivan opposed that culture with the authority of great ideas, appropriating noble cultural models like transcendental-

ism and rendering them up-to-date with his own irrepressible sensibilities and creativity.

Ambiguity, however, was a double-edged sword. The reductive meaning of Sullivan's formulation was not merely the agent of historiographical glory. Even Wright used a similarly reductive interpretation—so distant from the rich, multivalent one intended by its author—as late as 1935, when he wrote that Sullivan derived his mode of understanding architecture from Adler.[8] With this argument, anything but impartial, Wright reacted against the prevalent hagiographic attitude toward Sullivan, which coincided with a gradual waning of respect accorded to Adler. Adler, for that matter, had immediately busied himself, upon the publication of Sullivan's essay, with indirectly rectifying the theoretical system that his younger colleague had proposed, claiming authorship of it for himself.

Adler's lecture, delivered in Nashville in 1896, entitled "The Influence of Steel Construction and Plate Glass Upon the Development of Modern Style," was sufficiently noteworthy to prompt Lewis Mumford to republish it.[9] "But the architect is not only an artist, but also an engineer, a man of science and a man of affairs." Adler had this to say about Michelangelo, a hero of Sullivan's, who was undoubtedly first and foremost an artist: "An important [part of] his greatness as an architect was his familiarity with the techniques of the auxiliary and subsidiary arts, sciences and crafts. . . . " Great opportunities for design, Adler pointed out in a punctilious manner, derive from changes in the environment, which may be natural (as Sullivan claimed), but which are more often produced by artificial conditions and circumstances, like the development of metal structures, with their decisive influence upon new styles. Hence, Adler's new and improved version of Sullivan's great formula: "function and environment determine form."

In Adler's version, we can detect—as Narciso Menocal correctly notes[10]—the deterministic influence of Gottfried Semper, which reached the American engineer, and certainly John Root as well, with the 1889 English edition of *Der Stil in den Technischen und Tektonischen*, originally published in 1863. Adler, a German native, may even have read this book in the original language. It was precisely in the face of determinism that Sullivan found space to react, rebelling—in the name of individual creativity—against the circumscription of form solely by material and situational necessity. This was a particularly modest qualification for someone like Sullivan who, in the transcendentalist tradition of Leopold Eidlitz, sought the main path of human destiny, of truth and beauty, in the cosmic laws of nature. These were to be rediscovered in an anthropomorphic dynamic, an organic vitality.

1. See Paul Watzlawick et al., *Pragmatics of Human Communication: A Study of Interactional Patterns, Pathologies, and Paradoxes* (New York: W. W. Norton, 1967).

2. Robert Twombly, *Louis Sullivan: His Life and Work* (Chicago: University of Chicago Press, 1986), 325ff.

3. Wim de Wit, ed., *Louis Sullivan: The Function of Ornament* (New York: W. W. Norton, 1986), 104.

4. Ibid., 106–08.

5. Twombly, *Life and Work*, 324ff.

6. Louis H. Sullivan, *Louis Sullivan: The Public Papers*, ed. Robert Twombly (Chicago: University of Chicago Press, 1988), 103ff.

7. Ibid., 112.

8. Cited by H. Duncan, "Attualità di L. Sullivan," *Casabella* 2–3 (1954): 7.

9. Dankmar Adler, "The Influence of Steel Construction and Plate Glass Upon Style," excerpt reprinted as "Function and Environment" in Lewis Mumford, ed., *Roots of Contemporary American Architecture: 37 Essays from the Mid-Nineteenth Century to the Present* (New York: Dover, 1972), 247.

10. Narciso G. Menocal, *Architecture as Nature: The Transcendentalist Idea of Louis Sullivan* (Madison: University of Wisconsin Press, 1981), 44.

The success of the Guaranty Building, followed by the success (even more decisive for Sullivan's reputation) of the aphorism "form follows function," resulted in a revival of the great architect's cultural power, the effects of which persisted until the end of the century. This phase of restored credibility was marked by commissions from Schlesinger & Mayer, Bayard, and the Gage brothers, and was part of the general burgeoning of America's systems of production that brought about the ascendancy of large, depersonalized trusts. In architecture, this resulted in coordinated classical designs, even though the move to classicism was not yet truly underway. The working method for which Daniel H. Burnham became the standard-bearer—and for which the Columbian Exposition had been the programmatic forerunner—was slow in bearing professional and productive fruit, and only finally matured vigorously at the dawn of the new century.

In the final years of the nineteenth century, progressive entrepreneurs, who tended to employ designers like Sullivan, still possessed a certain amount of power, especially as they began to rebound from the serious depression of 1893. This elite believed that the intellectual avant-garde possessed the answer to their ambitions for quality. Although they failed to understand the intricacies of Sullivan's theoretical program—filled with radical observations, yet oriented toward the acceptance, in evolutionary terms, of capitalism—this class of enlightened businessmen intuitively grasped that his work was in tune with the indigenous values of American culture that formed their own elective identity. And yet it should remain clear that the complex set of problems linked to the anger and enthusiasm found in Sullivan's work was understood by official culture only in very generic terms.

The fragility of that understanding was demonstrated when Richard Morris Hunt died in the summer of 1895, and none other than Sullivan was selected as the ideal candidate to design the ornamental border of a memorial portrait to be published in Chicago's *Inland Architect*. As a justification for this choice, a muddled link was adduced between the Francophile aspect of the Eastern School's classicism with the recognition conferred upon Sullivan by the Union Central des Arts Décoratifs. In so doing, a blithe assumption was made of an exceedingly unlikely heritage from Hunt down to Sullivan.

The new commissions Sullivan received during the last three years of the century, referred by old clients of the firm of Adler & Sullivan such as David Schlesinger, were vital to the firm's survival, as they came during an exceedingly difficult time. Schlesinger had commissioned a residence from the firm as early as 1884. In 1890, when Schlesinger was working with Mayer, he had commissioned the firm to rebuild an existing department store at the corner of State and Madison Streets. Sullivan's office had overseen the transformation and enlargement of the structure, on behalf of a client that was indecisive and often changed its mind. In 1896, Sullivan was working for Schlesinger and Mayer once again, this time a project that involved raising and reconnecting the various areas of the block at State and Madison Streets, which the client had purchased over time. Quite soon, however, changes in the client's wishes forced Sullivan to redo the project entirely. The actual implementation of the plans, which had been redrawn repeatedly but which were fairly definitive by 1898, resulted in the construction of only three bays of nine floors overlooking Madison Street in 1899. In 1903, after some demolition, the façade overlooking Madison Street was enlarged by three more bays, while the elevation overlooking State Street was enlarged by seven bays; this new structure was raised to a height of twelve stories.

The solution that Sullivan adopted, right from the beginning, was conceived with a specific programmatic model in mind. How could the architect follow such a model when he was forced by hard times to work for a client who demanded constant rethinking and transformation? This was the central dilemma for Sullivan in planning this typical turn-of-the-century project. Sullivan certainly had the talent to formulate a response in terms of great architecture. Clearly, it would be impossible to use either a formally closed typological model or one that could be expanded only through adding floors and building upward, like the model for the Wainwright Building or the Guaranty Building. What was needed, instead, was a modular architecture like

Louis Henry Sullivan (with L. P. Smith), Bayard Building, New York City, 1897–99, views and typical floor plan.

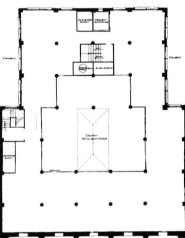

that of the Stock Exchange, but this time with the greater flexibility of a repetitive system. Sullivan made reference to the naturalistic metaphor of the beehive, which he may have borrowed from Leopold Eidlitz.[1] The key to a perfect beehive lies in the form of the repeatable cell. Hence, the highly functional design of the Chicago window, which served as the basis of the modular system.

Those who claim that Sullivan applied his dictate "form follows function"[2] to the Schlesinger & Mayer Department Store (from 1903 on, the Carson, Pirie, Scott Department Store) perhaps do not fully grasp that to consider form both a technical and an open linguistic system was unprecedented. Furthermore, form might follow the shifting demands of the client instead of a given function. While Sullivan's design process relied upon the teachings of Monsieur Clopet (the idol of his youth) for "demonstrations which were so simple . . . as to preclude exception,"[3] such a precedent did not necessarily presuppose the definition of an iconic model in the fashion of the classical temple (or the Wainwright Building). Instead, that rule might be tested, in this case in a dynamic way, upon an analogical model, such as a classicist building (or such as the Carson, Pirie, Scott Store).

Toward the end of the summer of 1897, Sullivan was in dire financial straits: the Schlesinger & Mayer project had once again come to a halt, while the various operating costs of his office and the many expensive clubs to which he belonged were draining him rapidly. He began to sell off real estate when, providentially it seems, he received his first New York City commission: the Bayard Building. Twombly hypothesized that it was Montgomery Schuyler who referred the project to him;[4] or it may have been another young architect, Lyndon Smith, who was in close contact with the client and was a great admirer of Sullivan.

Sullivan designed the Bayard Building—which came after the completion of the initial design for Schlesinger & Mayer, even though it was constructed earlier—at the same time that he wrote one of his most bitter essays, which remained unpublished until Twombly's anthology of 1988.[5] It might seem that

Louis Henry Sullivan, Gage and McCormick Building, Chicago, 1898–99, view of construction.

there was no connection between the building and the essay, since the New York skyscraper was one of Sullivan's most lavishly spectacular works. And yet a similar state of mind is evident in both the building and in the essay, and this might explain some aspects of Sullivan's behavior in this phase of his life, a phase that seems sadly and prematurely marked by mid-life crisis—he was, after all, only forty-one.

The essay, entitled "May Not Architecture Again Become a Living Art?"[6] soundly denounces the production of the time, which he decries as "a social evil; a flout and an insult to all that is noble, pure, and lofty in the human soul." In his view, this architecture was something like a battle against nature. In contrast, those with a true understanding knew that "the acme of life is beauty." This was followed in the text by the hope that "there may arise in the domain of art a man of whom it may be said, with truth, that his ruling passion is architecture," a phrase that, at this point, is clearly an allusion to himself.

It is, however, the beginning of the third paragraph that truly reveals Sullivan's state of mind, through a quote from Samuel Reynolds Hole: "He who would have beautiful roses in his garden must have beautiful roses *in his heart.*"[7] Here, a banal metaphor comes dangerously close to becoming a byword for hypocrisy. Finally, at the end of the text, the author's reference to himself becomes explicit, but it is a reference to the self of the past, conveyed in a tone of regret: "I who have loved my art with all my soul, with all my life, feel, more and more poignantly, year by year, as the hideous shape of it comes more fully, more clearly to my sight, how deep is the shame of it, how pitiful the humiliation!" There exists a gap—or conflict—between a pitiful, humiliating historical reality and the privileged standing of one who has "beautiful roses in his heart"—a gap that Sullivan seems eager to conceal by cultivating, despite everything, beautiful roses in the ornamental grace of his last few skyscrapers.

A great deal has been written concerning the Bayard Building as a model of Sullivan's work. Narciso Menocal has produced a structuralist, anthropomorphic reading of the building, based on the idea

Gage Building, ornamental design for a lunette, entrance façade detail, and view of the streetfront elevation.

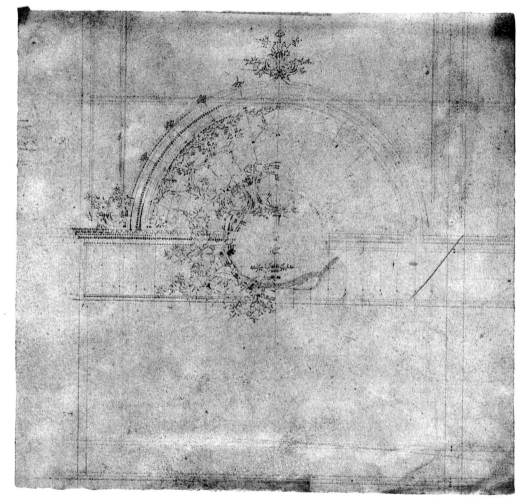

(certainly plausible) that the writings of Eidlitz directly and specifically influenced Sullivan.[8] Sullivan must have been aware of these writings, published in *Crayon* beginning in the mid-nineteenth century, and then anthologized in the volume *The Nature and Function of Art More Especially of Architecture*, dating from 1881. In any case, Sullivan is said to have adopted from Eidlitz the concept of two forces in equilibrium that substantiate the cosmic vital force: feminine emotion (expression), which can be found in intuition; and masculine reason (construction), which can be found in the intellect. In architecture, this equilibrium supposedly took form between the forces of ascension ("Rhythm of Life") and the forces of gravity ("Rhythm of Death"). On this basis, Menocal thought he could detect a sort of "anthropomorphic circuit" in the Bayard Building, in which the two opposite components merged in a closed diagram, which could be represented in quite a simple scheme: the ascending lines (feminine) would be those marked in the high section of the building by angels with spread wings; the gravitational lines (masculine), on the other hand, could be found in the outer and bottom pilasters.

Whether the conflict is between the "Rhythm of Life" and the "Rhythm of Death," as Menocal theorized it, or between the "beautiful roses" of the garden and the "social evil" to be excluded from it, we can be certain that the Bayard Building is the paradigm of an equilibrium that verges on paradox, attained with the vital support of a certain degree of cultural hypocrisy, or, at the very least, of a critical dimming of perception. If "the acme of life is beauty," then it is fair to rely upon an accredited and uncorrupted beauty, such as the carved lunette over the portal, in the style of fifteenth-century Florence; or the angels at the top of the building, in the Pre-Raphaelite style. And what does it matter if the mullioned windows on the top story undercut what could have been a great architectural moment, linked to a noteworthy typological innovation—the two-story space on the interior, which only later was divided by a loft structure?

If we set aside this shortcoming in the expression of a relationship between the interior and the exterior, the general proposal for the construction of

131

below: Gage Building, street façade.

*opposite: Louis Henry Sullivan, Schlesinger & Mayer
(later Carson, Pirie, Scott) Store, Chicago, 1898–99.*

this tall office building is unquestionably powerful: a triumphal base at street level, with rich ornamentation on the plate glass windows and the mezzanine; a repetitive vertical system, with the cells of the individual offices combined two-by-two within the primary load-bearing structure (pilasters), divided by a secondary upright structure (columns); and an ornamented cornice, also triumphal, not unlike the base. There was nothing new in this; but between the two extremes, on the ground and in the sky, the intermediate system expressed its theoretical strength, emphasizing the slenderness of the upright elements that extend in an elastic manner from one extreme to the other, as slim as the metal structure and the terra-cotta facing would allow. The tension

in this vertical system—which constituted a material expression of the economic investment on the site— was symbolized and rendered sublime by the large angels hovering in a rigid ascent toward the zenith.

The conclusion of this ascensional image—an angel atop each pilaster, with arms and wings spread wide—expressed its own contradiction. The very projection of the flat roof, which defined the building's height, was supported by these wings. Thus, the exceedingly long, ribbed pilaster strips were nothing more than a vertical extension of the tunic that draped the bodies of the angels, a parade of rockets thundering toward the clouds, leaving the building to its pragmatic and structural earth-bound destiny. Or was his use of the angels and the flora

*The two designs, at nine and twelve
stories, and view of the built version
of the Schlesinger & Mayer Store,
after later alterations to the cornice.*

design, instead, an effort to exorcise the masculine and real hegemony of quantity, in terms of the economic potential being created, with the feminine and ideal hegemony of quality? Or lastly, and more plausibly, was the building an authentic expression of a conflict whose dynamic cannot be reduced to any predetermined equilibrium?

Some critics have cited Art Nouveau as a reference for these angels.[9] This argument is unpersuasive considering the fact that in true Art Nouveau, the structural line underlying the entire architectural organism is first and foremost Symbolist in nature. The gestural fluidity of the Art Nouveau line allowed it to be easily assimilated into a load-bearing feature of construction, but its form could never be determined by structural considerations. Sullivan's understanding of load-bearing structure, on the other hand, adhered to the orthodox rules of structural technology, as followed by other Chicago School architects; the foundation of those rules in natural law, in fact, was a fundamental component of Sullivan's body of theory, and was necessary to the attainment—with organic decoration—of the most liberating potential of nature.

Sullivan's angels, of course, were also symbolic; the decorations were fluid and expressive. The formal role and the meaning that these angels took on in context, however, did nothing to undercut their structural function. On the contrary, the one served to validate and reinforce the other. Naturally, the levels of liberating symbiosis found in Art Nouveau design between formal elements and construction were unattainable here; and yet this made it possible to abandon eclecticism and make use of functionalist and rationalist visual language. And this language became all the more accessible as the role of decoration was made partial and limited. It is no accident that it was the Carson, Pirie, Scott Store, whose intense ornamentation was largely limited to the area around the display windows, that prefigured these new languages, as has generally been recognized.

It seems that the limit to Sullivan's reformist fantasy, in light of the real impotence apparent in the text of the unpublished essay of 1897, is reflected in a trend already operating in the design and construction of commercial buildings, which may be described as a reduction of connotative meaning. This tendency, evident even in the Gage Building (1898–99), which simply reiterates the typological and formal scheme of the Bayard Building, can be considered an inclination toward "styling," in the sense of an enrichment of exterior connotations, with a typological denotation that remains constant.[10]

Naturally, the exceedingly high quality of Sullivan's connotative apparatus, which benefited from his great creative and technical commitment, insured his works against reductivism and enhanced their enduring meaning. At such a difficult time, in the face of a prevailing attitude inclined to give priority to qualitative and functional value, Sullivan's pride in this endurance seems sufficient; it is, in any case, a less exhausting approach than that of the reformist creativity—sadly interrupted—that Sullivan had seemed determined to pursue courageously in a number of projects that were truly innovative in their methodology, such as the Chicago Stock Exchange.

But the master required support at this point. His financial troubles continued, making his solitude even harder to bear; he had cut off relations with Adler and Wright, but also with his brother and sister, Albert and May. Sullivan had also met a woman; Willard Connely's described her as "fairly tall with dark brown eyes like Sullivan's own, her face a bit rounded and her hair elaborately done up in the prevailing pompadour style." When the Architectural League of America held its convention in Cleveland, in June 1899, Sullivan was not present and his lecture, "The Modern Phase of Architecture," was read in his absence;[11] at the time, he was making preparations for his wedding, scheduled for July 1st.

The text, which was read by H. Webster Tomlinson (a collaborator of Wright's), conceals, beneath a paternalistic tone, a heartfelt appeal to the young in defense of Sullivan's own ideological standpoint. Perhaps this was an appeal to Sullivan's own youth, which he felt he abandoned early, and about which he harbored feelings of heartbreaking regret: "Youth is the most ambitious, the most beautiful, but the most helpless stage of life. It has that

View and details of the entrance façade of the Carson, Pirie, Scott Store.

immediate and charming idealism which leads in the end toward greatness. . . ." It is up to you, he exclaimed to the ninety-six members of the league, to demonstrate that "artistic pretension is not a synonym for moral irresponsibility. . . I am with you."

Margaret, Sullivan's new wife, was twenty, but she looked older, and claimed to be as well.[12] Sullivan's decision to marry her, and to thus begin the new century with a new personal life, came in the midst of deep existential turmoil. Historians have expressed skepticism as to the authenticity of the relationship—there was no honeymoon, and they set up housekeeping in a hotel suite (though it was certainly a luxurious one) at the Windermere Hotel. Biographers of Sullivan have worked to interpret the nature of this relationship, and the history of its development from a fairly frosty beginning; apparently, Sullivan spent his wedding night working to finish an essay. This seems to hint at an attitude resembling angry resignation on Sullivan's part—linked to great uncertainty about himself and his future—that pushed him to greater, more aggressive activity in his theoretical writings. It helped him to write and publish more widely.

Already, in early 1900, he responded to an article in *Brickbuilder* on the theme "Progress Before Precedent."[13] In his response, he denounced the work of his own generation, expressing the belief that the new generation might somehow offer greater hope. "I am an optimist," he wrote, and yet he was certain that the architecture of the time was "an art as yet without status in modern American life. Practically, it is a zero."[14] Was he speaking about himself? Certainly, he was talking of his own ideals. It was clear to him, at any rate, that these diatribes were his best hope of confirming and developing a role of some importance for himself—indeed, he was slowly building an audience and a following.

In the spring of 1900, the Architectural League held its convention in the Auditorium Building, Sullivan's own temple, as it were. When the time came for Sullivan to speak, after enjoying a triumphal explosion of applause, he began his long talk by claiming, rhetorically, to be surprised and unprepared. He then set off quite readily, sailing before the wind of his recollections: "When at three years of age I saw a storm dashing the waves over the rocks at Cape Ann, it left an impression which at that time I could not analyze. I realize it now, but I did not realize it then, that it was the Infinite spirit working in material forms as expressed in the form of that storm." He continued to speak of inspiration and of the soul. He also referred to the dynamics of history, distinguishing between high moments of architecture and long sloughs of depression, both the results of the worth of architects of the time. Finally, he came to the present day, addressing the issue of the values of American life: proud Americanism was at this point limited to nature and the spirit, and not found in art, which was wallowing in trickery and imitation.[15]

Once again, in June, he spoke at the banquet of the Architectural League, and his talk, "The Young Man in Architecture,"[16] which was later published in the *Inland Architect*, was a long, emphatic, and fairly pedantic one:

> American architecture is composed, on the hundred, of ninety parts aberration, eight parts indifference, one part poverty and one part Little Lord Fauntleroy. . . . Ninety-nine years of the hundred the thoughts of nine hundred and ninety-nine people of the thousand are sordid. This always has been true. Why should we expect a change? Of one hundred so-called thoughts that the average man thinks…ninety-nine are illusions, the remaining one a caprice.

The idea that Sullivan was trying to convey, then, was that art consisted of a magic moment, the rare product of a favorable social context and a tenacious, individual inspiration.

Sullivan "sings his song into your ears and, as by the cadence of a lullaby, objection is disarmed and opposition stilled,"[17] was the slightly sarcastic comment of the magazine *Architecture*.[18] The text, in fact, continued with a succession of short, repetitive, and rhythmic phrases—practically a devotional chant.

And, indeed, people listened raptly, perhaps even religiously. The depression had not abated; there was a high level of unemployment among architects and engineers. Sullivan had found a role as

the catalyst of dissatisfaction; it became his chosen task to give ideological form to the widespread apprehension, translating real anxiety into panicked protest. He delivered lashing rebukes to those who fit into a social climate that he deplored. He had no interest in whether those who listened to him were progressives or dreamers; he wished to have no say in the matter. Sullivan knew only that he was becoming a sort of messiah.

And he continued his crusade. In the summer, in the *Chicago Tribune*, and later, in *Interstate Architect and Builder*, he railed against the fact that "too many men live in a trance, stupor, or lethargy"; he attacked the educational system, "criminally false, bewildering, and destructive; and took particular aim at "the professors of architecture, brooding, like blight, over their schools,"[18] maintaining that with their attachment to the past, "they repress and prefer the spontaneity and charm of youth, the sanity, the higher usefulness of the future man." This hymn to youth, in which once again Sullivan lost all sense of proportion, seems to be linked to the sense of "unspeakably bitter hatred" that haunted him in this stage of his life. He clutched at "self-evident" remedies, such as a "return to natural, simple, wholesome, and sympathetic ways of thinking" in search of a complete "liberation of the creative impulse."

This statement caught the attention of the president of the American Institute of Architects, Robert S. Peabody, of the Boston architectural firm of Peabody & Stearns, who assumed that he was the target of the attack. And at the AIA conference in October, Peabody responded with overwrought sarcasm, deriding Sullivan's accusations of mediocrity and conservatism and defending the cultural and educational establishment. "Most of us shudder [at] what our land would be if subjected to 'a liberation of the creative impulse.'" This irony prompted a response from Sullivan, in turn; he dismissed Peabody's shudders, and arrogantly denounced the fact that "this stupid, paltry sentiment" should have been expressed in a presidential speech.[19]

Although the first year of the twentieth century was highly productive in terms of polemic and debate, it was not particularly rich in new design work by Sullivan. Perhaps the national slowdown

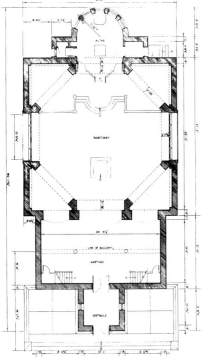

was in part responsible for this, or perhaps the anger unleashed during this exchange of attacks had negative repercussions on his practice. In November of 1899, Sullivan had been assigned the contract for the Russian Orthodox Congregation Holy Trinity Cathedral, his only major job during the year 1900. With so much free time, he attempted to deepen his understanding of the theology and history of Russian Orthodox churches. Some of what he learned appears in the structure: hence the octagonal shape of the hall of worship and the bell tower, and the square shape of the narthex and the vestibule. Aside from these few details, Sullivan seems to have been singularly uninspired—church architecture was a rare subject for him, and it apparently left him cold.

The handsome design of the roof, with broad geometric projections, is reminiscent of Wright, but the lack of inspiration is evident, and this effort to breathe new life into the project was clearly a failure. While designing this church, he had occasion to once again view the other house of worship he had designed ten years previously with Adler: the Kehilath Anshe Ma'ariv Synagogue. It is no accident that of all the buildings produced by the studio, this was the most redolent of Adler's style. The occasion of the visit was a painful one: Sullivan was invited by the Adler family to act as pallbearer at the burial of his partner. Adler had died suddenly, on 15 April, at the age of fifty-five. The comparison between the two houses of worship—one serious and foursquare, the other charming but unsure—may have increased the profound confusion hidden beneath Sullivan's behavior. And this comparison may have also reminded him of the contrast between two lives.

1. Narciso G. Menocal, *Architecture as Nature: The Transcendentalist Idea of Louis Sullivan* (Madison: University of Wisconsin Press, 1981), 64–65.
2. Ibid., 69.
3. Louis H. Sullivan, *The Autobiography of an Idea* (American Institute of Architects, 1924; reprint, New York: Dover, 1956), 223.
4. Robert Twombly, *Louis Sullivan: His Life and Work* (Chicago: University of Chicago Press, 1986), 339.
5. Louis H. Sullivan, *Louis Sullivan: The Public Papers*, ed. Robert Twombly (Chicago: University of Chicago Press, 1988), cited more than once.
6. Ibid., 113ff.
7. Samuel Reynolds Hole, *A Book About Roses: How to Grow and Show Them* (Edinburgh 1869), cited in Sullivan, *Public Papers*, 116.
8. Menocal, *Architecture as Nature*, 64.
9. Cited in Twombly, *Life and Work*, 342.
10. This is the definition of "styling" suggested by Umberto Eco.
11. Sullivan, *Public Papers*, 123.
12. Twombly, *Life and Work*, 357.
13. Sullivan, *Public Papers*, 125ff.
14. Ibid., 126.
15. Ibid., 126ff.
16. Ibid., 131ff.
17. Twombly, *Life and Work*, 367–68.
18. Louis H. Sullivan, "Reality in the Architectural Art," *Interstate Architect and Builder* 2 (11 August 1900), cited in Sullivan, *Public Papers*, 144–48.
19. Twombly, *Life and Work*, 369.

Toward the end of the year 1900, Sullivan had the most important opportunity of his career, or at least so he believed. It was at this time that he signed an agreement with *Inland Architect* to write a series of fifty-two articles, the "Kindergarten Chats." These were to be the forum in which he would hold forth, in prophetically didactic language, on an entire lifetime of ideas; here he would unpack his intellectual baggage, revealing his inspirations and regrets. Due to the continuing limitations on the construction of his designs, his emotional and mental spheres seemed to be in precarious states, racked by internal conflict. What drove him, and what determined the style of his essays—to which he devoted himself with incredible enthusiasm—was a powerful urge to speak to young architects, an urge already evident in his earlier writings. To Sullivan, the youthful architect represented the uncorrupted hope of a society and a world in which art and democracy were unwelcome visitors. Written in the traditional expository form of a philosophical dialogue between master and pupil, the style of the "Kindergarten Chats" emphasized the importance of his message and the sense of vital urgency with which it was delivered.

When the first article appeared on 16 February 1901, attacking the high tower of the Montgomery Ward Building as an "ill-compounded salad, with a rather rancid New-Yorky flavor," Sullivan had already written twenty-seven of the pieces; and the series continued for exactly one year, until 8 February 1902. The publisher was somewhat mystified by this series, which received many critical letters, few voicing approval. The letters were generally respectful in tone, but impatient. One—from 11 May 1901—responded to Sullivan's attack on the Chicago National Bank in the tenth installment, "A Roman Temple," pointing out the unfairness of describing as a crime what could at the very worst be lambasted as poor design. This type of response was in keeping with the general indifference that greeted Sullivan's year-long tirade.

Indeed, the ferocious polemics of the "Chats" met with little if any attention. Sherman Paul tells us of a letter that Sullivan wrote to Claude Bragdon, then a young admirer of the architect, expressing his disappointment: "I am amazed when I realize how insignificant... is the effect produced in comparison to cost, in vitality, to me... I shall never again make so great a sacrifice for the younger generation." He proceeds to explain, at some length, the purpose of his effort and to describe his rhetorical technique: to gradually introduce the logical and psychological sequence of "subjectivity, refinement, and altruism" in opposition to the "cynical, brutal, and philistine" positions of his opponents, thus bringing the young reader, with growing intensity of rhythm, "toward the noblest and purest of things."[1]

The "Kindergarten Chats" were unquestionably overwritten, tedious, and—above all—out of touch with reality. Reality, however, offered a variety of new opportunities to design and build that same year. And yet it was precisely here—in the pursuit of actual design projects—that Sullivan was unsuccessful; his slow explication of a complex message forced him to abandon the possibility of real commissions. And despite his best efforts, he failed to appeal even to the young architects of Stanway Hall, gathered around Frank Lloyd Wright.

However, Sullivan's writings offered new directions for the field, and enriched the wide array of ideas he outlined in his later years. He laid out a basic philosophical structure for his approach to design, noting the similarity between human creativity and natural creation, which was infallible in its "progression from function into form."[2] Here, he set forth a dynamic architectural vision in which his dictum—"Form ever follows Function"—was free of the deterministic connotations that it would acquire in the interpretation of Adler, and later in the functionalist reinterpretation of the modern movement.

In the twelfth "Chat," entitled "Function and Form," after a prolonged aside on the form and function of a lake, Sullivan went on to state: "and so on, and on, and on, and on—unceasingly, endlessly, constantly, eternally—through the range of the physical world... that world of the silent, immeasurable, creative spirit, of whose infinite function all these things are but the varied manifestations in form, in form more or less intangible, more or less imponderable... a universe wherein all is function, all is form.... All is function, all is form, but the fra-

Daniel H. Burnham & Company,
Flatiron Building, New York City,
1902, rendering.

grance of them is rhythm, the language of them is rhythm."[3] Here, once the cause-and-effect relationship between function and form had been lost, both function and form converged onto a single cognitive terrain, exchanging roles in the process of shaping and transforming the environment.

In his discourse on language Sullivan finally developed an idea of considerable interest; when his fictitious student asked him the meaning of the word "organic," the master invoked an array of related words: "organism, structure, function, growth, development, form." He then continued on to point out that "all of these words imply the initiating pressure of a living force and a resultant structure or mechanism whereby such invisible force is made manifest and operative."[4] Sullivan came close to the interesting result of giving one the definition of meaning, the other the definition of significance.

At the root of this philosophy was a notion of vital energy that Sullivan exhorted his young audience to seek and which, perhaps, he felt flagging in himself. Ironically, Sullivan was insistent on dismissing his enemies—the proponents of academic architecture—as old men. Of academic architecture he had this to say: "Its eye is lustreless." In contrast: "The architecture which we seek shall be as a man active, alert, supple, strong, sane. A generative man. A man having five senses all awake. . . knowing and feeling the vibrancy of that ever-moving moment, with heart to draw it in and mind to put it out: that incessant, that portentous birth, that fertile moment which we call Today!"[5]

That "today" seemed less than kind to Sullivan. The "Kindergarten Chats" left even the most advanced professional and cultural circles cold. Sullivan received few professional assignments, and those few did not turn out well. Two were residences: the first, a Wrightian design for a home in Lake Forest commissioned by Nettie McCormick, was rejected; the second, for Arthur Henry Lloyd of Chicago, also was not built. Commissions for Tusculum College and the Euston & Company Factory were fairly modest projects. An uninspiring balance sheet, and a truly disastrous state of affairs when compared—as Sullivan must have—with the brilliant success of the firm of his old rival, Daniel H. Burnham. Not

*Louis Henry Sullivan, National
Farmers Bank, Owatonna, Minnesota,
1906–1908, general views and façade
detail; commemorative stamp issued in
1981.*

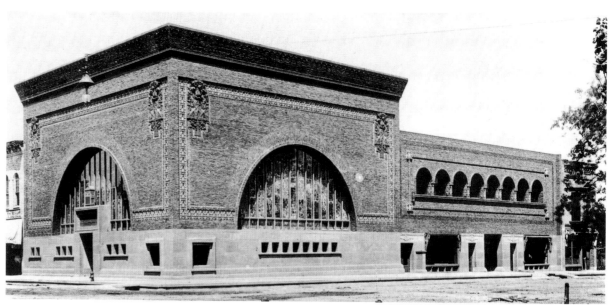

only did that firm design the splendid Flatiron Building on New York's Fifth Avenue, but Burnham himself was given the prestigious task of coordinating the design group for the city plan of Washington, D. C., laying the foundation for the doctrine and practice of the City Beautiful movement, which was to have profound and long-lasting effects on the renewal of major cities, both in America and around the world.

In May 1902, a speech written by Sullivan was read—in his absence—before the Architectural League of America, then assembled in Toronto. The talk had the distinct tone of a farewell, a lullaby that Sullivan had written for himself: "So would I nurse the dreamer of dreams, for in him nature broods while the race slumbers."[6] This speech also marked the end of his working relationship with *Inland Architect*, publisher of the "Kindergarten Chats."

Sullivan's survival, in 1902, was assured only by the job of enlarging the department store of Schlesinger & Mayer. However, this same company, when taken over by Carson, Pirie, Scott, assigned the next addition to its store to none other than Sullivan's rival Daniel Burnham, in 1905. Times were difficult for Sullivan; between 1903 and 1904, he posted a number of letters in search of work. In some of these, he went so far as to reassure the prospective client that he had sworn off the ornamental excesses of his past.[7] The Crane Company Building, which he was to finish in 1905, was in fact a building of great formal sobriety. Finally, he attempted to promote a real estate deal based on a speculative design of his own.[8]

Sullivan still enjoyed some standing in the Architectural Club, of which he was a patron. Outside of the United States, in the cultural climate of the Art Nouveau, he was also much admired. He continued to write articles, but the only magazine that would now publish his work was the *Craftsman*, a periodical founded in 1901 by Gustav Stickley, a leading figure of the American Arts and Crafts movement and follower of John Ruskin and William Morris. Stickley produced hand-crafted furniture, and Sullivan used his work in the National Farmers Bank in Owatonna, Minnesota—the project that was to revive Sullivan's practice and allow him to return

National Farmers Bank, views of the interior and ornamental design for a clock (drawing by George Elmslie, dated June 12, 1907), pencil, 11.8 x 7.8 in.

to formal experimentation. Morrison recounts the noteworthy events that led the founders of a small bank in the Midwest to decide, in 1907, to seek out the architect, now in his fifties, and rescue him from the oblivion beginning to enshroud him.[9]

The vice president of the bank, Carl K. Bennet, told his story in an account that the *Craftsman* lost no time in publishing. After deciding not to follow standard practice of the period and build in the form of a classical temple, the bank's administrators searched through architectural journals in search of an architect. Of course, Sullivan had addressed this very issue in one of his first "Kindergarten Chats," and he had also discussed the use of the classical style in his first article in the *Craftsman*, in 1905. Bennet, however, wrote as if he had come upon these ideas independently, and went on to describe how, after reading through all of the architectural publications available, the search committee had come across an issue of *American Contractor* dated January 1906. This issue included a long essay entitled: "What is Architecture: A Study in the American People of Today," and the committee found the ideas set forth in it to be powerful and persuasive. The author was Louis Sullivan.[10]

Sullivan began his collaboration with the *Craftsman* by returning to the themes and ideas set forth in the "Kindergarten Chats." These included the mirroring of architecture and society; the model of nature, with its evolutionary processes; the continuing decline in thought and education; and the epiphany of individual values. Sullivan distanced himself from what he felt to be the excessive social criticism of English thinkers, especially Morris and Walter Crane. An example can be seen in this aside: "I should add, perhaps, that, in speaking of the people, I do not use the word in the unhappy sense of the lower classes, so-called. I mean all the people; and I look upon all the people as constituting a social organism."[11] All the same, he did not shrink from using strong language in speaking of the educational system, stating that he felt that higher-education was "daily more reactionary, more feudal."[12] All of the elements of his Neo-Humanistic crusade were gradually and emphatically reiterated: "The heart is greater than the head. For, in the heart is

147

*Detail of a teller's window for the
National Farmers Bank.*

Desire; and from it, comes forth Courage and Magnanimity. . . . You have not thought deeply enough to know that the heart in you is the woman in man. You have derided your femininity, where you have suspected it; whereas, you should have known its power, cherished and utilized it, for it is the hidden wellspring of Intuition and Imagination." Sullivan proceeds to explain to his undoubtedly befuddled reader that he is talking about democracy; and derides the American people, saying "with what awful folly have you assumed selfish egotism to be the basis of democracy." Sullivan's solution is "individual honesty" leading in turn to "social equilibrium." The tool of this equilibrium is thought: "have thought for the integrity of your thought. . . . Naturally, then, as your thoughts thus change, your growing Architecture will change."

It is surprising that a country banker recognized in this text the ideas that convinced him that Sullivan was the perfect designer for a new bank building. We will probably never know which of Sullivan's numerous conceptual images persuaded the committee to award him the project. The fact remains, however, that it was a brilliant decision, and that Sullivan's building marked a high point in the search for an American language of architecture in the first decade of the new century, at least in terms of its autochthonous production. This part of the field neither sought nor allowed any comparison with the other main current in American architecture, that of classical town planning, led by Burnham and his plans for West Point (1903), Manila and Baguio (1905), San Francisco (1906), and Chicago (1908–09).

A qualitative comparison of the two architects is impossible, but not simply because there exists no radical difference between their skills; Burnham, like Sullivan, was a true master who had created at least two great works, the Monadnock Building and the Flatiron Building. What truly stands in the way of a comparison is the fact that the two architects employed fundamentally different methodologies and aspired to radically different objectives. Burnham worked on large-scale urban planning and redesign projects, and his chosen field of endeavor

*Louis Henry Sullivan, Euston &
Company Factory, Chicago,
1899–1902.*

*Virginia Hall, Greenville, Tennessee,
1901.*

relied heavily on the broad delegation of responsibility and the high-impact publicity provided by spectacular graphic displays. Burnham's attention was oriented toward final technical and formal solutions, and his prime focus often fell on extrinsic matters: the identification of economic and socio-cultural objectives, the organization of work, and the creation of consensus.

Sullivan worked within a radically different system of values and objectives, and the National Farmers Bank (1906–1908) is a perfect expression of his approach. This was the last project Sullivan designed with the assistance of George Elmslie; indeed, the fanciful elegance of much of the ornamentation, which was nonetheless rigorously architectural, is a clear legacy of Sullivan's faithful assistant, who seems to have given his all on this, his last project under Sullivan. Perhaps this generous effort was a way of taking leave from the exhausted but determined Sullivan during his leanest years of production. But, however great Sullivan's debt to Elmslie may have been, there can be no doubt that the clear and forceful design of the building, as well as the basic choices of material and color, came from Sullivan.

The bank was conceived as a single structure focused on a large public hall, which, as the dominant central feature, has the greatest visual impact. From the exterior, the volume of the hall, containing a vast square room (roughly 65 feet long on each side, 40 feet high), is striking. Large arches—enclosed with stained glass—overlooking the street recall great historical precedents; the four-sided loggia; the ancient Roman *"janus"* and its medieval and renaissance counterparts, such as the sedilia; and the Hispano-American tradition of the *"capillas posas."* The arches were chosen with an acute cultural sensitivity in an attempt to evoke the sense of "marketplace" or "meeting place" once associated with this form.

The two enormous arches give the building several pleasing features. On the interior, they provide abundant natural light, particularly useful in a building in which the public demands the ability to "see clearly" in all transactions. On the exterior, they give great force to the image of the building, set on the most important commercial street in Owatonna at the corner of its main square. In this prominent location, the building faced a rival bank across the street in the Kelly Building. The masonry structure of Sullivan's building rises from a solid base made of reddish Port Wing sandstone, clearly and deeply carved out by the confident geometric shapes of the entrance and large and small windows. Beyond the central arches, a series of semicircular arches, influenced in style by Adler, open onto an interweave of shaped bricks in various shades. This is "tapestry brick," as the terra-cotta facing so lovingly designed by Sullivan came to be known. As an accent of special architectural prestige, elegant terra-cotta panels of heraldry at the upper corners of the façade are joined to a decorative fascia by a dense network of green, glazed terra-cotta. This ornament all serves to affirm an ornamental system based on the geometry of the buildings volumes. Here Sullivan achieves a solid unity of taste with a precise stylistic identity.

The large cubic shell is interrupted by the small volume of the entrance vestibule, whose exterior door opens to the inside with a heavily decorated inner door. Entering the building from this smaller space, the exaggerated volume of the great hall comes as a surprise. Placed precisely across from the entrance is the vault room, in accordance with a well established typology expressing openness and reliability. The entire building is done in well-considered materials: terra-cotta, stucco, cast iron, and Italian marble, selected with a view to color coordination that Sullivan himself was to describe as a "symphony."

A complex array of values, therefore—all of them unquestionably artistic—house the most explicitly prosaic and alienating social activity of a human community. The final result, in any case, is so outstanding, even within the context of the intentional cultural hybridization of Sullivan's work, that the town of Owatonna has become famous, and, as Montgomery Schuyler wrote, a "Mecca of American architectural pilgrimages."[13] Sullivan enjoyed the positive repercussions of his new professional notoriety, even though there were few new assignments

Louis Henry Sullivan, Henry Babson Residence, Riverside, Illinois, 1907–1909 (demolished in 1960), front and rear views, and floor plans.

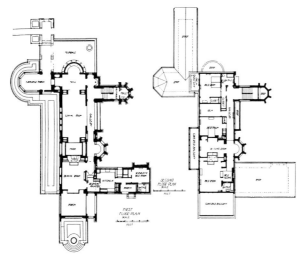

in the three years following the bank's completion—in part because of a financial panic in 1907 that drove up prices in the construction industry in concomitance with dangerously high unemployment.

These were years in which Chicago attempted to revive its manufacturing sector, then in the midst of bitter class conflict. This period followed the golden age of America's "open door" policy, when cities directly involved in international trade, such as New York and San Francisco, prospered most. When times are bad, the committed make preparations for a positive future, or so the tycoon Andrew Carnegie tirelessly preached. For Daniel Burnham, this message was clear, and it was at this time that he initiated large-scale planning efforts, upon which no expense would be spared. One result of this was the immense collective, intellectual, and technical effort lavished on the city plan of Chicago.

As for Sullivan, he had little room in which to maneuver. As a result, he assembled a different set of tools, ones with which he worked best. These included architectural language, understood as a summary of quality measured by and emphasizing the dimension of the individual.

The great Chicago project, though it was in part merely demonstrative, served to increase Burnham's fame and success, opening doors to power both within the United Stated and internationally. Sullivan, then, experienced the economic crisis alone, suffering from the depressed economy and his own growing state of existential panic.

We may consider as a mark of insecurity the apparently nonchalant manner in which Sullivan borrowed Wright's volumetric style in the plans for homes he had the opportunity to design. In the Henry Babson Residence of Riverside, Illinois, designed in 1907 but not completed until 1909, Sullivan's attempt to mediate the Prairie style with his own design method is clearly evident in the arched loggia on the façade and—above all—in a floor plan created by the aggregation of sharply defined systems, reassembled in a montage. Here, a series of symmetrically aligned rooms conclude in two hemicycles to which various irregular volumes are added, intersecting with the exterior space in typically Wrightian fashion. The other residence, to be

*Louis Henry Sullivan, Joseph Crane
Bradley Residence, Madison,
Wisconsin, 1908–1909, views and
floor plan.*

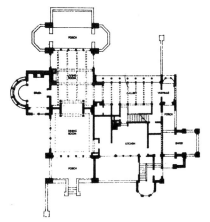

located in Madison, Wisconsin, was designed in 1908 for Harold Bradley in two different versions, both considered excessive by the client. It was finally built in what can be considered an interesting blend of the two manners—bombastic and inappropriately monumental.

The only project that seemed to break through Sullivan's defensive and despairing isolation was his design for Petty's Island in the Delaware River, where a consortium of investors planned to build an amusement park. This complex was to occupy roughly 250 acres, and if it had actually been built, it might have opened new territory for Sullivan's talent and vision. Unfortunately, the investors were unwilling or unable to follow through in the rough economic times between 1907 and 1909. Sullivan's passive approach did little to push things along, and it is instructive to note the difference between his mode of operations and the aggressiveness and capacity for self-promotion exhibited by both Burnham and Wright. The project, in the end, collapsed.

The hardest year for Sullivan was 1909, the year of Burnham's triumphant presentation of the city plan for Chicago. This plan went so far as to call for the widening of Congress Street, among an array of urban renovations, which would have resulted in the demolition of Sullivan's Auditorium Theater, specifically the section featuring the famous tower that housed Sullivan's desolate but still active office. Trusted George Elmslie left Sullivan to set up his own firm, with William Purcell, in Cincinnati. On 29 November, all of Sullivan's belongings were put up for auction, and a few days later, his wife Margaret left him. Last November's auction was "a slaughter,"[14] he wrote to Carl Bennett a month later, explaining that of the $2,500 that he had hoped to raise, he had only received $1,100, and that he had given $1,000 to Margaret. Taking that money, she had moved to New York, without any particular explanation.

The letter to Bennett is a dramatic document—a demonstration of self-awareness from Sullivan while he was attempting to get back on his feet. Twombly points out its cathartic and revelatory breadth: "I am glad to be left alone to work out my own destiny and start life all over again if I can."[15]

*Louis Henry Sullivan, design for the Island City
Amusement Park, Philadelphia, 1907, preliminary
studies.*

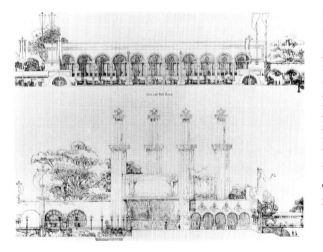

Sullivan speaks of poverty, worries, insomnia, somatic intestinal problems, and fears of madness and suicide. He tells how he was saved by the providential intervention of an acquaintance, a homeopathic physician named George Dute Arndt, who restored him to health over the course of two-and-a-half weeks by surrounding him with affection and by explaining to him the reasons for his crisis, which had developed over the previous seventeen years.

The reasons? "None other than my persistent lack of kindly feeling toward my fellow men."[16] This statement can be interpreted as unequivocal evidence of his homosexuality; especially as it is followed by this statement: "He is right and I intend to change."[17] Twombly takes this as a clear realization and acceptance of latent homosexuality, and therefore as the crowning evidence for his own (perhaps simplistic) thesis, based on a case-history approach: the identification with the father, more than with the mother (though which of the two was the more virile model?); the attraction to strong masculine figures, even the "Superman" recognized in the Michelangelo of the Sistine Chapel; his friends, always men; the use of the term "virile" to describe monumental buildings, such as the Marshall Field Store; the many references, in his "Kindergarten Chats," to "the real man" and "the whole man."

In this context, Sullivan's marriage would have been an extreme attempt to flee his own problems, especially those concerning emerging aspects of his own sexual identity, aspects that were coming forth in concomitance with his own professional decline. Twombly tends to think that this decline was a result of those problems: "It was not for loss of ability that he got fewer jobs," Twombly explains, "his genius never failed him." Twombly finally admits that "the explanation for Sullivan's decline is nevertheless extremely complicated," and he proceeds to list a number of possible causes, including: Sullivan's repeated attacks on the architectural establishment, his lack of institutional support, arrogant personality, rejection of compromise, reputation as an impractical artist, reluctance to design residences, and opposition to the classical revival that had been promoted by the Columbian Exposition of 1893.[18]

The causes that Twombly adduces could in fact be described as contributing factors, to some extent acceptable, in addition to a long-standing psychological disturbance variously expressed in Sullivan's interpersonal relationships. A further analysis, including historical factors, would lead us to concentrate upon the fascinating anachronism of the figure of Sullivan, an anachronism that (as is so often the case with artists) places him at the peak of his linguistic research during the time of his decline. In short, his professional success was being undermined by a disjunction that can be detected as far back as the late 1880s; right from the beginning of that seventeen-year period that Sullivan indicates as the period of incubation and development of his great crisis. Over this time, a full-fledged rift developed between the teleology that directed Sullivan's actions and writings, and the historical situation in America. Sullivan lacked the capacity and will—as did his colleague Root, whom it ultimately killed—to remain in step with real historical processes. But this was a non-complicity that, in the final analysis, will elude the grasp of those who fail to make use of those historical tools that allow one to examine relationships between artistic production and economic and social context.

1. See Sherman Paul, *Louis Sullivan: An Architect in American Thought* (Englewood Cliffs, NJ: Prentice-Hall, 1962), 58.
2. Louis H. Sullivan, *Kindergarten Chats and Other Writings* (1918; reprint, New York: George Wittenborn, 1947), chat 48, "On Poetry," 159.
3. Ibid., chat 12, "Function and Form," 44–45.
4. Ibid., chat 14, "Growth and Decay," 48
5. Ibid., chat 14, "Growth and Decay," 49.
6. Louis H. Sullivan, *Louis Sullivan: The Public Papers*, ed. Robert Twombly (Chicago: University of Chicago Press, 1988), 157.
7. Robert Twombly, *Louis Sullivan: His Life and Work* (Chicago: University of Chicago Press, 1986), 384.
8. Ibid.
9. H. Morrison, *Louis Sullivan: Prophet of Modern Architecture* (New York: W. W. Norton, 1935), 207ff.
10. Ibid., 207–08. The essay appears in Sullivan, *Public Papers*, 174ff.
11. Sullivan, *Public Papers*, 178.
12. Ibid., 190ff.
13. Montgomery Schuyler, "The People's Savings Bank of Cedar Rapids, Iowa," *Architectural Record* 1 (January 1912): 46.
14. Twombly, *Life and Work*, 407.
15. Ibid.
16. Ibid., 409.
17. Letter from Sullivan to Bennet, cited in R. R. Warn, "Bennet & Sullivan, Client & Creator," *The Prairie School Review* 10 (1973): 14–15.
18. Twombly, *Life and Work*, 403–06.

The final period of Sullivan's career is appraised by historians and critics in various ways; there is no question that the quality of his work was exceedingly high, but many critics fail to see a link to the previous development of his buildings, or to the complex intertwining of ideological motivations that accompanied his earlier work. There appear to be particular problems in establishing links between Sullivan's later work and its general historical and cultural context.

In his major theoretical essay, "What is Architecture?"[1] Sullivan's rediscovery of the feminine—to be understood as imagination and intuition—is expressed without qualification. At the close of the essay, Sullivan makes insistent efforts to penetrate the presumed barriers of indifference on the part of his bewildered readers. This "Hymn to Nature," taken as the inspirational mother of all building art in the machine age, leads us to think that Sullivan was addressing his audience as if from a pedestal of wisdom, exhorting them to break out of the narrow schemes of current thought, to activate liberating mechanisms based on a resonance with the external music of natural forces. It is as if he were a latter-day Ulysses, sailing with his mariners to the sound of the sirens' song. Here, this metaphor is transposed: while the Homeric hero forced his men to stop up their ears, allowing only himself the dangerous pleasure of hearing the song (though he was securely lashed to the mainmast), Sullivan, free of all inhibitions, seems to act as the mouthpiece of the sirens, offering his readers the dangerous invitation to plunge with him into the great bounding main of individualistic inspiration, far away from the sterile beaches of common sense and from all anchorage in concrete reality.

Nonetheless, the sirens' song, like its counterpart, the "Song of Nature," preserves the solitary attraction of a voice in the wilderness. But it can be applied only by those in power; such was the case with Carl K. Bennett, who entrusted the bank project at Owatonna to Sullivan. And Sullivan, in his growing isolation, seized on this project, lavishing upon it a disproportionate degree of symbolic and aesthetic wealth. No longer inspired by the virility of the likes of H. H. Richardson's Marshall Field Build-

ing, Sullivan aimed at a recovery of the feminine, in the sense that he himself had assigned to that term.

Sullivan thus entered a phase in which he repeatedly employed tapestry brick, as seen in two small banks and two residences. This technique, elucidated in an essay entitled "Artistic Brick,"[2] can be seen as early as the Monadnock Building—though he makes no reference to that building in the essay—in which bricks of various colors were used. If, however, the gradation ranged from dark to light and from purple to yellow in the Monadnock Building, it was nonetheless a continuous gradation (this may represent the contribution of John Wellborn Root to a design that on the whole should be attributed to Daniel Burnham).[3] Sullivan now introduced a new technique by mingling various shades of color, achieving an effect of diffuse irregularity, much like that seen in walls made with hand-made bricks. This effect could now be attained with cheaper, industrially made bricks, in the context of Sullivan's naturalistic inspiration. In the essay, Sullivan gave particular emphasis to the concept of "organic thought," allowing the use of this type of brick to take on an ideological dimension.

> This is nature's continuously operative law, whereby every single thing takes up its individual form in materials, and is recognizable as such. This law is not only comprehensive, but universal. It applies to the crystal as well as to the plant, each seeking and finding its form by virtue of its working plan, or purpose or utility; or if you choose to say so, by virtue of its desire to live and to express itself."[4]

This discourse became central in the last phase of Sullivan's production, finding almost messianic expression in an essay written by Sullivan in 1912 in regard to his project for the People's Savings Bank in Cedar Rapids, Iowa. This building clearly attracted notice, as Montgomery Schuyler was to speak of it as "the most interesting event . . . in the American architectural world to-day." Ironically, the critical success of the project came during the darkest period of Sullivan's own personal history. Sullivan, in fact, worked on this project beginning in the spring

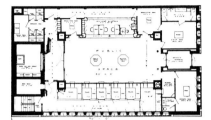

155

*People's Savings Bank, general view
and detail of the entrance.*

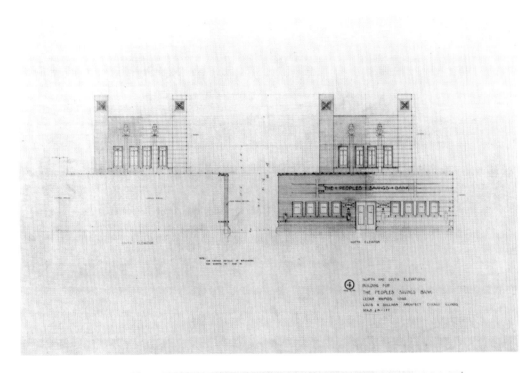

of 1909, and the plans, submitted at the end of the summer, had been rejected the day after the traumatic auction of all of his personal belongings. Still, his resilience, whatever its cause, was surprising; and it was this remarkable bank building that led to Sullivan's comeback, with all of his notorious—and to some extent accepted—contradictions.

Construction of the bank began in October of 1910, and the favorable moment was augmented by his simultaneous victory in the competition for St. Paul's Methodist Episcopal Church, also in Cedar Rapids. Sullivan won this competition over twelve rival architects, including Purcell & Elmslie. Still, it was the bank, much more than the church, that inspired Sullivan to fully commit himself to his work. In this building, he seems to attain some sort of apex, employing an exemplary, complete typology. Two rectangular volumes with carefully aligned proportions were employed here. The lower, larger one, served as a solid base atop which stood the smaller, a luminous volume supported by four projecting towers at its corners.

The bank presents a well balanced, turreted façade to the street, with many recondite iconic references. Completely devoid of the arches that were so essential to his building in Owatonna, this bank transcends its small size with a certain monumentality. A variety of lamps emphasize the extreme rigor of the layout on the exterior. Though it is a sacrosanct design with a distinct funerary aspect, it is also cheerfully adorned with a painstakingly composed tapestry of bricks.

Sullivan's work in these years, especially the bank in Cedar Rapids, made clear reference to his complex and ambiguous aphorism, which could not withstand the simple, performative logic of a thriving midwestern community. So it is perhaps not surprising that a large structural block was built in 1991 alongside Sullivan's remarkable structure. This new building usurps, with brutal indifference, the enchanted isolation of the latter. Most disquieting is the fact that the materials and plastic treatment of the awkward and cumbersome new building seek out an impossible dialogue with the earlier autonomous structure. Clearly, this was the architect's ingenuous intent.

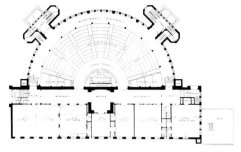

*Louis Henry Sullivan, St. Paul's
Methodist Episcopal Church, Cedar
Rapids, Iowa, 1910–14, exterior
view, elevation, and floor plan.*

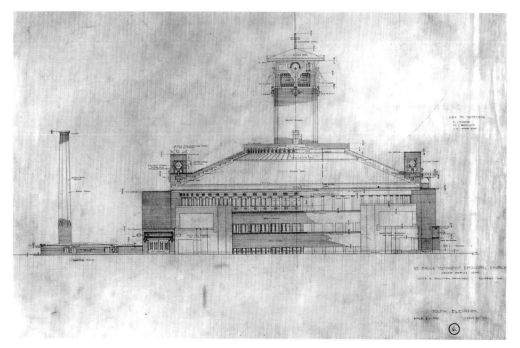

An ideological ambiguity is revealed when the physical project is compared to Sullivan's essay, "Lighting the People's Savings Bank, Cedar Rapids, Iowa: An Example of American Twentieth Century Ideas of Architecture and Illumination,"[5] in which he analyzes the work in detail. Twombly praises this essay highly, underscoring the integration of Sullivan's magical formula—"form follows function"— with Wright's famous slogan—"from the inside out." Sullivan's essay progresses from a strictly technical discussion concerning lighting to examine, in rapid succession and in minute detail: form, color, tactile values, and the variability of the terra-cotta facing. The essay notes that "the general effect is that of an antique oriental rug." Considering that the structure is a bank—a repository in which the public rituals of capitalism's financial mechanisms are enacted—one cannot help but be perplexed at the application of a precept that reads: "Form follows function, from within outward."

On the interior, the clarity of the geometric layout reveals, through the precision of the spatial arrangement, a qualitative potential in terms of luminous architectonic solemnity. Sullivan defines this space, sliding ineluctably into ideology, as democratic. For example: "the offices are in full view and easily accessible," and the materials are well chosen and elegant, "of the highest quality."[6] Thus, once again, he substitutes the appearance of democracy, understood as a humanistic utopia, for an impracticable realization of that utopia, a realization hoped for in vain (or perhaps never sincerely desired).

In any case, Sullivan had now entered his come-back period: the quality that he attained in these works is very high. The remarkable allure of these exquisite little buildings, erected in the depressing and unbroken banality of the North American heartland, also unquestionably resides—aside from the foreshadowing of Louis Kahn's work that can be seen in the People's Savings Bank—in the ambiguously anachronistic flavor conveyed by their comeliness.

It seems that at this point Sullivan, while he theorized on the elegance of nuanced color, also had unparalleled control of form in his work, in the

Louis Henry Sullivan, Henry C.
Adams Building, Algona, Iowa, 1913,
floor plans and view of the façade.

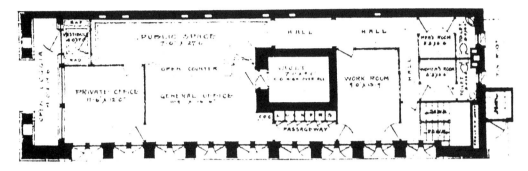

essential phase—which he called the "virile" phase—of creating a building's plan. Another example of this ability can be seen in St. Paul's Methodist Episcopal Church, also in Cedar Rapids. This was an occasion for typological invention that was a precursor to the clarity of Kahn's finest work; unfortunately, due to problems with costs that led to the abandonment of the finishings that Sullivan had planned to use, the building was completed in the banal style of W. C. Jones, the architect of the congregation.[7]

It is safe to say that the two areas of the senses, which Sullivan distinguished with the categories masculine and feminine, intimately coexist in the bank in Cedar Rapids (while in the church—though not through any fault of Sullivan's, as some have claimed—the latter seems to be entirely missing).

This perfect correspondence between the aesthetic treatment of the surfaces and the strength of the spatial and volumetric concept can be seen, in a particularly effective form, in the Henry C. Adams Building in Algona, Iowa (1913). There, the tapestry brick takes on a particular material sharpness due to the perfectly rectangular exterior, punctured by deep and well-defined openings.

In other cases, however, the two considerations—structural-functional and material-ornamental—prove to be oddly juxtaposed: this seems to be true in the Merchants National Bank in Grinnell, Iowa (1914), and especially in the John D. Van Allen & Sons Dry Goods Store in Clinton, Iowa, finished at the beginning of 1915.

In the first building, the masonry structure, divided into two cubes, is so compact and simple that it is visually perceived as spare, with an effect that unavoidably tends to render extraneous the emphatically decorative rose window and the elegant narrow windows carved into its side walls. At the same time, the (possibly feminine) element of the terra-cotta lacework, which serves as a cornice, softens the stereometric power of the top edge of the structure. It gives the impression of a genuine split of the project design into distinct phases, as if two separate personalities were overlapping. But in fact it is a further development of the method of assemblage evi-

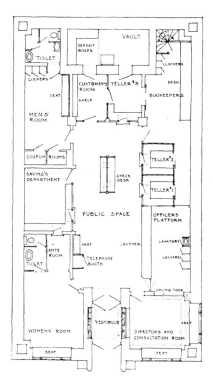

Louis Henry Sullivan, Merchants
National Bank, Grinnell, Iowa,
1913–14, floor plan, detail of the
entrance, and view of the interior.

dent in many different instances in Sullivan's best and most serious work, in which the heritage of Furness can be detected.

Similar observations can be made of a slightly later building: the People's Savings & Loan Association, Sidney, Ohio, inaugurated at the beginning of 1918. Here, once again, the corner location set between two major streets made Sullivan lean toward using a simple rectangular structure, almost a double-cube, whose geometric simplicity is assaulted, so to speak, by clamorous formal elements: a semicircular portal on axis, balancing the façade; a large and emphatic pattern of side windows that monumentalize the long side elevation of the building.

This time, the anchoring of the two values onto the solid structure of the building is emphasized by a string course on which rests both the semicircular triumphal arch at the entrance and, on the side, the remarkable fenestration. The string course continues on the low structure that is a continuation of the main building, there becoming the upper edge of a series of low windows. It is as if the feminine element of the imagination had developed into a fanciful and aggressive form encircling the masculine stereometry of the building.

In contrast, in the Van Allen stores in Clinton, the split between the two aspects in functional and structural terms took what was the common approach at this time: a traditional shape pierced by a regularly spaced rhythm of windows on three floors. The brickwork texture of the horizontal bands of the parapets and the vertical pilasters are enriched by an elegant tapestry brick accented by finely detailed terra-cotta reliefs. The structure is given verticality by three strong elements constituted of

Louis Henry Sullivan, John D. Van Allen & Sons Dry Goods Store, Clinton, Iowa, 1913–15, photographs of construction, general view, and façade details.

narrow pairs of small terra-cotta columns, stretched like elastic cables from the second floor almost to the cornice, anchored at top and bottom by two enlarged plant-like buckles in green ceramic. This vaguely Neo-Gothic plant theme, found in the Bayard Building and the Gage Building, here ushered in the new century with a charming, almost naive freshness.

The Home Building Association, in Newark, Ohio, perhaps the least known, least photographed, and worst cared-for of Sullivan's projects, expresses in the most surprising fashion the density and plurality of meaning evident in his oeuvre. Sullivan worked on this diminutive, small-town building between the springs of 1914 and 1915. Once again, the project was given to him by a small group of private investors who wished to construct an office building with a bank branch on the ground floor. The project was an unassuming one in an even more unassuming setting: on a corner lot between two main streets in the town. Yet there was an ambitious initiative underlying it and a willingness to engage

in cultural polemics, as seen in the investors choice of the most refined and controversial architect of the Chicago area. Evidently, they rejected the European-style homogeneity of the typical bank-building classicism that was so widespread throughout the United States.

This was the precise territory, marginal though it may have been, that Sullivan had carved out for himself and which he defended tooth and nail, though that territory was shrinking with the passage of time. Nevertheless, it is well known that the isolated master, although nearly destitute, was always willing to walk away from a project in the final phase, whenever questions or modifications threatened his work, even partially.

Embattled in the desolate but magical isolation of his tower, high atop the Auditorium, to which he clung over the years, Sullivan was now a free man. He was free to select forms, colors, symbolic accents, geometric experiments, various materials, and even nuance and shade. A small, three-story office and

Louis Henry Sullivan, People's
Savings & Loan Association Bank,
Sidney, Ohio, 1917–18, entry façade
and drawing of the main elevation.

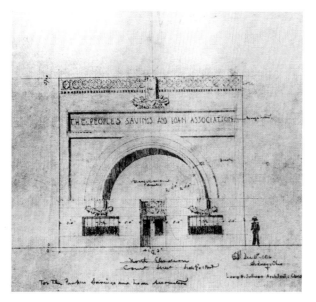

bank building on a fairly narrow, rectangular lot, a building that was destined to be oddly proportioned, taller than it was deep, was once again the subject of a powerful, perhaps excessive intellectual effort, which led him to invest a disproportionately large amount of creative energy in its design. He was able to do so because this was the one form of capital that had never failed him, a capital which, when invested in his later experimental bank projects, still remained his, and even increased in value—a value already high due to its scarcity. The worth of this connoisseur derived from his refusal to submit to the production of banally repetitious motifs.

In Newark, Sullivan made use of an elegant gray majolica against which he splashed the vivid colors of his most prominent elements, particularly the notable golden legend that stands out on the smaller elevation, overlooking a little park in front of a church. The division into three floors is concealed by the design of the building's two sharply differing elevations. The larger of these is marked by a thick, flat cornice that surrounds a broad opening occupying the entire elevation, containing all of its windows. This has the effect of transforming the entire building into a triumphal arch with a large, rectangular opening. This image was enhanced by the narrow side elevation, adjacent to the church and the gardens, which bore a panel notably inscribed, "The Old Home." The triumphal arch invests this humble urban setting with a contradictory but non-ironic monumentality, immediately softened by Sullivan's studied ornament. Colorful effects accompany the inscription, and two elegant majolica trees bracket the long elevation, on either side of the false opening, with another on the short elevation.

Such a decisive architectural array required certain sacrifices in terms of function. The clients were forced to accept two very small entrances, set at the corners, one of them square in the shoulder of the false arch. These entrances were so small that it later became necessary to form a new entrance by cutting off the corner and eliminating one of the small decorative trees, thus destroying the fine unified image that Sullivan had created.

During this period, Sullivan's design commitment was, as usual, inversely proportional to an ever

Side elevations and details.

165

*Louis Henry Sullivan, Home
Building Association Bank, Newark,
Ohio, 1914–15, general view and
detail of the ornamental frieze.*

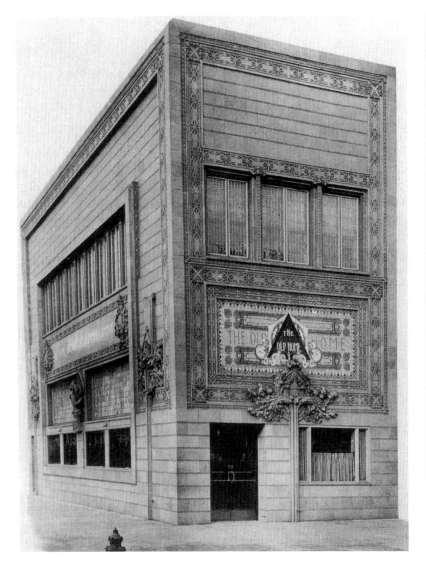

more meager professional niche. This brought him to the verge of bankruptcy. In 1918, after twenty-eight years, he was forced to leave his office in the Auditorium tower and move to a second-floor office with four rooms on South Wabash Avenue. The sense of isolation must have been excruciating for him, but he was working to understand his own past. One sign of this, after so many years of rancorous hostility, was an increasingly intense correspondence and friendship with Frank Lloyd Wright. Despite Sullivan's constant need for money, this friendship was a warm one on both sides. The restoration of an old and solid friendship between the sixty-two-year-old master and the now-famous former student, was triggered by a phone call from Sullivan to Wright in Taliesin; so happy was Wright to hear from him that he immediately came to visit Sullivan in Chicago.

Wright was now over fifty, and was in the heart of the eight-year project for the Imperial Hotel in Tokyo. Although he had offices in Tokyo, Los Angeles, Chicago, and Taliesin, his economic situation was likewise precarious. Still, he was able to respond fairly regularly to Sullivan's requests for money. The correspondence between the two, extending from 1918 until Sullivan's death, was painfully marked by Sullivan's recurring fear of poverty: "Now my dear Frank, I fancy you have troubles of your own and I hate to butt in, but I am terribly up in the air and I want to find out where I am." Wright answered, telling Sullivan about his work, both the good and the bad, enclosing an unmentioned check.[8]

Sullivan was becoming a pathetic figure. He had begun to smoke for the first time, and he drank increasing amounts of both coffee and alcohol. In 1919, he was awarded a final major bank design, oddly enough by clients who were great fans of Wright's work: Mr. and Mrs. J. R. Wheeler. They considered Sullivan's banks to be decidedly Wrightian in style, and they asked him to design the Farmers & Merchants Union Bank in Columbus, Wisconsin. Sullivan devoted himself wholly to this one project throughout the time of its design and construction; while doing so, he stayed in Columbus as a guest of the Wheelers. Wheeler and Sullivan became friends, and Wheeler, who was chairman of the bank, allowed Sullivan to lavish a decidedly large

Farmers & Merchants Union Bank,
preliminary sketches, view of the entry
façade, and general view.

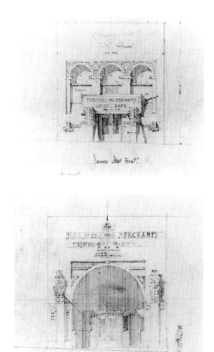

quantity of decoration on the bank building, causing construction costs to balloon. The warm friendship of the Wheelers made Sullivan's time in Columbus a period of prosperity and reminiscence: Sullivan's design featured notes of Wright's style (so dear to the Wheelers) and hints of Elmslie's work, as well as occasional self-quotations, as in the large lions rampant in the terra-cotta.

With his last project, the small façade for the Krause Music Store on North Lincoln Avenue in Chicago, Sullivan returned once again to the exquisite and entirely personal form of expression that had previously appeared in such clear form at the surprising building in Newark. His long-standing love for music helped him, perhaps, to joyfully yet powerfully balance shape, proportion, quality of ornamental style, and symbolic creativity. This façade's most striking element was an enormous key that, like a cross over an oratory, soared up the building on its central axis. This axis was further emphasized by a letter K set within a small triumphal arch above the cornice. The delicate balance of the façade is also evident in the building's fenestration—four identical windows, side by side, on the second floor, and one large central window on the ground floor that revealed a concert grand piano to the passersby.

Sullivan attained a remarkable, almost unprecedented equilibrium in his last project. This was an achievement, perhaps a last testament, that critics understood superficially, impressed only by the spectacular ornamentation.

The attraction of the decoration was in part distracting and misleading, a gross reduction of the complexity that Sullivan's work achieved on a connotative level. In the spring of 1922, on the occasion of the thirty-third annual exhibition of the Chicago Architectural Club, an entire wall was devoted to his work, with a special focus on ornamentation, beginning with the decorative exploit of the Golden Doorway of 1893 and leading up to his most recent bank buildings; among the latter, critics of the period were especially impressed with the Columbus bank, evidently swayed by the sheer weight of ornamentation in that project.

In January of 1922, A. N. Rebori had the idea of asking the elderly architect to write an autobiogra-

Louis Henry Sullivan, William P. Krause Music Store, Chicago, 1922.

phy, Sullivan accepted, and the two had signed a contract by 16 February. Sullivan was soon intent at work on the book, which he wrote while working on a commission that he had already accepted from the Chicago Art Institute's Burnham Library; twenty drawings for his *A System of Architectural Ornament According with a Philosophy of Man's Powers*. These two projects would carry him to the peak of a working fervor. In March, three chapters of *Autobiography of an Idea* were already complete, as were three plates for the Art Institute.

Thus, Louis Sullivan's role was determined—and circumscribed—by established culture. He was no longer the giant of American design, a role that had been inherited by Wright. Rather, he found a place in history through the renown of projects assigned to him during the last two years of his life: the writing of an ideological testament and the preparation of a linguistic bequest of decoration taken out of context. These two tasks placed him upon a historical pedestal while distancing him from his real legacy. In what spirit Sullivan renounced actual design work during his last two years we cannot say. Sullivan himself would not have answered such a question, absorbed as he was, at this point, in laborious self-contemplation, both verbal (with the *Autobiography of an Idea*) and non-verbal (with *A System of Architectural Ornament*).

In all likelihood he still nurtured the dream of triumphing over his long-time rivals—especially Burnham, the "big business man" already dead for ten years. This victory was to be achieved through the all-powerful and assertive instrument of his autobiography. He was to wait, however, for the insistence of his readers before proceeding to the final reckoning with his foes; tired after reading fourteen chapters on the subject of Sullivan's childhood, they pressed him to finally come to the subject of the Columbian Exposition—*apertis verbis*—to exhume his great anti-classicist polemic, and to deliver his final and lethal thrust against his old antagonists.

Perhaps this crusade, so dear to the hearts of the late ideologues of anti-classicism, was no longer at the center of Sullivan's thoughts, though he was not to renounce the opportunity of serving as its preeminent mouthpiece. He was an old man who

on this and on the following pages:
Louis Henry Sullivan, ornamental
designs from A System of
Architectural Ornament.

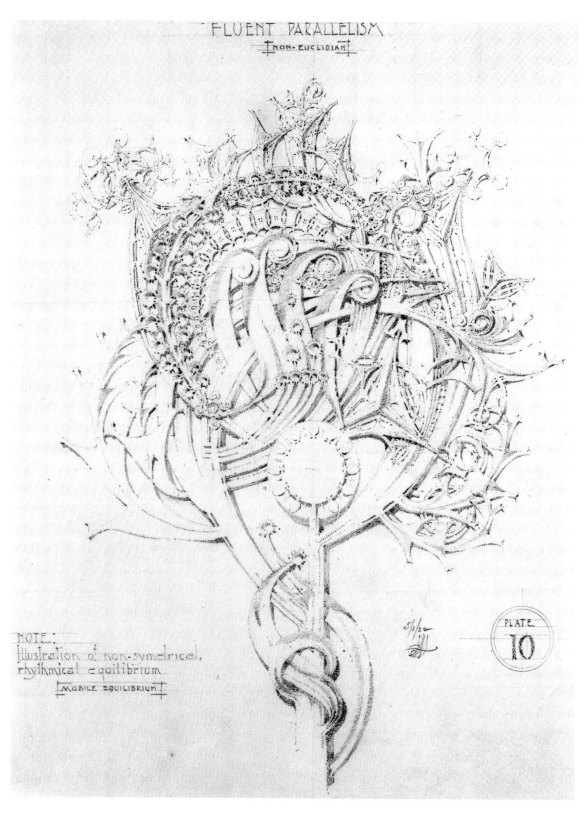

172

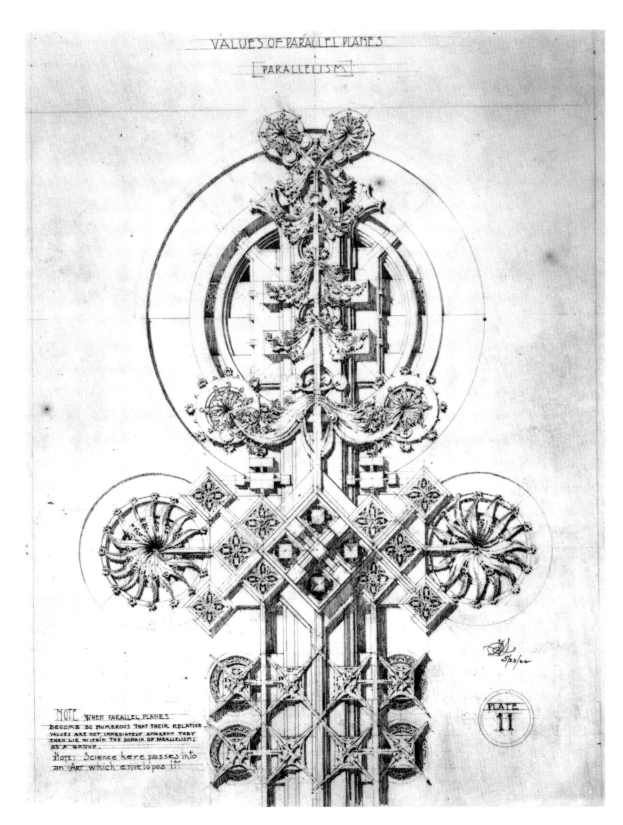

NOTE: WHEN PARALLEL PLANES
BECOME SO NUMEROUS THAT THEIR RELATIVE
VALUES ARE NOT IMMEDIATELY APPARENT THEY
THEN LIE WITHIN THE DOMAIN OF PARALLELISM
AS A GROUP.

NOTE: Science here passes into
an Art which envelopes it.

PLATE
11

173

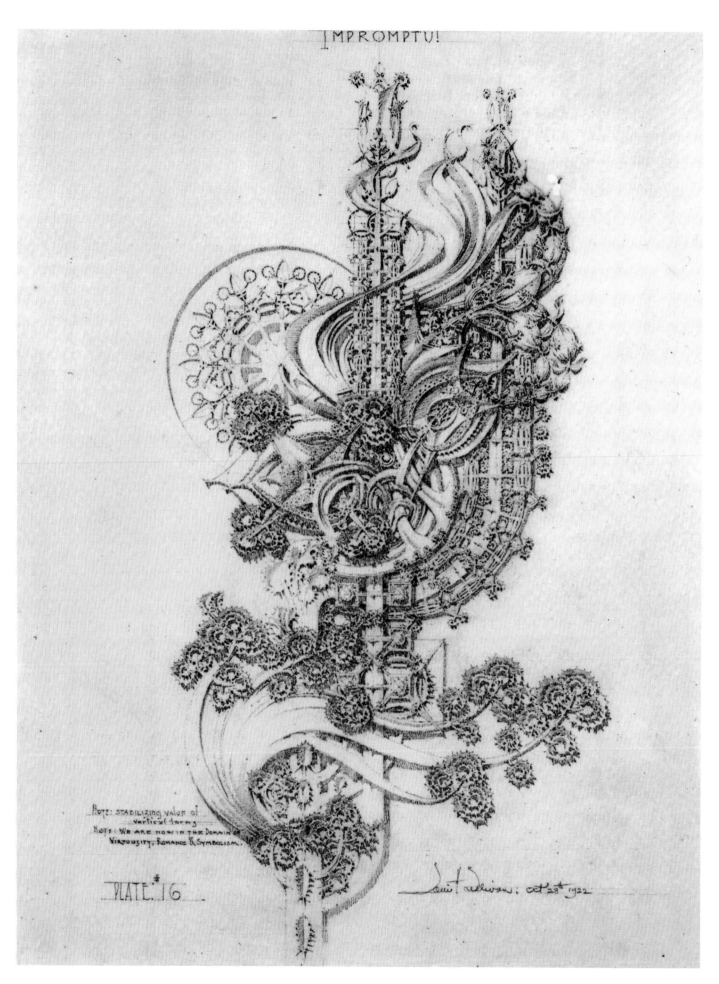

¡MPROMPTU!

NOTE: STABILIZING VALUE OF
VERTICAL FORMS
NOTE: WE ARE NOW IN THE DOMAIN
VIRTUOSITY, ROMANCE & SYMBOLISM.

PLATE #16

Louis H. Sullivan: Oct 28th 1922

174

needed the security of popular support at a time when his exquisite and subtle late work comprised a stylistic language too complex for the facile enthusiasms of the moment. A confusedly allusive language can be found, for that matter, in his *Autobiography of an Idea*. Regardless, he anxiously awaited the publication of the work in book form and when it arrived, he presented Wright a copy with a trembling hand, no longer able to write out a dedication.

Still, Sullivan's testament did not consist solely of the lengthy revisitation of a childhood that was perhaps merely imagined. He supposedly admitted to Wright during their last meeting, on 11 April 1924 that, although it was Wright who had created a new architecture in America, he could not have done it without Sullivan. That, at least, is how Wright reports the master's final farewell, and Sullivan may indeed have said these words, laying the foundation of an opinion that his student would in time develop. Sullivan died three days later, with many doubts (like anyone) concerning the meaning of his relationship to the world. But perhaps he had no doubts about his own architecture.

1. Louis H. Sullivan, "What is Architecture? A Study in the American People of Today" (1906) in Louis H. Sullivan, *Louis Sullivan: The Public Papers*, ed. Robert Twombly (Chicago: University of Chicago Press, 1988), 174ff.

2. Ibid., 200ff.

3. This thesis, in its strongest form, is mine; see Mario Manieri Elia, "Per Una Città Imperiale, D. H. Burnham E Il Movimento City Beautiful," In *La Città Americana Dalla Guerra Civile Al "New Deal"* (Rome: Laterza, 1973), 14ff and note 19.

4. Sullivan, *Public Papers*, 202.

5. Ibid., 205ff.

6. Ibid.

7. Robert Twombly, *Louis Sullivan: His Life and Work* (Chicago: University of Chicago Press, 1986), 413, examines this phenomenon and states that George G. Elmslie, on that occasion, stated that Sullivan should have refused to allow his name to be linked to that work.

8. B. Brooks Pfeiffer, ed., *Letters to Architects. Frank Lloyd Wright* (Fresno: California State University Press, 1984).

APPENDICES

compiled by Susanna Pasquali

1876–82

From 1879 until the first half of 1881, Sullivan worked as an outside consultant for the architect Dankmar Adler; from the second half of 1881 until 30 April 1883, he worked as a partner in the studio of Adler & Co.

1876

Interior ornamentation of the Chicago Avenue Church (Moody Tabernacle), Chicago; architecture by the studio of Johnson & Edelmann.

Interior ornamentation of the Sinai Synagogue, Chicago; architecture by the associated studios of Johnson & Edelmann and Burling & Adler.

1878–80

Interior ornamentation of the Central Music Hall, Randolph and State Streets, Chicago; with D. Adler.

1880

John Borden Residence, 3949 Lake Park Avenue, Chicago; with D. Adler (dem).

Renovation of the interior of the Grand Opera House, Chicago; with D. Adler.

1880–81

Max M. Rothschild Store, 210 West Monroe Street, Chicago; with D. Adler (dem. in 1972).

1880–82

John Borden Block, Randolph and Dearborn Streets, Chicago; with D. Adler (dem. in 1916).

1881–82

Jeweler's Building, 15–19 South Wabash Avenue, Chicago; with D. Adler (extant, the ground floor has been modified).

1881–83

John M. Brunswick & Julius Balke Factory, Orleans and Sedgwick Streets, Chicago; with D. Adler (enlarged in 1891 and dem. in 1989).

Revell Building, Adams and Wabash Streets, Chicago; with D. Adler (dem. in 1968).

1882

Academy of Music, Kalamazoo, Michigan; with D. Adler (dem.).

1883–95

From May 1883 until June 1895 Sullivan worked with the architect D. Adler, founding the studio of Adler & Sullivan; Frank Lloyd Wright worked in the studio from the beginning of 1888 until May 1893, George Elmslie worked there from 1889 or 1890.

1883

Max M. Rothschild Flats, Chicago (dem.).

Ann Halsted Residence, 440 West Belden Street, Chicago (extant).

Morris Selz and Charles H. Schwab Residences, 1715 and 1717 Michigan Ave., Chicago (dem.).

1883–85

Modernization of the J. H. McVicker's Theater, 25 West Madison Street, Chicago (dem. in 1925).

1884

Leon Mannheimer Residence, 2147 North Cleveland Avenue, Chicago (extant).

Solomon Blumenfeld Flats, Chicago (dem.).

A. F. Troescher Building (later the Chicago Journal Building), 15–19 South Market Street, Chicago (dem.).

Martin A. Ryerson Building, 16–20 East Randolph Street, Chicago (dem.).

1884–85

Ann Halsted Flats, 1826–34 Lincoln Park West, Chicago (extant).

1885

Partial renovation of the Interstate Exposition Building, on behalf of the Chicago Opera Festival (dem.).

Zion Temple, Chicago.

Fanny Kohn Residence, Chicago (dem.).

Dankmar Adler Residence, Chicago (dem.).

1885–86

Eli B. Felsenthal Residence, Chicago (dem.).

1886

Ryerson Charities Trust Building, Chicago.

1886–89

Auditorium Building, Michigan and Wabash Avenue, Congress Street, Chicago (extant, property of Roosevelt University since 1946).

1887

Wirt Dexter Building, 630 South Wabash Avenue, Chicago (extant).

Selz, Schwab Factory, Chicago (dem.).

Martin A. Ryerson Tomb, Graceland Cemetery, Chicago (extant).

1887–88

Standard Club House, Michigan Avenue and 24th Street, Chicago (dem. in 1931).

1888

Victor Falkenau Flats, Chicago (dem.).

1888–89

Walker Warehouse, Adams and Market Streets, Chicago (dem. in 1953).

1889–90

Opera House Block, Pueblo, Colorado (dem. in 1922).

1889–90 (*cont.*)

Kehilath Anshe Ma'ariv Synagogue, 3301 South Indiana Avenue, Chicago (extant as the Pilgrim Baptist Church).

1890

Chicago Cold Storage Exchange Warehouse, Chicago (partly built).

Ontario Hotel, 2nd South Street, Salt Lake City, Utah (only the foundation was built).

Design of the Opera House Block, Seattle, Washington.

Carrie Elisabeth Getty Tomb, Graceland Cemetery, Chicago (extant).

Helen and James Charnley and L. H. Sullivan Cottages, Ocean Springs, Mississippi.

Renovation of the interior of the Grand Opera House (or Das Deutsche Haus Stadt Theatre), Milwaukee, Wisconsin.

1890–91

Dooly Block, 111 West 2nd South Street, Salt Lake City, Utah (dem.).

Second renovation of the J. H. McVickers Theater, 25 West Madison Street, Chicago (dem. in 1925).

1890–92

Wainwright Building, 7th and Chestnut Streets, St. Louis, Missouri (extant).

1891

Illinois Central Railroad Station, New Orleans, Louisiana (dem.).

Design of the Mercantile Club Building, St. Louis, Missouri.

Design of the Odd Fellows Fraternity Temple Building, site not determined, Chicago.

1891–92

James Charnley Residence, 1365 Astor Street, Chicago (extant).

1891–92 (*cont.*)

Sullivan House, 4575 Lake Park Avenue, Chicago (dem. in 1970. Built for Sullivan's mother, who died before it could be completed; Sullivan lived there until 1896, after which his brother Albert occupied the house.)

1891–93

Schiller Building, 64 West Randolph Street, Chicago (dem. in 1961).

Transportation Building, World's Columbian Exposition, Chicago (dem).

1892

Charlotte Dickson Wainwright Tomb, Bellefontaine Cemetery, St. Louis, Missouri (extant).

Design of the Portland Building, St. Louis, Missouri.

1892–93

Two designs of the Trust Savings Building, St. Louis, Missouri.

St. Nicholas Hotel, Locust and 8th Streets, St. Louis, Missouri (renovated 1903; dem. in 1973).

Union Trust Building, Oliver and 7th Streets, St. Louis, Missouri (modified on the ground floor and mezzanine in 1924; extant).

Victoria Hotel, Chicago Heights, Illinois (built for the World's Columbian Exposition in 1893; dem. in 1961).

William Mayer Warehouse, Van Buren and Franklin Streets, Chicago (dem. in 1969).

Chicago Stock Exchange Building, La Salle and Washington Streets, Chicago (dem. 1970s, Trading Room installed in the Chicago Art Institute).

1894

Herman Braunstein Store and Flats, Chicago.

1894 (*cont.*)

Chicago Dock Company Warehouse, Chicago.

Design of the Burnet House Hotel, Cincinnati, Ohio.

Design of the Chemical National Bank Building, St. Louis, Missouri.

1894–95

Guaranty (later Prudential) Building, Pearl and Church Streets, Buffalo, New York (extant).

1895–1922

In July 1895 Sullivan ended his partnership with D. Adler; Sullivan worked as an independent architect; George Elmslie left the studio in 1909.

1897–99

Bayard (later Condict) Building, 65 Bleecker Street, New York; with L. P. Smith (extant).

1898

Design for the A. W. Goodrich Residence, Harbor Springs, Michigan.

1898–99

Gage and McCormick Building façades, 18 South Michigan Avenue, Chicago (extant).

Schlesinger & Mayer (later Carson Pirie Scott) Store, State and Madison Street, Chicago (for the headquarters on Madison Street, design for a twelve–story building, later reduced to nine stories. For the wing on Wabash Street, , planned to be ten stories tall, only two stories were built; extant.)

1899–1900

Holy Trinity Cathedral, 1121 North Leavitt Street, Chicago (extant).

1899–1902

Euston & Company Factory (or Riverside Seed & Cleaning Company), Chicago (extant in 1985).

1901

Virginia Hall, Tusculum College, Greenville, Tennessee (extant).

1902–03

Schlesinger & Mayer (later Carson Pirie Scott) Store, State and Madison Street, Chicago (twelve–story building; in the same year and for the same site, plans for a twenty–story building; modified in 1948; extant).

1904

Crane Company Office, Chicago.

1906

Eli B. Felsenthal Store and Flats, Chicago.

1906–08

National Farmers Bank, Broadway and Cedar Streets, Owatonna, Minnesota (extant).

1907

Design of the Island City Amusement Park, Petty's Island, Philadelphia.

1907–09

Henry Babson Residence, 230 Riverside Drive, Riverside, Illinois (dem. in 1960).

1908–09

Harold Bradley Residence, 106 North Prospect Street, Madison, Wisconsin (extant).

1909–11

People's Savings Bank, 3rd Avenue and 1st Street, Cedar Rapids, Iowa (extant).

1910–14

St. Paul's Methodist Episcopal Church, 3rd Avenue and 14th Street, Cedar Rapids, Iowa (design partially completed; extant).

1911

Design for the Carl K. Bennet Residence, Owatonna, Minnesota.

1913

Henry C. Adams Building, Moore and State Streets, Algona, Iowa (extant).

1913–14

Merchants National Bank, 4th and Broad Streets, Grinnell, Iowa (extant).

1913–15

John D. Van Allen & Sons Dry Goods Store, 5th Avenue and 2nd Street, Clinton, Iowa (extant).

1914

Purdue State Bank, West Lafayette, Indiana (extant in 1985).

1914–15

Home Building Association Bank, West Main and North 3rd Streets, Newark, Ohio (extant).

1917–18

People's Savings & Loan Association Bank, Count Street and Ohio Avenue, Sidney, Ohio (extant).

1919–20

Farmers & Merchants Union Bank, James and Dickson Streets, Columbus, Wisconsin (extant).

1922

William P. Krause Music Store, 4611 North Lincoln Avenue, Chicago (extant; now houses the Kelmscott Gallery).

GENERAL WORKS AND ARTICLES

Adler, D. *Autobiography.* Manuscript, Chicago, Newberry Library.

———. "The Influence of Steel Construction and Plate Glass upon the Development of Modern Style," *Inland Architect* 28 (November 1896): 34–37.

———. "Light in Tall Office Buildings," *Engineering Magazine* 4 (November 1892): 171–86.

———. "The Tall Business Building," *Cassier's Magazine* 12 (November 1897): 193–210.

———. "The Tall Office Building. Past and Future," *Engineering Magazine* 3 (September 1892): 765–73.

Andrews, W. *Architecture, Ambition and Americans: A Social History of American Architecture.* 1947; reprint, London: Collier Macmillan, 1964.

American Institute of Architects. *Guide to Chicago.* Introduction by P. R. Duis. San Diego: Harcourt Brace, 1993.

Baker, R. *Richard Morris Hunt.* Cambridge: MIT Press, 1980.

Banham, R. "The Wilderness Years of Frank Lloyd Wright," *Royal Institute of British Architects Journal* 76 (December 1969).

Baron, R. "Forgotten Facets of Dankmar Adler," *Inland Architect* (April 1964): 14–26.

Barth, G. *City People: The Rise of Modern City Culture in Nineteenth-Century America.* New York: Oxford University Press, 1980.

Beard, C. and M. Beard. *A Basic History of the United States.* New York: Doubleday.

Behrendt, W. C. *Modern Building.* New York: Harcourt, Brace, 1937.

Boyer, O. M. and H. M. Morais, *Labor's Untold Story.* United Electrical, Radio & Machine Workers of America, 1955.

Bragdon, C. "Architecture in the United States, III. The Skyscraper," *Architectural Record* 26 (August 1909).

Brooks, H. A. " 'Chicago School,' Metamorphosis of a Term," *Journal of the Society of Architectural Historians* 25 (May 1966): 115–118.

———. "La Prairie School," *Edilizia Moderna* 86 (1965).

———. *The Prairie School: Frank Lloyd Wright and His Midwest Contemporaries.* Toronto: University of Toronto Press,1972.

Brown, M. T. "Greenough, Paine, Emerson and the Organic Aesthetic," *Journal of Aesthetic and Art Criticism* 14 (1956): 304.

Burchard, J. and A. Bush Brown. *The Architecture of America: A Social and Cultural History.* Boston: Little, Brown & Co., 1961.

Chai, L. *The Romantic Foundation of the American Renaissance.* Ithaca: Cornell University Press, 1987.

Ciucci, G., F. Dal Co, M. Manieri Elia, and M. Tafuri, *La città americana dalla guerra civile al "New Deal."* Rome-Bari: Editori Laterza, 1973.

Cohen, J. L. and H. Damisch, eds. *Américanisme et modernité: L'idéal américain dans l'architecture.* Paris: Flammarion, 1993.

Coles, W. A., ed. *Architecture and Society: Selected Essays of Henry Van Brunt.* Cambridge: Belknap Press at Harvard University Press, 1969.

Coles, W. A. and H. H. Reed Jr., eds. *Architecture in America: A Battle of Styles.* New York: Appleton, Century, Croft, 1961.

Collins, P. *Changing Ideals in Modern Architecture.* Montreal: 1967.

Condit, C. W. *The Chicago School of Architecture: A History of Commercial and Public Building in the Chicago Area: 1875–1925.* Chicago: University of Chicago Press, 1964.

———. *Chicago 1910–1929: Building, Planning, and Urban Technology.* Chicago: University of Chicago Press, 1973.

David, A. C. "L'architettura delle idee," *Edilizia Moderna* 86 (1965).

De Feo, V. "La tesi 'organic' in architettura," *Rassegna dell'Istituto di Architettura e Urbanistica 2* (December 1966).

Edelmann, J. "The Pessimism of Modern Architecture," *Engineering Magazine* 3 (April 1892): 44–54.

Egbert, D. D. and P. E. Sprague. "In Search of John Edelmann: Architect and Anarchist," *American Institute of Architects Journal* 45, (February 1966) 35–41.

Eidlitz, L. *The Nature and Function of Art, More Especially of Architecture.* London: 1881.

Elia, M. Manieri. "Per una città imperiale: D. H. Burnham e il movimento City Beautiful." In G. Ciucci et. al., *La città americana dalla guerra civile al "New Deal."* Rome-Bari: Editori Laterza, 1973.

Elmslie, G. "The Chicago School: Its Inheritance and Bequest," *Journal of the Society of Architectural Historians* 18 (July 1952).

Elstein, R. S. "The Architecture of Dankmar Adler," *Journal of the Society of Architectural Historians* 26 (December 1967): 242–249.

Fitch, J. M. *American Building: The Historical Forces that Shaped It.* Boston: 1962.

———. *Architecture and the Esthetics of Plenty.* New York: Columbia University Press, 1961.

Fitzpatrick, C. W. "Chicago," *The Inland Architect and News Record* 45 (June 1905).

Frank, E. "Filosofia organica, architettura organica" *Architettura: Cronache e storia* 15, no. 7 (November 1969).

Giedion, S. *Space, Time and Architecture: The Growth of a New Tradition.* Cambridge: Harvard University Press, 1941.

Greenough, H. *Form and Function: Remarks on Art,* ed. H. A. Small. Berkeley: 1949.

Griswold Van Rensselaer, M. *Henry Hobson Richardson and His Works.*1888. Reprint, New York: Dover, 1969.

Hines, T. S. *Burnham of Chicago: Architect and Planner.* New York: Oxford University Press, 1974.

Hitchcock, H. R. *Architecture: Nineteenth and Twentieth Centuries.* New York: Penguin Books, 1958.

———. *The Architecture of H. H. Richardson and His Times.* New York: Museum of Modern Art, 1936. Reprint, Cambridge: MIT Press, 1966.

———. *Modern Architecture: Romanticism and Reintegration.* New York: Payson and Clarke, 1929.

———. *In the Nature of Materials: The Buildings of Frank Lloyd Wright, 1887–1941.* New York: Duell, Sloane and Pearce, 1942.

Jordy, W. H. *American Buildings and Their Architects.* Vol. III, *Progressive and Academic Ideals at the Turn of the Twentieth Century.* Garden City: Anchor Books, 1976.

Karlowicz, T. M. "D. H. Burnham's Role in the Selection of the Architects for the World's Columbian Exposition," *Journal of the Society of Architectural Historians* 29 (October 1970): 247–254.

Kaufman, E. Jr., ed. *The Rise of an American Architecture.* New York: Praeger Publishers, 1970.

Kimball, F. *American Architecture.* New York: Bobbs Merril, 1928.

McLean, R. C. "Dankmar Adler," *Inland Architect and News Record* 35 (May 1900): 26.

Mayer, H. M. and R. C. Wade. *Chicago: Growth of a Metropolis.* Chicago: University of Chicago Press, 1969.

Matthiessen, F. O. *American Renaissance.* New York: 1949.

Metzger, C. O. "Whitman on Architecture" *Journal of the Society of Architectural Historians* 16 (March 1957).

Monroe, H. *John Wellborn Root: A Study in His Life and Work.* Boston: Houghton, Mifflin & Co., 1896. Reprint, Park Forest: Prairie School Press, 1966.

Moore, C. *Daniel H. Burnham: Architect Planner of Cities.* Boston: Houghton, Mifflin & Co., 1921.

Mumford, L. *The Brown Decades: A Study of the Arts in America: 1865–1895.* New York: Harcourt Brace, 1931. Reprint, New York: Dover Press, 1955 and 1971.

———. "Form Follows Nature: The Origin of American Organic Architecture," *Journal of Aesthetic Education* 42 (1989).

———. *The Roots of American Architecture.* New York: Reinhold, 1952.

———. *Stick and Stones: A Study of American Architecture and Civilization.* New York: 1924.

Nelson, L. H. "White, Furness, McNally and the Capital National Bank of Salem, Oregon," *Journal of the Society of Architectural Historians* 19 (May 1960): 57–61.

O'Gorman, J. F. *The Architecture of Frank Furness.* Philadelphia: Philadelphia Museum of Art, 1973.

Parsons, W. E. "Burnham as Pioneer in City Planning," *Architectural Record* 38 (July 1915): 13–31.

Peisch, M. L. *The Chicago School of Architecture: Early Followers of Sullivan and Wright.* New York: Random House, 1965.

Pennsylvania Railroad Co. *Guida alla Esposizione colombiana.* Philadelphia: Ferrovia della Compagnia, 1892.

Pevsner, N. *Pioneers of Modern Design from William Morris to Walter Gropius.* New York: Museum of Modern Art, 1949.

Phillips, "Organicism in the Late Nineteenth and Early Twentieth Centuries," *Journal of History of Ideas* 21 (1970): 413.

Randall, F. A. *History of the Development of Building Construction in Chicago.* Urbana: University of Illinois Press, 1949.

Reps, J. W. *The Making of Urban America: A History of City Planning in the United States.* Princeton: Princeton University Press, 1965.

Root, J. W. "Architects of Chicago," *Inland Architect and News Record* 16 (January 1891): 91–92.

———. *Building and Writings*, ed. D. Hoffmann. New York: Horizon Press, 1967.

Saltzstein, J. W. "Dankmar Adler: The Man, the Architect, the Author," *Wisconsin Architect* 38 (July/August 1967): 15–19; (September 1967): 10–14; (November 1967): 16–19.

Schuyler, M. *Studies in American Architecture.* New York: Harper & Bros., 1892. Reprinted in *American Architecture and Other Writings*, eds. W. Jordy and R. Coe. New York: Atheneum, New York 1964.

———. "The Art of City Making," *Architectural Record* 12 (May 1902): 1–26.

———. "The 'Skyscraper' Up To Date," *Architectural Record* 8 (January–March 1899): 231–257.

Scully, V. *American Architecture and Urbanism.* London: Thames and Hudson, 1969.

Tafuri, M. and F. Dal Co. *Architettura contemporanea.* Milan: Electa, 1976.

Tallmadge, T. E. *Architecture in Old Chicago.* Chicago: 1941.

———. "The Chicago School," *Architectural Review* 15 (April 1908).

———. *The Story of Architecture in America.* New York: W. W. Norton & Co., 1927.

Tallmadge, T. E., et al. *Architectural Essays from the Chicago School*, ed. W. R. Hasbrouck. Park Forest: 1967.

Tselos, D. "The Chicago Fair and the Myth of the 'Lost Cause,' " *Journal of the Society of Architectural Historians* 26 (December 1967) 259–268.

Turak, T. "The École Centrale and Modern Architecture: The Education of William Le Baron Jenney," *Journal of the Society of Architectural Historians* 29 (March 1980): 40–47.

Winter, R. W. "Fergusson and Garbett in American Architectural Theory,"

Journal of the Society of Architectural Historians 17 (December 1958) 25–30.

Woltersdorf, A. "A Portrait Gallery of Chicago Architects, II: Dankmar Adler," *Western Architect* 37 (July 1924): 75–79.

Wright, F. L. *An Autobiography.* New York: Horizon Press, 1932.

———. *Genius and the Mobocracy.* New York: Duell, Sloane & Pearce, 1949.

———. *Letters to Architects*, ed. B. Brooks Pfeiffer. Fresno: California State University Press, 1984.

Zevi, B. *Architettura e storiografia.* Milan: 1950.

———. *Frank Lloyd Wright.* Milan: 1947.

———. *Storia dell'architettura moderna.* Turin: Einaudi, 1950.

Zueblin, C. *A Decade of Civic Development.* Chicago: 1905.

Zukowsky, J., ed. *Chicago Architecture: 1872–1922.* Chicago: 1987.

WRITINGS ON LOUIS HENRY SULLIVAN

American Architect and Architecture. "Sullivan's Letters at Columbia," *American Architect and Architecture* 149 (November 1936): 100–101.

American Magazine of Art. "Memorial to Louis H. Sullivan," *American Magazine of Art* 19 (May 1928): 276–277.

Andrew, D. S. *Louis Sullivan and the Polemics of Modern Architecture: The Present Against the Past.* Chicago: University of Illinois Press, 1985.

Barker, A. W. "Louis H. Sullivan: Thinker and Architect," *Architectural Annual* 2 (1901): 49–66.

Bragdon, C. "An American Architect, Being an Appreciation of Louis H. Sullivan," *House and Garden* 7 (January 1905): 47–55.

———. "Louis Sullivan, Prophet of Democracy." In *Architecture and Democracy.* New York: A. W. Knopf & Co., 1918.

———. "Letters from Louis Sullivan," *Architecture* 64 (July 1931): 7–10.

———. "Louis H. Sullivan," *Journal of the American Institute of Architects* 12 (May 1924): 241.

Brown, A. Bush. *Louis Sullivan.* New York: George Braziller, 1960.

Caffin, C. "Louis H. Sullivan, Artist among Artists, American among Americans," *Criterion* 20, (28 January 1899): 20.

Chapman, L. L., ed. *Louis H. Sullivan Architectural Ornament Collection.* Edwardsville, Il: Southern Illinois University Office of Cultural Arts and University Museums, 1981.

Connely, W. "The Last Years of Louis Sullivan," *Journal of the American Institute of Architects* 23 (January 1955) 32–38.

———. "Louis Sullivan and His Younger Staff," *Journal of the American Institute of Architects* 22 (December 1954): 266–268.

———. *Louis Sullivan as He Lived: The Shaping of American Architecture.* New York: Horizon Press, 1960.

———. "The Mystery of Louis Sullivan and His Brother," *Journal of the American Institute of Architects* 20 (November 1953) 226–229.

———. "New Sullivan Letters," *American Institute of Architects Journal* 20 (July 1953).

Dal Co, F. "Louis Henry Sullivan: la qualità nell'epoca del sorgere della metropoli. Appunti su 'Autobiografia di un'idea,' " *Rassegna dell'Istituto di Architettura e Urbanistica* 7, no. 19 (April 1971): 69–86.

De Nevi, D. "Louis Sullivan on Art Education," *Art Journal* 20 (1970).

Desmond, H. W. "Another View: What Mr Sullivan Stands For," in *Architectural Record* 16 (July 1904).

Duncan, H. D. "Attualità di L. Sullivan," *Casabella* 2–3, no. 104 (February–March) 1954): 7–32.

———. *Culture and Democracy: The Struggle for Form in Society and Architecture in Chicago and the Middle West During the Life and Times of Louis H. Sullivan.* Totowa, N. J.: Bedminster Press, 1965.

Eaton, L. K. *American Architecture Comes of Age. European Reaction to H. H. Richardson and Louis Sullivan.* Cambridge: MIT Press, 1972.

Elia, M. Manieri. "L. H. Sullivan, epigono di un'ideologia." In *L. H. Sullivan, Autobiografia di un'idea, Officina.* Rome: 1970.

———. "Scuola di Chicago: il mito e la realtà," *Rassegna dell'Istituto di Architettura e Urbanistica* 7, no. 19 (April 1971).

Elmslie, G. G. "Sullivan's Ornamentation," *Journal of American Institute of Architects* 6 (October 1946): 155–158.

Frazier, N. *Louis Sullivan and the Chicago School.* New York: Crescent Books, 1991.

Frei, H. *Louis Henry Sullivan.* London: Artemis Verlag, 1992.

Gebhard, D. "Louis Sullivan and George Grant Elmslie," *Journal of the Society of Architectural Historians* 19 (May 1960): 62–68.

Hitchcock, H. R. "Sullivan and the Skyscraper," *Journal of the Royal Institute of British Architects* 60 (July 1953): 353–361.

Hope, H. R. "Louis Sullivan's Architectural Ornament," *Architectural Review* 102 (October 1947): 111–114.

Ison, M., ed. *Buildings Designed by Louis Sullivan, Recorded by the Historic American Buildings Survey.* Washington: Library of Congress, Prints and Photographs Division, 1981.

Kaufman, E. Jr., ed. *Louis Sullivan and the Architecture of Free Enterprise.* Chicago: Art Institute of Chicago, 1956.

Kaufman, M. D. *Father of Skyscrapers: A Biography of Louis Sullivan.* Boston: Little, Brown and Co., 1969.

Kennedy, R. W. "Form and Function, and Expression. Variation on a Theme by Louis Sullivan," *Journal of the American Institute of Architects,* 14 (November 1950): 198–204.

Kimball, S. F. "Louis H. Sullivan, His Work," *Architectural Record* (July 1924): 28–32.

———. "Louis Sullivan: An Old Master," *Architectural Record* 57 (April 1925): 289–304.

———. "Louis Sullivan, the First American Architect," *Current Literature* (June 1912): 703–707.

Johnson, P. "Is Sullivan the Father of Functionalism?" *Art News* 55 (December 1956): 44–57.

Louis Sullivan in the Art Institute of Chicago. An Illustrated Catalogue of Collections, edited by S. C. Mollmann, Garland, New York-London 1989.

"Louis Sullivan, the First American Architect," *Current Literature* 52 (June 1912): 703–707.

McCoy, E. "Letters from Louis H. Sullivan to R. M. Schindler," *Journal of the Society of Architectural Historians* 20 (December 1961): 179–184.

McLean, R. C. "Louis Henry Sullivan, Sept. 3, 1856–April 14, 1924: An Appreciation," *Western Architect* 33 (May 1924) 53–55.

Manson, G. "Sullivan and Wright, an Uneasy Union of Celts," *Architectural Review* (November 1955): 297–300.

"Memorial to Louis Sullivan," *Western Architect* 38 (June 1929): 100.

Menocal, N. G. *Architecture as Nature: The Transcendentalist Idea of Louis Sullivan.* Madison: University of Wisconsin Press, 1981.

Morrison, H. *Louis Sullivan: Prophet of Modern Architecture.* New York: W. W. Norton & Co.,1935 . Reprint: Mew York: P. Smith, 1952 and 1963.

———. "Louis Sullivan Today," *Journal of the American Institute of Architecture* (September 1956).

Office of Cultural Arts and University Museums. *Louis H. Sullivan: Architectural Ornament Collection, Southern Illinois University at Edwardsville.* Edwardsville: Southern Illinois University, 1981.

O'Gorman, J. *Three American Architects: Richardson, Sullivan, and Wright: 1865–1915.* Chicago: University of Chicago Press, 1991.

Peisch, M. L. "Letter of George Grant Elmslie to Frank Lloyd Wright: 12 June 1936," *Journal of the Society of Architectural Historians,* 20 (October 1961): 140–141.

Pettengill, G. E. "The Biography of a Book: Correspondence Between Sullivan and 'The Journal,' " The American Institute of Architects Journal 63 (June 1975): 42–45.

I. K. Pond, "Louis Sullivan's The Autobiography of an Idea: A Review and an Estimate," in *Western Architect* 33 (June 1924): 67–69.

Purcell, W. G. "Louis H. Sullivan, Prophet of Democracy" *Journal of the American Institute of Architects* 16 (December 1951): 256–268.

———. "Sullivan at Work," *Northwest Architect* 8 (January–February 1944): 11.

———. "What is Architecture. A Study of the American People of Today: An Interpretation," *Journal of the Society of Architectural Historians* 4 (April 1944).

Rebori, A. N. "*Louis H. Sullivan, an Obituary,*" Architectural Record 55 (June 1924): 586–587.

Rice, W. "Louis Sullivan as Author," *Western Architect* 33 (June 1924): 70–71.

Robertson, H. "The Work of Louis Sullivan," *Architect's Journal* 59 (18 June 1924): 1,000–1,009.

Ryckwert, J. "Louis Sullivan and the Gospel of Height," *Art in America* (November 1987): 158–195.

Sherman, P. *Louis Sullivan: An Architect in American Thought.* Englewood Cliffs: Prentice Hall, 1962.

Schuyler, M. "Architecture in Chicago: A Critique of the Work of Adler & Sullivan," *Architectural Record* special series, 4 (December 1895): 3–48.

Scully, V. "Louis Sullivan's Architectural Ornament: A Brief Note Concerning Humanistic Design in the Age of Force," *Perspecta* 5 (1959): 73–80.

Sprague, P. E. "The European Sources of Louis Sullivan's Ornamental Style," *Journal of the Society of Architectural Historians* 23 (May 1974): 167.

———, ed. *The Drawings of Louis Henry Sullivan. A Catalogue of the Frank Lloyd Wright Collection at the Avery Architectural Library.* Princeton: Princeton University Press, 1979.

Severens, K. W. "The Reunion of Louis Sullivan and Frank Lloyd Wright," *Prairie School Review* 12 (April–June 1975): 5–21.

Starret, T. "The Architecture of Louis H. Sullivan," *Architect's and Builder's Magazine* 44 (December 1912): 469–475.

Sturgis, R. "Good Things in Modern Architecture," *Architectural Record* 8 (July–September 1898): 92–110.

Sullivan, L. "Drawings of Louis Henry Sullivan from the Frank Lloyd Wright Collection, Avery Library, Columbia University," *Architectural Record* (March 1966): 147.

———. *The Public Papers,* ed. R. Twombly. Chicago: University of Chicago Press, 1988.

"Sullivan Seen by his Contemporaries in his Centennial Year: Another Look," Architectural Record 120 (September 1956): 18.

Szarkowski, J. *The Idea of Louis Sullivan.* Minneapolis: University of Minnesota Press, 1956.

Turak, T. "French and English Sources of Sullivan's Ornament and Doctrines," *Prairie School Review* 11 (October–December 1974): 5–30.

Twombly, R. *Louis Sullivan: His Life and Work.* Chicago: University of Chicago Press, 1986.

Weingarden, L. S. "The Colours of Nature: Sullivan's Polychromy and 19th Century Colour Theory," *Winterthur Portfolio* 20 (1985) 243.

———. Louis H. Sullivan. "Investigation of a Second French

Connection," *Journal of the Society of Architectural Historians* 39 (December 1980): 297–303.

———. "Naturalised Technology," *Centennial Review* 30 (1986) 480.

Weisman, W. "Philadelphia Functionalism and Sullivan," *Journal of the Society of Architectural Historians* 20 (March 1961): 3–19.

Wit, W. de, ed. *Louis Sullivan. The function of Ornament.* New York: W. W. Norton & Co., 1986.

Wright, F. L. "Louis H. Sullivan, Beloved Master," *Western Architect* 33 (June 1924): 64–66.

———. "Louis H. Sullivan: His Work," *Architectural Record* 56 (July 1924): 28–32.

———. "Sullivan Against the World," *Architectural Record* 105 (June 1949): 295–298.

Zevi, B. "Il pensiero di Louis Henry Sullivan." In *Pretesti di critica architettonica.* Turin: 1960.

WRITINGS ON INDIVIDUAL PROJECTS
Texts cited here are for books and articles that have appeared in journals of architecture and engineering. For news articles from the contemporary press, see especially R. Twombly, Louis Sullivan: His Life and Work, *(Chicago: University of Chicago Press,1986). Parenthetical notes following the citations indicate the project referenced, when necessary.*

Adler, D. "The Auditorium Tower," *American Architect and Building News* 32 (April 1891): 15–16.

———. "The Chicago Auditorium," *Architectural Record* 1 (April–June 1892): 415–434.

———. "Foundation of the Auditorium," *Inland Architect* 2 (March 1888): 31–32.

Andrew, D. S. "Adler and Sullivan's 'Other' Skyscraper in St. Louis: The Unacclaimed Union Trust Building," *Architectura* 2 (1972): 153–166.

"Architectural Drawings at Chicago," *Builder* 65 (2 September 1893): 167–170. (Union Trust Building)

"The Auditorium Building," *American Architect and Building News* 26 (28 December 1889) 299–300.

"Bayard Building, Bleecker Street, New York City," *Brickbuilder* 7 (June 1898) 127–128.

Bennett, C. K. "A Bank Built for Farmers: Louis Sullivan Designs a Building Which Marks a New Epoch in American Architecture," *Craftsman* 15 (November 1908): 176–185. (National Farmers Bank)

"Brick and Terra Cotta in American and Foreign Cities," *Brickbuilder* 8 (December 1899): 253–254. (Gage Building)

"A Chicago Architect's Winter Retreat," *American Architect and Building News* 55 (23 January 1897): 31. (Sullivan Cottage)

"The Chicago Auditorium," *American Architect and Building News* 26 (9 November 1889): 223–234.

"Colour Decoration at the Chicago Exhibition," *Builder* 65 (26 August 1893): 151–152.

Commission on Chicago Historical and Architectural Landmarks. *Carson Pirie Scott & Company Building.* Chicago: City of Chicago Press, 1979.

———. *Holy Trinity Orthodox Cathedral and Rectory.* Chicago: City of Chicago Press, 1978.

———. *Krause Music Store.* Chicago: City of Chicago Press, 1977.

Condit, C. W. "The Structural System of Adler and Sullivan's Garrick Theatre Building," *Technology and Culture* 5 (1964): 523–540.

Crook, D. H. "Louis Sullivan and the Golden Doorway," *Journal of the Society of Architectural Historians* 26 (December 1967): 250–258.

"A Departure from Classical Tradition: Two Unusual Houses by Louis Sullivan and Frank Lloyd Wright," *Architectural Record* 30 (October 1911): 327–338.

Ferree, B. "Architecture at the World's Fair," *Engineering Magazine* 5 (August 1893): 651–659.

Fletcher, B. "American Architecture Through English Spectacles," *Engineering Magazine* 7 (June 1894). (Ryerson Tomb, Transportation Building)

Greengard, B. C. "Sullivan 'Presto:' The Krause Music Store," *Prairie School Review* (July–September 1969): 5–10.

Gregerson, C. "Early Adler & Sullivan Work in Kalamazoo," *Prairie School Review* 11 (July–September 1974): 5–15.

Hallberg, L. G. "Untitled Letter Concerning the Central Music Hall," *American Architect and Building News* 6 (1879): 174–175.

Hasbrouck, W. R. "Chicago's Auditorium Theater," *Prairie School Review* 4, (July–September 1967): 7–19.

"How the Rich Are Buried," *Architectural Record* 10 (July 1900): 23–54. (Getty Tomb, Ryerson Tomb, Wainwright Tomb)

Johnson, R. D. "The Gage Panels. From Contractor's Scrap to Museum Display," *Prairie School Review* (July–September 1964): 15–16. (Gage Building)

"Making a Monument Work: How Sullivan's Minnesota Bank Was Remodeled and Restored to Its Original Beauty and Grace," *Architectural Forum* 109 (July 1958): 99–106.

"The Merchants National Bank, Grinnell, Iowa," *Western Architect* 23 (February 1916): 20.

Millet, L. J. *The Curve of the Arch: The Story of Louis Sullivan's Owatonna Bank.* St. Paul: Minnesota Historical Society Press,1985.

———. "The National Farmers Bank of Owatonna, Minn.," *Architectural Record* 24 (October 1908): 249–254.

Millet, L. J. and H. W. Desmond, "The Schlesinger and Mayer Building," *Architectural Record* 16 (July 1904): 53–67.

"The New Schlesinger and Mayer Building," *Brickbuilder* 12 (May 1903): 101–104.

Orr, G. "*The Collaboration of Claude and Starck with Chicago Architectural Firms,*" *Prairie School Review* 12 (October–December 1975): 5–12. (H. C. Bradley House)

Pearlman, D. H. *The Auditorium Building: Its History and Architectural Significance. Chicago:* Roosevelt University Press, 1976.

Handbook of the World's Columbian Exposition. Chicago: Rand McNally & Co., 1893.

Randall, J. D. *The Art of Office Building: Sullivan's Wainwright and the St. Louis Estate Boom.* Springfield: J. D. Randall, 1972.

Rebori, A. N. "*An Architecture of Democracy: Three Examples from the Work of Louis H. Sullivan,*" Architectural Record 39 (May 1916): 437–465. (Algona Land and Loan Office, Merchants National Bank, Home Building Association Bank)

"Restoration of the Harold C. Bradley House," *Wisconsin Architect* (October 1975): 13–14.

"St. Paul's Methodist Episcopal Church," *Western Architect* 20 (August 1914): 85–88.

Sabine, P. E. "Acoustics of the Chicago Civic Opera House," *Architectural Forum* 2 (April 1930): 599–604.

Schuyler, M. "The Last Words About the World's Fair," *Architectural Record* 3 (January–March 1894).

———. "The People's Savings Bank of Cedar Rapids, Iowa," *Architectural Record* 31 (January 1912): 45–56.

Severns, K. W. "Louis Sullivan Builds a Small-Town Bank," *Architectural Association Journal* 65 (May 1976): 68–71.

Siry, J. *Carson Pirie Scott: Louis Sullivan and the Chicago Department Store.* Chicago: University of Chicago Press, 1988.

Smith, L. P. "The Home of an Artist-Architect: Louis H. Sullivan's Place at Ocean Springs," *Architectural Record* 17 (July 1905): 471–490.

———. "The Schlesinger & Mayer Building: An Attempt to Give Functional Expression to the Architecture of a Department Store," *Architectural Record* 16 (July 1904): 53–60.

Sprague, P. "Adler & Sullivan's Schiller Building," *Prairie School Review* 2 (April–June 1965): 5–20.

———. "The National Farmers Bank, Owatonna, Minnesota," *Prairie School Review* 4 (April–June 1967): 5–21.

———. "Sullivan's Scoville Building: A Chronology," *Prairie School Review* 11 (July–September 1974): 16–23.

"The Standard Club's New Building," *American Architect and Building News* 25 (23 March 1889): 137.

"Store for Martin Ryerson" *American Architect and Building News* 17 (March 1885): 127.

"Sullivan in the West," *Western Architect and Engineer* 218 (November 1959): 34–37. (Dooly Block)

Tallmadge, T. E. "The Farmers & Merchants Bank of Columbus, Wisconsin," *Western Architect* 29 (July 1920): 63–65.

———. *"The People's Savings & Loan Association Building of Sidney, Ohio,"* American Architect 114, no. 23 (October 1918): 477–482.

Turak, T. "A Celt Among Slavs: Louis Sullivan's Holy Trinity Cathedral," *Prairie School Review* 9 (October–December 1972): 5–23.

Twose, G. "Steel and Terra Cotta Buildings in Chicago," *Brickbuilder* 3 (January 1894): 1–5. (Schiller Building)

Twyman, J. "Decoration of the McVicker's Theatre, Chicago," *American Architect and Building News* 23 (March 1888): 118.

"A Unique Church Building," *American Contractor* 32 (4 November 1911): 92–93. (St. Paul's Methodist Episcopal Church)

Vinci, J. *The Art Institute of Chicago: The Stock Exchange Trading Room.* Chicago: Art Institute Press, 1977.

Warn, R. R. "Bennet and Sullivan, Client and Creator," *Prairie School Review* 10 (July–September 1973): 5–15. (C. K. Bennet House)

———. "Two House Projects for the Carl K. Bennet Family by Louis Sullivan and Purcell and Elmslie," *Northwest Architect* 36 (March–April 1972): 64–72.

Waughn, E. J. "Sullivan and Elmslie at Michigan," *Prairie School Review* 6 (April–June 1969): 20–23.

Weingarden, L. S. *Louis H. Sullivan: The Banks.* Cambridge: MIT Press, 1987.

Wight, P. B. "Country House Architecture in the Middle West," *Architectural Record* 38 (October 1915): 385–421.

Wright, F. L. "Chicago's Auditorium is Fifty Years Old," *Architectural Forum* 73 (September 1940): 10.

In addition to their original places of publication, many of the following references can be found in Louis Sullivan: The Public Papers, *ed. R. Twombly (Chicago: University of Chicago Press, 1988). For covenience, in the following citations, references to this volume are provided following the abbreviation* PP. *Additionally,* LHSA *indicates The Louis H. Sullivan Archive, The Burnham Library, The Art Institute, Chicago.*

1872–82

"Lotus Club Notebook," compiled by Sullivan, J. Edelmann, et. al. Avery Library, New York.

1885

"Characteristics and Tendencies of American Architecture," *Inland Architect and Builder* (November 1885): 58–59; *PP*: 2–8.

Response to "We Are All Jolly Good Fellows," *Inland Architect and Builder* (November 1885): 86–87; *PP*: 8–10.

1886

"Inspiration," *Inland Architect and Builder* (December 1886): 61–64.

Inspiration: An Essay by Louis H. Sullivan, Architect. Chicago: R. F. Seymour, 1964; *PP*: 10–28.

1887

"What are the Present Tendencies of Architectural Design in America?" *Inland Architect and News Record*, (March 1887): 26; *PP*: 28–29.

"What is the Just Subordination, in Architectural Design, of Details to Mass?" *Inland Architect and News Record* (April 1887): 52–54; *PP*: 29–35.

As the chairman of the "Committee on a Standard of Professional Requirement," Sullivan authored a text for *Inland Architect and News Record* (November 1887): 252–253; *PP*: 36–39.

1888

"Remarks on an Architects' Code of Ethics," *Inland Architect and News Record* (November 1888): 64 ; *PP*: 40–41.

"Letter to the Editor" signed jointly by Sullivan and Adler concerning credit for the decoration of McVicker's Theater in Chicago: *American Architect and Building News* 11 (February 1888): 70–71; *PP*: 41–45.

"Style," *Inland Architect and News Record* (May 1888): 59–60; *PP*: 45–52.

Essay concerning the advisability of establishing an Architect's Protective League: *Inland Architect and News Record* (June 1888): 76; *PP*: 53–56.

Proposal for establishing an Architect's Protective League: *Building* 25 (August 1888): 64; *PP*: 56–59.

Essay concerning the impending merger of the Western Association of Architects with the American Institute of Architects: *Inland Architect and News Record* (November 1888): 68; *PP*: 60–61.

1888–1904

Plans for a book of poetry to be entitled *Nature and the Poet*; this unpublished text was comprised of four parts: "Nature and the Poet: A Prose Song," 1888–89; "Inspiration," 1886; "Sympathy: A Romanza," c. 1904; "The Master," 1 July 1899. LHSA.

1889

"The Artistic Use of Imagination," *Building* 19 (October 1889): 129–130; *PP*: 62–67.

1890

Essay on the advisability of the practice of subcontracting: "Shall the National Association Recommend That It Be Encouraged?" *Inland Architect and News Record* 15 (February 1890) 18–19; *PP*: 67–72.

1891

"Plastic and Color Decoration of the Auditorium," *Industrial Chicago* 1 (1891): 490–491; *PP*: 73–76.

"The High Building Question," *Graphic* 5 (December 1891): 405; *PP*: 76–79. See also: D. Hoffmann, "The Setback Skyscraper of 1891: An Unknown Essay by Louis H. Sullivan," *Journal of the Society of Architectural Historians* 29 (May 1970): 181–187.

1892

"Ornament in Architecture," *Engineering Magazine* 3 (August 1892): 633–634; *PP*: 79–85.

1893

Letter addressed to D. Burnham, 11 November 1893. LHSA.

"Polychromatic Treatment of Architecture," lecture delivered to the World Congress of Architects, Chicago, 5 August 1893. Text quoted in *Inland Architect and News Record* (August 1893): 11. Now lost, see: R. Twombly, *Louis Sullivan: His Life and Work*, (Chicago: University of Chicago Press,1986): 463.

Description of the Transportation Building jointly written by Sullivan and Adler: *Handbook of the World's Columbian Exposition*, (Chicago: Rand, McNally & Co., 1893): 30–34; *PP*: 85–87.

1894

"Emotional Architecture as Compared with Intellectual: A Study in Subjective and Objective," *Inland Architect and News Record* (November 1894): 32–34; *PP*: 103–113.

1896

"The Tall Office Building Artistically Considered," *Lippincott's Magazine* 57 (March 1896): 403–409; *PP*: 88–103.

1897

"May Not Architecture Again Become a Living Art?" manuscript, c.1897. LHSA; *PP*: 113–118.

1898

"On the Use of Burned Clay for Fire–Proof Building," *Brickbuilder* (September 1896): 189–190; *PP*: 118–121.

1899

"An Unaffected School of Modern Architecture: Will it Come?" *Artist* 24 (January 1899): XXXIII–XXXIV; *PP*: 121–122.

"The Modern Phase of Architecture," *Inland Architect and News Record* (June 1899): 40; *PP*: 123–125. For a complete version of the manuscript, see: LHSA.

"The Master," manuscript, 1 July 1899. LHSA.

1900

Opinion concerning the slogan "Progress Before Precedent," adopted by the periodical *Brickbuilder*: *Brickbuilder* 9 (May 1900): 96; *PP*: 125–126.

Lecture on the occasion of the Architectural League of America Convention, Chicago: *Inland Architect and News Record* (June 1900): 42–43; *PP*: 120–131.

"The Young Man in Architecture," *Inland Architect and News Record* (June 1900) 38–40; *PP*: 131–144.

"Reality in the Architectural Art," *Interstate Architect and Builder* 2 (11 August 1900): 6–7; *PP*: 144–149.

"Open Letter on Plagiarism," *Interstate Architect and Builder* 2 (8 August 1900): 7; *PP*: 149–150.

1901–1902

From 16 February 1901 through 8 February 1902 Sullivan published fifty-two essays, on a weekly basis, in *Interstate Architect and Builder*. Collected and published in book form in 1918 under the title *Kindergarten Chats.*

1901

Letter in response to a reader in regard to "Kindergarten Chat 10: A

1901

Roman Temple," *Interstate Architect and Builder* 2 (18 May 1901): 6; *PP*: 149–150.

Telegram to the Architectural League of America Convention, Philadelphia: *Brickbuilder* 10 (June 1901): 2; *PP*: 152.

"Architectural Style," *Inland Architect and News Record* (September 1901): 16; *PP*: 153.

1902

Text addressed to the Architectural League of American Convention, Toronto: "Education," *Inland Architect and News Record* (June 1902): 41–42; *PP*: 153–157.

1903

"Sub–Structure at the New Schlesinger & Mayer Store Building, Chicago," *Engineering Record* 47 (21 February 1903): 194–196; *PP*: 158–167.

1904

Lecture read to the American Institute of Architects' Illinois Chapter: "Basement and Sub–Basements," *Economist* 31 (20 February 1904): 254; *PP*: 167–169.

1905

"The Modern Use of the Gothic: The Possibilities of a New Architectural Style," (in response to F. Stymez Lamb) *Craftsman* 8 (June 1905): 336–338; *PP*: 170–173.

"Letter to the Editor," *Craftsman* 8 (July 1905): 453; *PP*: 173–174.

1906

"What is Architecture? A Study in the American People of Today," *Craftsman* 10 (May 1906): 145–149; (June) 352–358; (July) 507–513. See also: *Journal of the Society of Architectural Historians* 4 (April 1944); *PP*: 174–196.

1908

"Letter to the Editor" concerning sculptor G. Borglum: *Craftsman* 15 (December 1908): 338; *PP*: 196–197.

Democracy: A Man–Search, essay begun in 1905 with the title "Natural Thinking: A Study in Democracy." Completed in 1908 and published posthumously: E. Hedges ed., (Detroit: Wayne State University Press, 1961).

1909

"Is Our Art a Betrayal Rather than an Expression of American Life?" *Craftsman* 15 (January 1909): 402–404; *PP*: 197–200.

1910

"Artistic Brick," preface to the catalog *Suggestions in Artistic Brick*, (St. Louis: Hydraulic–Press Brick Co., c. 1910). See: *Prairie School Review*, 4 (April–June 1967) 24–26; *PP*: 200–205.

1912

"Lighting the People's Savings Bank, Cedar Rapids, Iowa: An example of American Twentieth Century Ideas of Architecture and Illumination," *Illuminating Engineer* 6 (February 1912): 631–635; *PP*: 205–208.

"The People's Savings Bank, Cedar Rapids, Iowa," *Banker's Magazine* 84 (March 1912): 415–426.

1915

Commemoration of the architect Solon S. Beman, delivered to the Illinois Chapter of the American Institute of Architects on 8 June 1915. LHSA; *PP*: 208–211.

1916

"Development of Construction," *Economist* 55 (24 June 1916): 252; 56 (1 July 1916): 39–40; *PP*: 211–222.

1918

Kindergarten Chats and Other Writings, author's revision 1918. First published and edited by C. Bragdon (Lawrence: Scarab Fraternity Press, 1934). Reprint, New York: G. Witterborn Inc., 1947 and 1955.

1922

Paper appearing in the *Proceedings of the Fifty-fifth Annual Convention of the American Institute of Architects*, (New York: American Institute of Architects Press, 1922): 63.

1922–23

From June 1922 through September 1923 Sullivan published his autobiography in sixteen installments on a monthly basis in the *Journal of the American Institute of Architects*.

1923

"The Chicago Tribune Competition," *Architectural Record* 5 (February 1923): 151–157; *PP*: 223–232.

"Concerning the Imperial Hotel, Tokyo, Japan," *Architectural Record* 53 (April 1923): 332–352; *PP*: 233–244.

1924

"Reflections on the Tokyo Disaster," *Architectural Record* 55 (February 1924): 113–117; *PP*: 244–251.

The Autobiography of an Idea. New York: American Institute of Architects Press, 1924. Reprint, New York: W. W. Norton & Co., 1934; New York: P. Smith, 1949; New York: Dover Press, 1956 and 1980.

A System of Architectural Ornament According with a Philosophy of Man's Powers. New York: American Institute of Architects Press, 1924. Reprint, New York: The Eakin Press, 1967; Chicago: Art Institute of Chicago, 1990.

Harold Allen
Art Institute of Chicago
Avery Architectural and Fine Arts
    Library
Avery Architectural Library, Columbia
    University
Joseph Barron
Patricia L. Bazelon
Bostonian Society
Chicago Architectural Photographing
    Company
Chicago Historical Society
Emil Lorch Collection, Bentley
    Historical Library, University of
    Michigan
Historic American Buildings Survey
Lewis Kostiner
Library of Congress, Historical
    American Buildings Society,
    Washington, D.C.
Giovanni Manieri Elia
Manuela Morresi
Missouri Historical Society
Museum of the City of New York
People's Savings Bank
David Phillips
Richard Nickel Committee, Chigago
Cervin Robinson
Tim Samuelson
J. W. Taylor
The Art Institute of Chicago Avery
    Architectural Library
Tusculum College Archives
Robert Twombly
University of Chicago Library
Vinci/Hamp Architects